Praise for *Strategic Planning for Nonprofit Organizations, Third Edition*

"Strategic planning is key to strong and successful nonprofits but   also be intimidating. Allison and Kaye demystify this important work   l and manageable steps, help people and organizations move   en if you have done strategic planning before, you   v I have, and I heartily recommend it."

—**Kevin Cathcart**,   ..ula Legal

"*Strategic Planning for Nonprofit Organizations* is the b   ..egic planning book in our industry. The third edition is even better and I look forward to sharing it widely!"

—**Robert Walker**, Executive Director,
The Frank H. and Eva B. Buck Foundation

"A much needed detailed walk through of the process of constructing and using a strategic plan."

—**Sharon Oster**, Frederic D. Wolfe Professor of Management
and Entrepreneurship and Economics, Yale School of Management

"*Strategic Planning for Nonprofit Organizations* is a great resource! It is accessible, practical, and user-friendly, and will help address important questions about direction and possibilities. I recommend this to any organization that wants to engage in a fun and productive planning process."

—**Akaya Windwood**, President, Rockwood Leadership Institute

"Strategic planning can be esoteric, daunting, and subjective, but it doesn't have to be. Allison and Kaye provide the framework and tools to help any organization's leadership team create a clear, concise, and compelling plan that can be understood and operationalized by all key stakeholders. Time and again, I have turned to *Strategic Planning for Nonprofit Organizations* as both the chart and compass to navigate our planning process, and time and again, it has led us to mission fulfillment."

—**Roslyn Quarto**, Executive Director,
Empowering and Strengthening Ohio's People

Strategic Planning for Nonprofit Organizations

A Practical Guide for Dynamic Times

THIRD EDITION

MICHAEL ALLISON

JUDE KAYE

WILEY

Published by John Wiley & Sons, Inc., Hoboken, New Jersey.
Published simultaneously in Canada.

For general information on our other products and services or for technical support, please contact our Customer Care Department within the United States at (800) 762-2974, outside the United States at (317) 572-3993 or fax (317) 572-4002.

Wiley publishes in a variety of print and electronic formats and by print-on-demand. Some material included with standard print versions of this book may not be included in e-books or in print-on-demand. If this book refers to media such as a CD or DVD that is not included in the version you purchased, you may download this material at http://booksupport.wiley.com. For more information about Wiley products, visit www.wiley.com.

ISBN 978-1-118-76814-3 (Paperback)
ISBN 978-1-118-76986-7 (ePDF)
ISBN 978-1-118-76815-0 (ePub)

Printed in the United States of America

10 9 8 7 6

For my parents Lee and Margot
who welcomed me, for Jennifer my partner in life,
for my daughters Sarah and Madeline who give me faith
in the future . . . and for all of the incredible people
doing the work every day.

—Mike Allison

I dedicate this third edition
to my wife, Linda Van Sciver,
who I believe personifies the values and beliefs
of the nonprofit sector: a commitment to helping others;
believing in the goodness of people and their capacity
to grow and learn; and always striving to help make the
world a better place.

—Jude Kaye

Contents

About the Third Edition

In the 18 years since we wrote the first edition of this book, the two of us have been astounded and delighted by the reception it has received. We have heard from people all over the country and from abroad, who have let us know that the book was helpful to them in various ways—leading their own organizations through planning, as consultants to nonprofit organizations, and as university instructors at both the undergraduate and graduate levels.

Strategic planning continues to be the most common organization development activity undertaken in the nonprofit and private sectors. This is because it works and is necessary for organizations to succeed. Strategic planning is alive and well, and the practice continues to evolve. Hence a third edition!

In the past two decades, the nonprofit sector has grown enormously in scale and in sophistication. Expectations of nonprofits have grown for better measures of impact, financial transparency and integrity, and increased collaboration. Social media, economic recessions, globalization, and income inequality all can make the seas that nonprofits navigate choppy. In these dynamic times, having a clear *strategy* helps nonprofits keep their eyes on the horizon and successfully adapt their *plans* to stay focused on accomplishing their mission.

In this new edition, we have provided additional guidance on the specific steps in strategic analysis and priority setting, and we have included more discussion about how to use your strategic plan effectively. All worksheets and other related resources are now online, and we point you toward several valuable assessment and management tools that are now widely available.

Our basic principles and insights about the strategic planning process have withstood the review of thousands of readers and the test of time. We remain dedicated to the principle that the best results come from sustained, intentional efforts, and we have found time and again that the process guidelines for strategic planning we describe in this book can contribute to just such efforts and results.

We welcome comments from readers and colleagues, and we are always looking for opportunities to improve our tools, add new ones, and share our passion for supporting the world-changing work of nonprofit organizations.

We are proud to be colleagues with you in working for a better world!

MIKE ALLISON
JUDE KAYE

Preface

*S*trategic Planning for Nonprofit Organizations, Third Edition, offers a conceptual framework and detailed process suggestions for strategic planning by nonprofit organizations. For readers of one of the first two editions, much will look familiar, but much is new as well. The logic and flow of the process are the same, but we have broken out the middle section into a few more specific steps. In particular, we have added more detailed guidance on developing the program strategy and business model.

The book is the product of the authors' experience as planning and organization development consultants. The concepts, process design, and language presented here have been shaped by our strategic planning work with hundreds of nonprofit organizations. Many of the worksheets and approaches to formulating strategy were developed while working with individual clients in response to particular situations. Our approach is informed by the work of many published authors and dozens of colleagues, including in particular the wisdom and experience of our colleagues at CompassPoint Nonprofit Services, where we both worked for many years.

We hope that this book provides you with a practical approach that is comprehensive, without being either overly complex or unduly simplistic. The user-friendly tools and techniques will help you put the framework into action. Those who have experience with strategic planning will find the book a useful refresher and a one-stop source book of fundamental concepts and techniques; those without such experience will find it a valuable introduction to what strategic planning is—and is not—and how to make the best use of the process.

When done well, strategic planning is a creative and a participatory process that engenders new insights and helps an organization focus its efforts in pursuit of its mission. It is an important tool that can help nonprofit organizations achieve their goals. A tool's effectiveness, though, ultimately depends on how well it is wielded. With this book, we hope to help others understand enough about the potential and the pitfalls of this particular management tool to create sound strategic plans that contribute to the viability and success of their organizations' work.

INTENDED AUDIENCE

This book was written to help the board and staff of nonprofit organizations—and other planning practitioners—to produce powerful strategic plans. The book was written with medium-size organizations (that is, organizations with budgets from several hundred thousand dollars to those with budgets of several million dollars) particularly in mind. However, the general nature of much of the discussion will also serve the smallest nonprofits as well as larger organizations, consultants working with nonprofit organizations, teachers and students of nonprofit management, and others interested in this area. We have heard from many readers who have used our methodology with larger nonprofits, governmental entities, and even in the private sector.

STRUCTURE OF THE BOOK

The book is organized so that it can be easily followed and referenced during the course of strategic planning. The first chapter provides an introduction to strategic planning. It outlines the conceptual framework, offers guidance on managing the planning process, and examines how strategic planning in nonprofit organizations relates to other topics. Chapters on each step in the process follow the Introduction.

SUPPORTING RESOURCES

Cautions for Facilitators are tips, included throughout the book, for anyone leading a strategic planning process to avoid pitfalls. A supplementary resource section provides suggestions and instruments to assist with strategic planning. The book contains several features—worksheets, sidebars, and a case study that unfolds in the completed worksheets—to help explain concepts and to help readers work through the various planning steps.

Worksheets

Worksheets associated with each step in the planning process are an integral feature of this book. The worksheets help planners structure and focus their work on each planning step. Each worksheet is discussed in the text and includes process notes. Blank worksheets are included on the companion website for this book. The worksheets provide helpful structure for a planning committee to write a strategic plan, but not all of the worksheets are necessary in every situation. Completed worksheets for the Case Study are included at the end of each chapter to illustrate the use of the worksheets.

Case Study

We use a fictitious organizations "County Legal Aid Society (CLAS)" to illustrate how each of the worksheets are used in the text. Completed worksheets are included at the end of each chapter.

The "story" of the Case Study organization follows:

County Legal Aid Society's (CLAS) mission is to promote equal access to justice by providing counseling and legal representation for disenfranchised and low-income people in Central County. CLAS operates from two offices and has 21 staff attorneys, 9 other staff members, and 105 volunteer lawyers. With an annual budget of $2,200,000, CLAS's support comes from federal, state, and local government grants, private foundations, law firms, and private donors. Last year County Legal Aid Society provided assistance to 3,500 individuals.

CLAS provides free civil legal services in the areas of housing, public benefits, health care, and family law. CLAS does not handle criminal law cases. In addition to representation, CLAS offers advice and counsel to the county's vulnerable populations as well as providing referrals to other sources of assistance. CLAS helps people whose household incomes are at or below 125 percent of the federal poverty guidelines and works with a wide variety of low-income populations in the county. Its four main programs are:

- *Housing:* CLAS work in this area includes helping individuals resolve landlord-tenant disputes, assisting renters facing eviction, and helping people maintain housing subsidies.

- *Public Benefits:* CLAS assists people in obtaining and maintaining government assistance such as Social Security, General Assistance (GA), Supplemental Security Income (SSI), and so on.

- *Health Care:* CLAS has always been committed to helping individuals access timely, affordable, and quality health care.

- *Family Law:* CLAS assists victims of domestic violence by obtaining restraining orders, helping parents obtain and keep custody of their children, and assisting family members in obtaining guardianship for children without parents.

CLAS was founded in 1977 by a group of attorneys who were concerned about the lack of quality representation for low income individuals in Central County. Issues CLAS has identified for strategic planning include: significant growth demands organizational changes, pressure to expand service to adjacent regions, need to rebalance business model, and the announced departure of long term Executive Director.

Sidebars

Short commentaries drawn from real-life experience with nonprofit organizations are included throughout the book to illustrate situations that may arise during a planning process. In some cases, the name of the organization is used, but in others, the name has been changed for purposes of confidentiality.

Additional Resources

Additional resources to support strategic planning are included in the Appendices. Included are: sample workplans, tools to assist with various steps in the strategic planning process, and a list of selected references for more information on the topics covered. Resources include books and articles on strategy, competition, business models, organizational capacity, leadership, and governance.

HOW TO USE THIS BOOK

For anyone who is looking for an overview of the strategic planning process, the introductory chapter should suffice. There are points in the process at which different options are possible, depending on the organization's specific goals and circumstances. Anyone leading a strategic planning process for the first time will want to read the entire book through before initiating the planning process.

A WORD ABOUT WORDS

We want to clarify the terms we've chosen to describe three groups of people about whom we will be speaking a great deal. For simplicity's sake, we have chosen one term for each group.

Clients. The beneficiaries or consumers of the goods and services nonprofit organizations produce are called by many names: clients, patients, arts patrons, constituents, customers, members, and so on. In some cases, beneficiaries are the general public, animals, or the global environment. We have chosen the term *client* as a representative name for the primary beneficiaries or consumers of the goods and services produced by nonprofit organizations.

Executive director. President and CEO are other frequently used titles for the most senior staff person selected by the board of directors and to whom all staff ultimately report. We use the term *executive director* for this person, because it is the most commonly used term.

Stakeholders. Nonprofit organizations are not owned in the way private corporations are owned, nor are they subject to the electoral process, as government organizations are. Nonetheless, nonprofit organizations are accountable to many parties for their work, in addition to their clients. As with the word *clients,* the individuals and groups of people to whom nonprofit organizations are accountable are called by many names. We have chosen to call funders, clients, the general public, other organizations, regulators, and so on *external stakeholders,* and to call board members, staff, and volunteers *internal stakeholders.* Simply stated, a stakeholder is anyone who cares, or should care, about the organization—anyone who has a stake in the success of its mission.

Acknowledgments

The origins of this book were the worksheets Jude created for a training at the National Minority AIDS Coalition in the early 1990s. Although the ideas and presentation of the strategic planning process have been put to paper by the two of us, we gratefully acknowledge our debt to the many other consultants, writers, and friends who have kept us sane and contributed to our learning and to the field of planning over the past many years.

We think of all of our colleagues through the many years we both worked at CompassPoint as contributors to this book. We especially thank Jan Masaoka, long-time executive director for her creativity and innovative thinking about nonprofit management.

We are grateful to be able to share a series of cartoons, alternately ironic, playful or fanciful, from a collection titled "Planet 501c3; Tales from the Nonprofit Galaxy." These cartoons were created by a now deceased very dear colleague, Miriam Engleberg.

A big thank you to Richard Fowler who created the new artwork for the planning framework and planning process.

Julia Wilson, executive director at OneJustice, gave us many, many hours over a period of months to make a major contribution to this edition by helping us draft the unfolding of the case study in the worksheets.

We acknowledge and appreciate the generosity of The Evelyn and Walter, Jr. Haas Fund for allowing us to share their Leadership Assessment Tool.

We thank Jennifer Chapman and Todd Manza, who provided invaluable editorial input.

We have benefited greatly from all of the authors whose work we reference.

In the list of people to whom we are intellectual heirs, we would like to acknowledge a special debt to the late Jon Cook, founder of the Support Centers of America and a pioneer in bringing the practice of strategic planning to the nonprofit sector. Jon was an important teacher to both of us, and many of our best ideas originally came from him.

Perhaps our most far-reaching debt of gratitude is to all of our clients who have helped us to develop and refine much of our thinking over the last several years and continually inspire us to make our written materials as user-friendly as possible.

Introduction

Strategic planning helps organizations achieve two critical outcomes: clear *decisions* about purpose and strategy and *commitment* to those decisions. It is a process designed to support leaders in being intentional rather than reactive. Simply stated it is a management tool, and as with any management tool, it is used for one purpose only–to help an organization do a better job.

We define strategic planning as *a systematic process through which an organization agrees on and builds key stakeholder commitment to priorities that are essential to its mission and responsive to the organizational environment. Strategic planning guides the acquisition and allocation of resources to achieve these priorities.* Several key concepts in this definition are expanded on below.

1. The process is *strategic* because it involves choosing how best to respond to the circumstances of a dynamic and sometimes hostile environment. Non-profit organizations have many choices in the face of changing client or customer needs, funding availability, competition, and other factors. Being strategic requires recognizing these choices and committing to one set of responses instead of another. The most difficult choices often involve what *not* to do.

2. Strategic planning is *systematic* in that it calls for following a structured, driven process. The process raises a sequence of questions that helps planners examine history and performance, test assumptions, gather and incorporate new information, anticipate the environment in which the organization will be working, and decide how best to respond going forward.

3. The process is about *building alignment and commitment.* A well-crafted plan without alignment of people, systems, and structures will not be successful. Taking the time to engage stakeholders, including clients and the community, in the process of identifying priorities allows disagreements to be voiced and constructively resolved. Putting the time and effort into getting agreement and thinking through implications pays huge dividends down the road.

4. Strategic planning guides the *acquisition and allocation of resources.* A sound strategic plan helps leaders make proactive and realistic choices between competing funding strategies and between spending for various program and administrative

needs. Balancing resource acquisition with spending plans is the essence of the business discipline of strategic planning.

STRATEGY AND PLANNING

There is much debate in the field about whether a three- or five-year strategic plan can remain relevant in a dynamic environment. The first answer is that a plan can remain relevant as long as it deals with the most important questions and issues. This takes both honesty and work, because the real issues are often partially obscured by observable problems, group dynamics, or inherent uncertainties. Second, it is important to keep in mind that strategic planning combines two distinct types of thinking: strategy and planning. Strategy is aspirational in setting direction and is focused on broad, fundamental choices. Planning involves translating the strategy into concrete goals and guidance for how to achieve them. Strategic direction will help navigate changing circumstances, whereas implementation plans will often need to be adapted.

We look at it this way: Most organizations develop an annual budget (and more and more frequently, two- or three-year forecasts), with monthly updates using the original budget as reference. Everyone expects that some changes and surprises will occur during the course of the year. That doesn't keep people from making a budget, but it does require vigilance and a willingness to adapt to the unexpected. Organizations don't throw out the budget in response to new information; they continually update projections. But without a budget (which is a plan in the language of dollars), how would any organization know how to interpret and respond to changes?

Because organizational aspirations and broad strategic directions don't often change fundamentally in the period of a few years, purpose and strategy are less subject to short-term shifts in the environment—even, and sometimes especially, big shifts. Adjustments in the annual organizational and department workplans, similar to annual budgets, will almost certainly be needed along the way. What is needed to keep the strategic plan relevant and current is a process for regular (at least quarterly) adaptation of operational plans in response to a continually evolving understanding of the environment. This is not difficult to operationalize for most organizations.

WHY PLAN?

Why should an organization undertake a strategic planning effort? After all, planning consumes time and money—precious commodities for any nonprofit—and defining the direction and activities of an organization in an ever-changing environment is daunting and can almost seem futile. The evidence of success for nonprofits is not primarily financial (profit); it is accomplishment of mission. The answer to why strategic planning should be done is that it helps an organization to increase the impact of its work—to accomplish more of its mission—by helping leaders be intentional about priorities and proactive in motivating others to achieve them.

INCREASING IMPACT

To increase impact is to grow in one or more ways. There are two major ways to grow:

1. More: The easiest way to increase your impact is to do more of what you are already doing—to increase *scale*—which requires an increase in budget and other resources.

2. Different: Another option is to do your work differently. The three main ways to do work differently are through:
   - *Process improvement*—doing the same work more efficiently and getting better results by doing more with (proportionately) less
   - *Design improvement*—doing the same work in new and better ways to get better results
   - *Strategic improvement*—doing different work, changing your mix of programs to get better results

---

Leadership guru Warren Bennis wrote "Managers are people who do things right, and leaders are people who do the right thing."[1] Strategic planning is both a leadership tool and a management tool. As a leadership tool, a successful planning process encourages the organization to look at the question, Are we doing the right thing? As a management tool, an effective planning process focuses on whether the organization is "doing things right."

Planning alone does not produce results; it is a means, not an end, and plans must be implemented to produce results. However, well-developed plans increase the chance that the day-to-day activities of the organization will lead to desired results. Planning does this in two ways: it helps the members of an organization bring into focus the organization's priorities; and it improves the process of people working together as they pursue these priorities.

Successful strategic planning improves the *focus* of an organization by generating:

- An explicit understanding of the organization's mission, strategy, and organizational values among staff, board, and external constituencies

- A blueprint for action based on current information

- Broad milestones with which to monitor achievements and assess results

---

[1] Warren Bennis, *On Becoming a Leader* (New York: Perseus Publishing, 2003).

- Information that can be used to market the organization to the public and to potential funders

Successful strategic planning improves the *process* of people working together by:

- Creating a forum to discuss why the organization exists and the shared values that should influence decisions

- Fostering successful communication and teamwork among the board of directors and staff

- Laying the groundwork for meaningful change by stimulating strategic thinking and focusing on what's most important to the organization's long-term success

- Bringing everyone's attention back to what is most important—seeking opportunities to better accomplish the organization's mission

- Encouraging thinking about how to use the strategic plan to adapt to changing circumstances

WHAT STRATEGIC PLANNING IS NOT

Everything that has been said to describe what strategic planning *is* also informs an understanding of what it is *not*:

1. *Strategic planning does not predict the future.* Although strategic planning involves making assumptions about the future environment, the decisions are made in the present. As George Steiner (considered by many to be the father of current-day strategic planning) put it, "Planning deals with the futurity of current decisions. Forward planning requires that choices be made among possible events in the future, but decisions made in their light can be made only in the present."[2] An organization must monitor changes in its environment over time and assess whether its assumptions remain valid.

2. *Strategic planning is not a substitute for the ongoing judgment of leadership.* A strategic plan does not and cannot provide, let alone activate, an autopilot switch. There is no substitute for the exercise of judgment by an organization's leadership. Leaders of any enterprise must continually ask, "What are the most important issues we face?" and "How shall we respond?" However, the clarity of mission and the fundamental priorities of a plan provide a frame of reference that helps leaders respond effectively to an ever-changing environment.

3. *Strategic planning is not a math problem; there is no right answer.* Both rational analysis and creative sense-making are required. The search for opportunities and the internal negotiations leading to truly shared commitment are what

---

[2] George Steiner, *Strategic Planning* (New York: Free Press, 1979), pp. 14–15.

make the process challenging and, if it is done well, incredibly meaningful and rewarding.

4. *Although it is structured and systematic, strategic planning is not completely linear.* It is a creative process, requiring flexibility. The fresh insight arrived at today might very well alter the decisions made yesterday. Inevitably, the process moves forward and backward several times before the group arrives at the final set of decisions. No one should be surprised if the process feels less like a comfortable trip on a commuter train and more like a ride on a roller coaster, but remember that even roller coaster cars arrive at their destination, as long as they stay on track.

KEYS TO EFFECTIVE STRATEGIC PLANNING

The elements highlighted previously in our definition and approach speak to those characteristics of strategic planning that we believe are most necessary for success. In addition, we can offer prospective planners a few other thoughts about our approach:

1. *Focus on the most important issues during your strategic planning process.* It may take a while to become clear, but inevitably there are only a few critical choices that the planning process must address. These choices define an organization's strategy. (If you don't have any really important choices to make about your organization's future, you don't need strategic planning.) Resist the temptation to pursue all of the interesting questions. You simply won't have the time, energy, or resources to do it all.

2. *Don't let yourself avoid the difficult or sensitive questions.* Be willing to question both the status quo and sacred cows. In order to understand what is most important in the current atmosphere and in the expected future, old assumptions about what is important must be challenged. It is possible, and necessary, to honor the past and still make new decisions. Don't allow new ideas to be characterized as inherent criticisms of the past.

3. *Produce a document.* Whether an organization engages in an abbreviated process or an extensive strategic planning process, a planning document should be created. A useful strategic plan can be only a few pages long—clarity, not length, determines usefulness. The document is a symbol of accomplishment, a guide for internal operations, and a marketing tool for current and future supporters.

4. *Make sure the strategic plan is linked to annual workplans and the annual budget.* One test of a good strategic plan is that the operational implications are clear. Without a practical operating plan that articulates short-term priorities—and clearly identifies who is responsible for implementation—a strategic plan cannot be implemented. Writing the first year's annual operating plan and

supporting budget with the strategic plan in mind ensures that your strategic plan passes this test.

Summary of Key Concepts

Strategic planning:

- *Is strategic.* It intentionally responds to the current environment, including competition.
- *Is systematic and data based.* It gathers new information to make decisions.
- *Builds alignment.* It engages appropriate stakeholders.
- *Guides resource acquisition and allocation.*

Strategic planning is *not*:

- *A prediction of the future.* Instead, it is a plan based on current information.
- *A substitute for judgment.* Instead, it is a vehicle for informed decision making.
- *A math problem.* There is no right answer.
- *A linear process.* Instead, it is iterative; insights at one stage may change earlier conclusions.

Keys for effective planning:

- Focus on the most important issues.
- Don't let yourself avoid the difficult or sensitive questions.
- Produce a document.
- Make sure the strategic plan is linked to annual workplans and the annual budget.

WHAT IS STRATEGY?

To boil it down to the most basic elements: Your mission is your purpose, and your strategy is "how" you will accomplish your mission. Part of the problem with the word *strategy* is that it is a very general term and is defined by different practitioners in a variety of ways. A simple dictionary definition is "a careful plan or method for achieving a particular goal."

For our purposes, a strategic plan articulates a sound strategy when an organization has made clear choices about its highest-level goal—the impact the organization seeks to make through pursuit of its mission—and its "plan" for achieving that goal. This "plan" using our strategic planning framework, requires attention to five dimensions: the competitive environment, programs, funding, capacity, and leadership. Strategy at this level, for the organization as a whole, is overarching. But because there are many levels of goals, there are also many levels of strategy. These subordinate level strategies are simply called Program Strategies, Revenue Strategies, Capacity Strategies, and Leadership Strategies. In all cases, however, we are using strategy to mean fundamental choices about *how* specific goals will be achieved, choices that will drive implementation plans for the life of the strategic plan.

> Strategy is not a response to short-term fluctuations in operations or the environment . . . . Strategy deals with the predetermined direction toward which these quick responses are pointed. It is concerned with the longer-term course that the ship is steering, not with the waves.[3]

In the final strategic plan, a very few "core strategies" will make clear what the organization sees as its top priorities to achieve success. (We have a sample strategic plan for the case study included at the end of Chapter 9 in which four core strategies are identified.)

Sample Program Strategy

After many years spent caring for neglected animals, one chapter of the American Society for the Prevention of Cruelty to Animals (ASPCA) shifted its organizational strategy from primarily focusing on the care and adoption of neglected animals to include an explicit focus on prevention. This shift incorporated keeping programs providing shelter and adoption at current levels while adding prevention program strategies to conduct education and advocacy, and to aggressively grow their existing spay and neuter program. Among the steps taken to implement the strategy, all programs were instructed to develop and implement an education component, and the staff increased its efforts to pass legislation designed to prevent unwanted pets and animal abuse.

The strategy implies a plan with goals and objectives. A long-term goal to support this strategy is: "Within the next five years, reduce by 50 percent the number of animals that have to be put to sleep." Sample short-term objectives to support this strategy include the following:

- Within the next year, have each department develop and implement a plan for adding an education component to its scope of work.
- Hire an education director to coordinate education efforts.
- Significantly expand our animal spay and neuter campaign.

Sample Revenue Strategy

In pursuit of its mission to "increase opportunities to experience world-class art in our community," a new museum without a big endowment chose an innovative

---

[3] Boris Yavitz and William H. Newman, *Strategy in Action: The Execution, Politics, and Payoff of Business Planning* (New York: The Free Press, 1984), p. 4.

resource acquisition strategy. Rather than primarily raising money to increase its art collection it chose to rent a significant portion of its collection and to host traveling exhibitions from other museums. This would allow them to attract visitors right away, while taking time to build up endowment funds for art purchase. Although this strategy did not directly affect all departments, it did have a major impact on the use of resources, freeing up funds for programming.

Sample long-term goals to support this strategy include the following:

- Acquire at least 50 percent of exhibitions from other museums' collections.

- Focus art collecting on 20th-century California artists.

A sample short-term objective to support this strategy includes "Within the next year, collaborate with three other museums to put on one exhibition that highlights 19th-century Japanese drawings and one exhibition that highlights French impressionists."

Sample Organizational Strategy

During its planning process, an organization received feedback that although clients valued its services, most people—referral agencies, potential donors, and so forth—knew little about the organization's work. This information was important for fund development purposes, as well as marketing of some of its services. One of its core future strategies, therefore, was "greater emphasis on visibility." Each department was asked to add a visibility component to its long-term objectives and annual workplan.

A sample long-term goal to support this strategy includes "Increase by 25 percent the number of referrals received from government and community organizations." Sample short-term objectives to support this strategy include the following:

- Contract with a public relations firm to assist in the development of a marketing campaign.

- Update website, online communications, and printed collateral to be used by the board and staff to publicize services.

- Focus visibility efforts with key referral sources, and expand the number of agencies prepared and committed to referring clients to us.

Sample Leadership Strategy

The board of directors of a volunteer-run organization played both an administrative and a governance role: They ran the organization (made all of the day-to-day decisions) and governed the organization (protected the public interest by making conducted oversight and decided mission, strategy, and business model. The board decided to start hiring staff to run the programs and to change its role from an administrative *and* governance board to a primarily governance board.

Sample long-term goals to support this strategy include the following:

- Focus board committees primarily on governance (i.e., fundraising, finance, and planning), as opposed to organizational operations.
- Increase the board to 18 members, with particular attention to individuals with fundraising experience and interest.

Sample short-term objectives to support this strategy include the following:

- Train board members on the roles and responsibilities of a governance board.
- Develop a decision-making grid to clarify the decision-making roles of the staff and board.

In each case, the organization made a clear choice among competing options about how best to pursue its mission. Organization-level strategies either affect every department or use a considerable amount of an organization's resources. It is easy to see how each of these core strategies might be translated into specific goals and objectives over a period of several years and for the immediate future, with sufficient resources allocated in the yearly budget to support the accomplishment of those strategies. What is not easy to see is how much effort, experimentation, and discussion were required to find these successful strategies.

THE STRATEGIC PLANNING PROCESS

Our planning model is designed to address five interrelated dimensions of strategy. Each dimension frames an important component of the resulting strategic plan:

- *Environmental Scan.* What are the most important competitive and other external forces to which you must respond?
- *Theory of change and program portfolio.* How should your overall program strategy, known as a theory of change, and your mix of programs evolve?
- *Business model.* What should your business model be going forward?
- *Organization capacity.* In what ways do organizational resources, systems, and structures need strengthening?
- *Leadership.* How will you optimize staff and board leadership and governance?

These five areas encompass the content of the strategic plan. This model also provides the conceptual framework for organizing the process and the work of the strategic planning committee. This model is shown in Figure I.1.

FIGURE I.1   STRATEGIC PLANNING FRAMEWORK

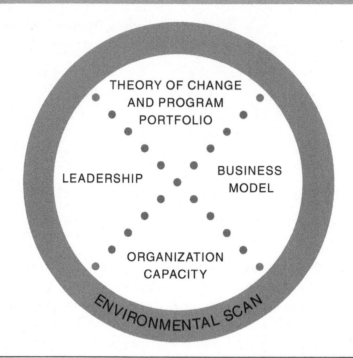

The strategic planning *process* is designed to thoroughly cover each of these dimensions and to develop a plan that recognizes the interconnections among all five. The process is organized as a series of 10 steps grouped in three sections, as shown in Figure I.2. The order of these steps is sequential, but in practice the process is iterative, with each step sometimes providing new insights for the step before.

Section One: First Steps

Organizing the planning process, getting input from stakeholders and articulating foundational ideas of mission, vision, and values ground and launch the effort.

Set Up for Success

The first question in getting ready for strategic planning is to assess whether it is the right time for your organization to engage in a planning process—and to envision what that planning process might look like. Although several issues must be addressed in assessing readiness, that determination essentially comes down to whether an organization's leaders are truly committed to the effort and are able to devote the necessary attention to the big picture at the time. If a funding crisis

FIGURE I.2   STRATEGIC PLANNING PROCESS

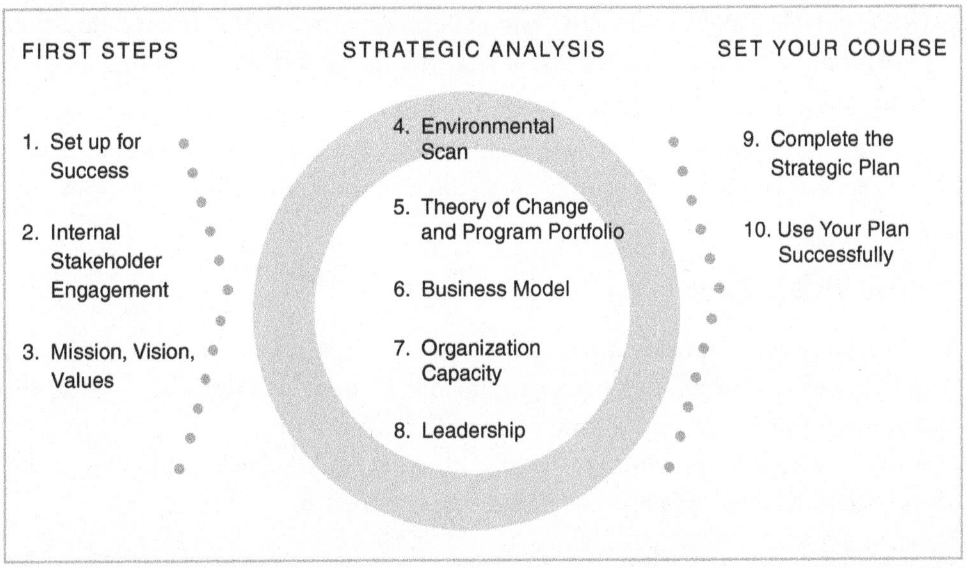

FIRST STEPS

1. Set up for
   Success

2. Internal
   Stakeholder
   Engagement

3. Mission, Vision,
   Values

STRATEGIC ANALYSIS

4. Environmental
   Scan

5. Theory of Change
   and Program Portfolio

6. Business Model

7. Organization
   Capacity

8. Leadership

SET YOUR COURSE

9. Complete the
   Strategic Plan

10. Use Your Plan
    Successfully

looms, if the founder is about to depart, or if external demands are so turbulent that everyone is putting out fires, then it doesn't make sense to engage in strategic planning.

An organization that determines it is ready to begin strategic planning must then complete the following tasks to pave the way for an organized process:

- Identify specific issues or choices that should be addressed.
- Decide on the basic process to use, including roles and participation (e.g., who does what in the process, whether to use a planning committee, whether to hire a consultant).
- Determine the information needed to help make sound decisions.

The product developed by the end of Step 1 is a strategic planning workplan—a guiding document for planning.

Stakeholder Engagement

Strong organizations have highly engaged stakeholders. A tightly developed plan with impeccable logic is worthless unless the people who need to act on the plan are committed to the vision and strategy. Internal stakeholders are board, staff, and often, volunteers. External stakeholders include funders, partner agencies, experts in the field, community members, elected officials and so on. In this step, strategic planners reach out to stakeholders for two reasons:

1. *Planners seek to get stakeholder input.* Their opinions and the information they have are an important ingredient in the strategic analysis to come.

2. *Reaching out early in the process helps to build buy-in and increase interest in the strategic planning process.* It is very difficult to enlist support for a plan later if there has been no opportunity for stakeholders to be heard early on.

Mission, Vision, Values

A *mission statement* communicates your purpose—the impact you want to have in the world. Some organizations choose to include a brief description of what the organization does—and for whom—to fulfill that purpose.

A *vision statement* presents an image of what success will look like if the organization achieves its purpose. As Nanus described it,

> A vision is a mental model of a future state . . . built upon reasonable assumptions about the future . . . influenced by our own judgments about what is possible and worthwhile . . . . A vision is a mental model that people and organizations can bring into being through their commitment and actions.[4]

Finally, most nonprofit organizations are driven by—and grounded in—*values* and beliefs about why they exist and how they want to operate in support of those values. The more those values are made explicit, the more likely it is that those values will be put into action.

With mission, vision, and values statements in hand, an organization knows why it exists, what success will look like, and what it stands for. The products developed in this step are draft statements of mission, vision, and values.

Section Two: Strategic Analysis

In these five interrelated steps, planners spend the most time and complete research analysis and develop preliminary proposals for the plan.

Environmental Scan

All nonprofit organizations are subject to environmental forces, both favorable and unfavorable. Political, economic, social, technological, demographic, and other forces can play an enormous role in how successful a nonprofit will be in

---

[4] Burt Nanus, *Visionary Leadership* (San Francisco: Jossey-Bass, 1995), p. 25.

achieving its mission. The task in this step is not to develop a treatise on how the world is changing around us; it is a much more nuanced assignment. Instead, we are looking for the *most relevant* environmental forces. As a starting point, it is helpful to take a broad view of changes taking place, but then it is important to decide which are the few environmental trends or forces to which your strategic plan must respond.

Theory of Change and Program Portfolio

Now the rubber hits the road. You have clarified your mission and values and have drafted a vision of success. You have solicited input from stakeholders and assessed the external environment. At this point, strategic planners must look squarely at *how* they plan to succeed. What is the theory of change? What is the overall program strategy? What business are you in? And finally, what is the right mix of programs— the program portfolio—to act on this strategic framework?

This step can be as simple as evaluating the strengths, weaknesses, opportunities, and threats involved with all programs (SWOT analysis) and making adjustments. Or it can involve careful analysis of program evaluation information, competitive analysis, and financial sustainability implications. The product of this step is an initial formulation of the heart of your strategic plan—what your organization is going to do to accomplish its mission. The program portfolio is not finalized until it is closely balanced in relationship to the opportunities and constraints of the business model.

Business Model

Financial sustainability is fundamental to success. In this step you will look at historical trends at your organization and assess the current financial health of your organization. One important objective of this step is for planners to clearly understand the revenue and costs associated with each program activity, as well as fundraising and other support costs. The business model of your nonprofit is an overall description of how it attracts funding. Clearly, the business model is intimately interdependent with the program portfolio. Different programs will have access to different revenue streams and different levels of support over time.

Organization Capacity

Organization capacity encompasses the many dimensions of staffing, systems and structures that support the delivery of mission-driven programs. Human resources, facilities, financial management, technology, communications, and marketing, as well as less tangible dimensions such as organizational culture, are all necessary functions. As with the other aspects of research and analysis, this step can be done in a way that is very limited or very comprehensive. An organization may have recently assessed one or more of its organizational systems, in which case this task is already partly done.

Leadership

The most successful nonprofits function with a leadership team, including top staff and the board. Assessing the effectiveness of the senior staff and the board and, importantly, assessing their working relationship helps identify opportunities to strengthen and focus leadership across the organization. Senior staff drives and manages the work of the organization, and a nonprofit board is ultimately responsible for the success of the organization. It can either greatly enhance the effectiveness of an organization or serve as a major drain on its resources and energy. Many of our clients consider strengthening leadership through additional analysis or additional negotiation among key parties the Strategic Planning Committee must find a way to finalize remaining decisions.

Section Three: Set Your Course

This is the home stretch, and these two last steps cannot be shortchanged. Making final decisions, building agreement and planning for implementation, and monitoring take place complete your process.

Complete Your Strategic Plan

In the previous steps, the strategic planning committee not only will be doing research but also will develop proposals for action. At this point it is time to finalize decisions about the direction of the organization, the broad approach to be taken (core strategies), and the general and specific results to be sought (the long-term and short-term goals and objectives). Leadership is also the time to test and strengthen commitment and alignment to these decisions. The team also creates the final document in this step.

This step can take considerable time. Discussions at this stage may require additional information or a reevaluation of conclusions reached during earlier discussions. It is possible that new insights will emerge that change the understanding of the mission statement. In order to create the best possible plan, planners must be willing to go back in the process to an earlier step to use new information. The following tasks are included in this step:

- *Finalize decisions.* Many of the most important decisions will have become clear. It is absolutely necessary to ensure that these decisions work *together*. There will almost certainly still be a few decisions where more than one option is quite viable. One way or another, through additional analysis or additional negotiation among key parties, it is time for the Strategic Planning Committee to get the thinking done.

- *Ensure alignment,* especially among board and staff. A final round of input, or testing nearly final ideas may be useful to give the team confidence that this plan has the enthusiastic support of your internal stakeholders.

- *Write the plan.* This task involves creating one coherent document. A member of the planning committee, the executive director, or a consultant typically drafts a final plan document utilizing the contributions of the full committee and then submits it for review by all key decision makers. The reviewers should make sure that the plan answers the key questions about priorities and directions, and in sufficient detail to serve as a guide for action. Revisions should not be dragged out for months, but action should be taken to answer any important questions raised.

    Surprisingly, many important choices are made during the writing stage, as questions surface about what will be required to succeed. These choices may appear to be semantics or minor nuances, but they can be important choices nonetheless. If a choice arises that really needs the explicit endorsement of key internal stakeholders to be implemented, do not hesitate to pause and check. The end result will be a concise description of where the organization is going, how it should get there, and why it needs to go that way—ideas that are widely supported by the organization's staff and board. The product of Step 9 is the strategic plan.

Using Your Plan Successfully

The strategic planning process culminates in the creation of a written plan, but the strategic thinking related to strategic planning is never finished. There are cycles and periods of more or less intense activity, but the process of responding to a changing environment is ongoing. Each organization needs to choose the appropriate length of time for planning and reevaluating. Many nonprofits use a three- or five-year planning cycle. For a three-year plan, the first strategic plan is completed with a three-year time horizon and a one-year annual operating plan. At the end of years one and two, progress toward the priorities of the strategic plan is assessed and adjustments made as necessary, and a new annual operating plan is developed. During year three, a renewed strategic planning process is undertaken. Depending on the extent of change in the organization's internal and external environment, the subsequent strategic planning workplan is more or less intensive. By the end of year three, a new three-year plan and a new annual operating plan are approved, and the cycle begins again.

A few key tasks are included in this step.

- *Sync strategic planning with annual workplans and budget planning.* Syncing the strategic plan with annual planning and annual budgeting begins with the early discussions about what the resulting plan will look like, but this connection must be tight to get the full value of the plan. All of the work described so far is for naught if it doesn't align the day-to-day work with the strategic priorities that have been so carefully chosen. The interface between the strategic, directional thinking embodied in the strategic plan and day-to-day work is a concise and easy-to-use operating plan. It should coincide with the organization's fiscal year and accommodate the need for other, more detailed program planning related to funding cycles or other reporting cycles.

  An organization's strategic priorities, its organizational structure, and its previous planning process will influence the nature of a particular organization's operating plan. The essence of the operating plan, though, remains the same: a document that defines the short-term, concrete objectives leading to achievement of strategic goals and objectives and that is easy to use and monitor. Ironically, the level of detail is not the deciding factor in how useful the operating plan is (more is not always better!); the most important factors are the clarity of guidelines for implementation and the precision of results to be monitored.

- *Plan for the change required during implementation.* Even with substantial involvement and preparation, confusion and resistance may surface during implementation of the plan, in response to the changes that need to occur. To help ensure successful implementation of the plan, leaders must anticipate and plan for the management of required change and support organization members in successfully executing those changes.

- *Develop a nonprofit dashboard* will help the board and staff track implementation at a level of detail that is specific enough to be meaningful and yet broad enough to be focusing on important dimensions of organizational performance.

- *Decide how the organization will monitor* ongoing changes in the environment and what its process will be for responding as needed.

Your staff and board are engaged in ongoing discussions with colleagues, are going to conferences, or are participating in regional and field-oriented task forces, so you are not working for three years without an ongoing flow of new information. In addition to this predictable cycle of planning, we advocate the creation of ongoing scanning capability, which will enable you to respond to changes and keep your strategic plan relevant.

If the core strategies and priorities agreed to remain valid, which is not uncommon, then the time frame previously outlined works well. However, if the environment changes in ways that are fundamentally different from the assumptions underlying the strategic plan, then it is necessary to regroup and re-strategize earlier. The products of Step 10 are four key mechanisms to make successful use of your plan: a tight connection to operational planning, a plan for managing change, a tracking mechanism known as a dashboard, and a schedule for ongoing assessment of the validity of decisions made during the strategic planning process and revision of the plan as needed.

OTHER CONSIDERATIONS IN STRATEGIC PLANNING

Of Means and Ends: Language of Strategic Planning

Language is fairly well defined in professions such as accounting and law. Every accountant knows what a *debit* is. Every lawyer knows what a *tort* is. Unfortunately, there is no such agreement on the definitions of planning words used by planners. Is there a difference between *mission* and *purpose*? Why distinguish between *external* and *internal vision*? What is a *strategy*? What distinguishes *goals* from *objectives* and *programs* from *activities*?

We believe two things are important about strategic planning terms. The first is that it doesn't really matter what you call certain concepts, as long as everyone in your group uses the same definitions. The definitions we use are spelled out in the next couple of pages. The second point relates to the fundamental distinction between means and ends. One of the key purposes of language clarity is to support this conceptual clarity.

A successful strategic planning process supports an organization in involving its stakeholders in reaching agreement about what end results they are trying to achieve (i.e., external vision, purpose, goals, and objectives) and the means to accomplish those results (i.e., internal vision, core services, specific programs and administrative functions, and activities). An organization's strategic plan is not an end, but rather is a means of achieving its purpose. Peters and Waterman, John Carver, and many others have emphasized the need for the people implementing a strategic plan to have enough flexibility and authority to be creative and responsive to new developments—without having to reconstruct an entire strategic plan.[5] This flexibility is required most in adjusting means. In other words, the purpose of an organization and the priority goals are much less likely to change than are the programs and activities necessary to achieve them.

---

[5] See Thomas J. Peters and Robert H. Waterman Jr., *In Search of Excellence: Lessons from America's Best-Run Companies* (New York: HarperCollins, 1982) and John Carver, *Boards That Make a Difference* (San Francisco: Jossey-Bass, 1997).

FIGURE I.3   MEANS AND ENDS

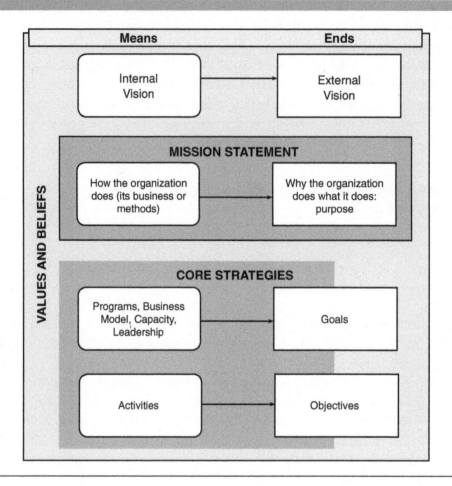

For example, perhaps an organization decides it wants to achieve a particular goal and sets up a program to achieve that goal. If another organization later decides to set up a similar program, the first organization may collaborate with the second organization or adjust its program plan without changing its original goal and overall strategy. Peters and Waterman call this being "tight on ends" (i.e., building strong commitment to the purpose and goals of an organization), while allowing the people in the organization to creatively adapt their methods to best achieve the goals, or staying "loose on means."[6]

The planning process presented in this book is built on the important relationship between ends and means. Figure I.3 and Table I.1 define the language we prefer, to help make the thinking behind this process clear and useful.

---

[6] Peters and Waterman, *In Search of Excellence.*

TABLE I.1   MEANS AND ENDS CONCEPTS

Means	Ends
Internal vision: A description of the organization operating at its most effective and efficient level.	**External vision:** A statement that describes how the world will be improved, changed, or different.
Business: What the organization does; the primary method(s) used by the organization to achieve its purpose.	**Mission:** One sentence that describes an organization's purpose—the ultimate result an organization is trying to achieve.
Programs and internal management functions: Programs an organization offers and the necessary internal operations.	**Goals:** Outcome statements that define what an organization is trying to accomplish both programmatically and organizationally.
Activities: The specific actions required to produce services and products.	**Objectives:** Precise, measurable, time-phased results that support the achievement of a goal.

Key terms can be defined as follows:

- *Core strategies* are broad, overall priorities or directions adopted by an organization.

- A *mission statement* is a succinct statement that articulates an organization's purpose (ends) and may include what the organization does (its programs, or the means).

- *Values* are the basic guiding principles and commitments that guide and inspire the board and staff.

Remember, when implementing your strategic plan, you should stay tight on ends and loose on means.

Long-Range Planning, Business Planning, and Strategic Planning

Although many people use the terms *long-range planning* and *strategic planning* interchangeably, the two differ in their emphasis on the assumed environment. Long-range planning generally assumes that current knowledge about future conditions is sufficiently valid to ensure the plan's reliability over the duration of its implementation. In the 1950s and 1960s, for example, the U.S. economy was seen as relatively stable and somewhat predictable; therefore, long-range planning was both fashionable and useful. It was not uncommon for U.S. corporations to have large planning staffs developing long-range plans with highly detailed goals and strategies and with operational objectives identified over a 20-year time period or even longer. These days, only organizations that make enormous capital investments (i.e., corporations, governments, and the largest nonprofits) formulate plans that cover a period of several decades.

As it is typically thought of in the private sector, the third category of planning, *business planning*, assumes a flow of revenue that is predictable enough to borrow against. The traditional business plan sought to convince potential investors and lenders that a business activity would generate enough money to pay a return or to repay a loan. Today, business planning has become much more popular in the nonprofit sector as well, although rarely for the purpose of taking on debt. Instead, it is used for basic managerial discipline. A business plan must be grounded in strategy, but the emphasis of the document is weighted toward execution and includes more detail about the process of growth. A strategic plan may not include all of this detail, but it is nonetheless important for nonprofits to answer most of the questions answered in a business plan.

Strategic planning assumes that an organization must respond to an environment that is dynamic and difficult to predict. Although strategic plans are grounded in a long-term vision, they must position an organization to successfully respond to changes in the environment, including changes by competitors and collaborators. The emphasis is on overall direction, including milestones, rather than on drafting detailed multiyear implementation plans. In addition, the strategy for funding the organization is a fundamental element of a sound strategic plan.

We see strategic planning as the most comprehensive of the three kinds of planning. Strategic plans are grounded in a long-term vision, require a clearly articulated business model, and provide additional flexibility by articulating midterm goals and objectives, with annually updated operational plans.

Incorporating a Business Planning Approach into Your Strategic Plan

Traditionally, few nonprofits have been able to borrow money to fund operations, largely because their operations did not generate predictable revenue streams. Non-profits did not spend money they did not have; rather, they raised money from grants and contributions and then spent it. However, as more nonprofits have begun to manage revenue-generating activities and the demand for more visibility into the finances of nonprofits has increased, the use of a business planning orientation has increased.

Most nonprofits are unable to provide the kind of detail forecasts anticipated in private-sector business plans because of the unpredictability of many of their revenue streams. Even so, business planning—that is, thinking of operations in terms of financial sustainability should be incorporated into a strategic plan. Organizations should ask such questions as, Do we have a sustainable business strategy? What are the assumptions on which our strategy is based? Do the current and future political, economic, social, technological, and demographic trends support the sustainability of our current business strategy?

Part of strategic analysis is to define the organization's business model, which articulates the organization's business strategy—how it plans to fund itself. An organization that plans to continue receiving 90 percent government funding for its services might articulate its business model as "Delivering X services, subsidized primarily by government funding, supplemented by a modest amount of foundation and private contributions." A business model requires a clear understanding about both where money comes from and where it goes. Many organizational budgets break out expenses by salaries, rent, and so forth, for the organization as a whole, but don't have a clear idea of how much is spent on each program individually. Such clarity is required to articulate a business model that matches funding sources to the services provided. In Step 6 we focus in depth on the business model of a nonprofit in the context of strategic planning.

Strategic Planning Is Organization Development

Capacity Building   In the past two decades, we have seen enormous growth in attention to capacity building for nonprofit organizations. Strategic planning has long been one of the most common and most impactful of the various capacity-building activities undertaken by nonprofits.[7] Other activities include strengthening internal management (such as through new information technology), reorganization, team building, leadership development, and board development. Organizations employ many external resources, including books, training programs, conferences, learning communities, and consultants, in order to build their capacity.

Moreover, studies show that nonprofits use these various capacity-building activities nearly as often as do private-sector companies. For example, the 2011 management tools survey by the global consulting firm Bain & Company found that 89 percent of its private sector clients had conducted strategic planning within the previous year or two. And in the first of its kind study of nonprofit organizations, modeled after the Bain & Company study, The Bridgespan Group found that 89 percent of its respondents used strategic planning.[8]

Strategic planning builds capacity in three ways: First, a clear direction supports the intentional use of resources, making the best use of capacity. Second, strategic planning often calls for investment in various dimensions of an organization's capacity, such as program evaluation, financial management, personnel training, or capital improvements. Finally, and just as important, strategic planning actually improves nonprofit functioning. It does this by strengthening communication, building confidence in shared values, and employing the entire organizational

---

[7] Paul C. Light, "The Case for Capacity Building and the National Infrastructure to Support It," Working paper, Wagner School of Public Service, New York University, 2004.

[8] Carttar, Paul, Chris Lindquist, Amy Markham, *Nonprofit Management Tools and Trends 2014*, The Bridgespan Group, Boston, MA, 2015.

system to make the most important decisions, building greater investment and buy-in from all concerned.

Change Management When an organization pivots to a new strategy, the strategic planning process sets the stage for successful change. Core principles of successful change management are inherent in strategic planning. One of the early and still most prolific researchers and authors on change management is John P. Kotter, author of the seminal book *Leading Change*. In this book, Kotter names eight stages in the change process, beginning with Establishing a Sense of Urgency and ending with Anchoring New Approaches in the Culture.[9] Strategic planning as we describe it encompasses each of these eight principles.

Systematically engaging internal stakeholders in the process informs and helps create credibility for the resulting strategies. An organization actually begins the process of moving in new directions even before the plan is completed, as understanding and agreement are built through the leadership and the rest of the organization.

Time and Money Required for Strategic Planning

A useful strategic plan may be sketched out in a few hours at no cost, may be completed at a one- or two-day retreat for several hundred or a few thousand dollars, or may take six to nine months to create and cost more than $100,000. Many factors influence the cost and time required for an organization to do strategic planning. (In fact, sometimes it is more expensive to take less time, because more of the work needs to be outsourced.) Taken together, these factors can be weighed and balanced to develop an appropriate planning process:

1. *The level of complexity and the depth of the questions to be answered.* The larger the organization and the more dynamic its environment, the more in-depth planning is required.

2. *How much time and money is available or can be made available for planning.* It pays to be realistic. The ranges of available money and time are usually relatively narrow, and these ranges should be respected and used as meaningful constraints.

3. *Familiarity and comfort with planning.* The strategic plan of a relatively large organization that has undergone a major leadership change or has not done formal strategic planning in many years is likely to require more work. However, if leadership is comfortable with planning and an organization has a well-developed annual program and budget planning routine, much of

[9] John P. Kotter, *Leading Change* (Boston: Harvard Business School Press, 1996). The eight stages of the change process are (1) establishing a sense of urgency, (2) creating the guiding coalition, (3) developing a vision and strategy, (4) communicating the change vision, (5) empowering employees for broad-based action, (6) communicating the change vision, (7) consolidating gains and producing more change, and (8) anchoring new approaches in the culture.

the information needed for strategic planning may be readily available, thus shrinking both the time and cost of a strategic planning effort.

4. *Type of organization.* Although strategic planning is often supported through technical assistance grants, it is simply more useful and appropriate for some organizations than others to invest a lot of money in strategic planning. One 50-year-old organization with a multimillion-dollar budget had not deeply examined its mission and program mix in decades. It received a $100,000 grant to support a two-year planning process that also covered the cost of staff time devoted to the planning process. A small and/or young organization may not be comfortable spending even $5,000 for a planning process lasting a few months, when its entire operating budget is less than $200,000.

Other factors that will affect the amount of time needed to do strategic planning are as follows:

- *The degree of commitment to the current mission statement.* Is there a fundamental agreement about the purpose, mission, and guiding principles of the organization? Is there a shared vision of the impact the organization wants to have in the world and what the organization would need to do to accomplish that result? If so, then the mission statement may only need polishing; if not, a full day or more may need to be devoted to this task.

- *The amount of new information that needs to be gathered in order to make informed decisions.* How well do planners currently understand the strengths, weaknesses, opportunities, and threats facing the organization? How current is feedback on the organization's programs and services from outside stakeholders, such as clients, funders, or community leaders? What information is needed to assess the competitive environment and the effectiveness of current programs?

- *The level of agreement on priorities.* How much agreement or disagreement currently exists with regard to the overall direction and allocation of resources? Is there agreement about which clients to serve and which services are most important? Are there power struggles over competing internal resource needs for program services, facilities, development, staff, and so on?

- *The level of trust among and between the staff and board.* The level of trust among all of the key stakeholders involved in the planning process can significantly hinder, or greatly support, the discussion of differences and the management of conflict.

- *Involvement of key stakeholders.* How much time and energy needs to be spent involving key stakeholders in the planning process in order to get both their input and their support for decisions made during the planning process?

- *The size of the organization.* Is there only one service provided, or does the organization provide a variety of services that need to be assessed? Does the organization have one department, or do many departments need to be involved in the planning process?

STRATEGIC PLANNING IS ALIVE AND WELL!

After a newspaper obituary reported him dead, Mark Twain famously responded wryly, "The report of my death was an exaggeration."

It is popular now to say that strategic planning is dead, no longer relevant, the world is changing too fast, and that even a three-year plan is unrealistic. In 1994, the year before the first edition of this book was published, Professor Henry Mintzberg published his book *The Rise and Fall of Strategic Planning* and ushered in a steady stream of articles and books joining this chorus.

So why all of this hand-wringing? Two primary and legitimate, complaints surface most. The first is that strategic planning is difficult and is sometimes not done well. The process requires not just time and money but also skill and meaningful leadership, a willingness to make difficult decisions, and the stamina to develop in sufficient detail the operational implications of an inspiring vision. The second problem is that many things in the world around us are changing at breakneck speed. It is tempting to declare that developing a meaningful strategic plan is impossible because it will be out of date by the time it is completed.

To say that because strategic planning is difficult and the world is rapidly changing the process is *fundamentally* no longer relevant or useful is a logical fallacy. In fact, research reveals that a great majority of organizations are ignoring these prognostications. The Bain & Company's 2011 Management Tools survey of 1,230 businesses in 70 countries found that two thirds of respondents used strategic planning (second highest) and that it had the highest satisfaction rating among the 25 most used management tools.[10] And a recent national study among 1,000 US nonprofits found that the more effective an organization, the more value it reports getting from strategic planning.[11] Why are leading nonprofits and large businesses continuing to use strategic planning when it is so maligned?

The short answer is that creating change and accomplishing important things, rather than responding to change, doesn't happen overnight. People need to know where they are headed for more than three or six months at a time. It usually takes years of hard work to launch a new company or nonprofit. Increasingly

---

[10] Rigby, Darell and Barbara Bilodeau. Management Tools and Trends 2011. Bain and Company. 2011.

[11] D. McNerney, D., Perri, and M. Reid, *Strategic Planning Practices in High Performing Nonprofit Organizations (501c3)*. Research results from national survey sponsored by Association for Strategic Planning (ASP) with University of Arkansas. Presented April 23, 2013, at the ASP National Conference, Atlanta, GA.

organizations are doing multiyear budgeting. Thirty-year mortgages remain the norm in residential real estate. While the world changes people continue to make long-term plans.

In a recent *Wall Street Journal* bestseller, *Playing to Win: How Strategy Really Works*, eminent business leaders A.G. Lafley and Roger Martin writing about naysayers declare: "They deny that long-term (or even medium-term) strategy is possible. . . . Emergent strategy has become the battle cry of many technology firms and startups, which do indeed face a rapidly changing marketplace. Unfortunately, such an approach places a company in a reactive mode, making it easy prey for more-strategic rivals."[12]

Organizations understand that moving from good to great demands both great focus with regard to *strategy* and clear *plans* to guide execution. While a specific path to be taken by an organization—the plan—will need to be adapted as the situation inevitably changes, a clear vision and strategy will endure and is often critical to navigating changing conditions successfully.

The practice of strategic planning in the nonprofit sector has, without a doubt, become more sophisticated and nuanced in the past two decades as expectations of organizational performance, management, and governance have steadily increased. However, the fundamentals of strategic planning have not changed dramatically, nor have they become any less useful. The death of strategic planning is an exaggeration.

STRATEGIC PLAN GUIDES ORGANIZATION THROUGH THE GREAT RECESSION

In June of 2008, the board of the San Diego Museum of Art (SDMA) adopted a strategic plan that included significant investments in art and facilities from their endowment and a major capital campaign for a new building. Two and a half months later, on September 15, came the collapse of Lehman Brothers Holdings and the start of the "Great Recession." SDMA's endowment lost 40 percent of its value within the next six months and major gifts disappeared. This turn of events, shall we say, was not part of the plan. Would they throw the plan out the window?

SDMA was created after the 1915 Panama Exhibition and had become a well respected museum with a good collection and strong endowment. The board and Executive Director had bold dreams of becoming one of the best museums in the country built around an international perspective, taking full advantage of being on the border of Mexico, a gateway to Asia and their strong partnerships with leading museums in Italy, France and Russia. To accomplish this vision would require investing several million dollars from the endowment in immediate upgrades, a signature art purchase

---

[12] Lafeley, A.G., Roger L. Martin. *Playing to Win: How Strategy Really Works*. Boaton, MA: Harvard Business Review Press. 2013. A.G. Lafley is the former Chairman and CEO of Proctor and Gamble. Roger L. Martin is the Dean of the Rotman School of Management.

and new staffing as well as the capital campaign to modernize and expand their beautiful, but aging facility.

By the end of 2008, rather than investing in growth, the board and staff agreed they needed to cut more than two million dollars from their operating budget for the next fiscal year. Great uncertainty prevailed and projections for when the economy might turn up again ranged from 6 months to 5 years!

The board and staff created a transitional planning group to assess their options. This board-staff leadership body had an impressive level of sophistication, perseverance and general good will. They did not look for people to blame; they sought solutions. Remarkably, this group did not see their plan as irrelevant in light of this dramatic change in the environment—*they simply realized that some of the specific planned actions as well as the time frame for their plan would need to be adjusted.* Their commitment to the fundamental vision and strategy had been fire tested and came out as polished and strong as one of their ancient pieces of ceramic pottery.

In the end, rather than being made obsolete by the dramatic turn of events, the strategic plan drove these tough decisions *because they had established clear direction and priorities.* Plans to phase out certain programs were made. Staff and volunteer roles were carefully rebalanced. While painful, in some ways the cuts in staff and programming moved SDMA toward their vision more quickly by accelerating planned changes that would have been made more methodically. Urgency demanded action.

Just a few years later, with a new executive director (hired from a prestigious museum in Mexico), an endowment that had substantially recovered and a rejuvenated board, SDMA was again moving full steam toward their vision of nationally recognized excellence with an international perspective. And, according to the chairperson of the Strategic Planning Committee, the strategic plan remains as the guidebook to their future!

First Steps

In Section 1: First Steps, the first three steps of the strategic planning process take place and get things off to a solid start. In Step 1: Set Up for Success, readiness is assessed, planning outcomes are identified, and a workplan for the strategic planning process is completed. In Step 2: Stakeholder Engagement, the planning process is grounded in the input from internal stakeholders (primarily board and staff) and input is sought, or planned for, from external stakeholders. In Step 3: Mission, Vision, Values, the strategic planning committee clarifies its guidance with respect to organizational purpose, its vision of success, and the core organizational values. At the conclusion of these three steps strategic planners should have clear focus for the work to do during Section 2: Strategic Analysis.

CHAPTER 1

Step 1: Set Up for Success

FIRST STEPS	STRATEGIC ANALYSIS	SET YOUR COURSE
1. Set up for Success	4. Environmental Scan	9. Complete the Strategic Plan
2. Stakeholder Engagement	5. Theory of Change and Program Portfolio	10. Use Your Plan Successfully
3. Mission, Vision, Values	6. Business Model	
	7. Organization Capacity	
	8. Leadership	

Strategic planning is a good idea in theory, but it is only a good idea in practice if the right people in an organization believe it is a good idea and the organization is ready. The initial worksheets to be used in Step 1 specify prerequisites for successful planning, as well as potential pitfalls to avoid. Chief among the prerequisites is a true commitment to the planning process by the executive director and board leadership. In other words, regardless of how much an organization needs to do some strategic planning, a sole program manager or board member will not be able to initiate a planning process alone or see that it happens successfully.

This does not mean that a lone visionary on the staff or board has no opportunity to initiate a strategic planning process, but it does mean that such an individual must actively recruit support from leaders by identifying the potential benefits to the organization and helping them see the need for planning. For example, is the staff aware of all the big changes happening in the program environment? Does the board shy away from seeking community support for the organization because it's unclear how it should measure the success of its efforts? Has the organization grown or shrunk significantly over the past few years? If the answer to these kinds of questions is yes, and it has been some time since any structured strategic planning has been done, then a compelling case for doing strategic planning can be made to the organization's leadership. Similarly, an enthusiastic executive director working with staff and board members who are reluctant to commit their time, energy, or money to strategic planning must look for ways to understand the organization's needs from their perspective.

Whoever initiates the strategic planning process must recognize that its success lies in building broad-based commitment, and this takes involvement from all parts of the organization. Therefore, the executive director and board president must be committed to planning, and must be willing to participate fully and invest the necessary organizational resources (time and money) to support the planning process. These two individuals, at a minimum, need to be clear on what they would like the planning process to accomplish, and they must assess the organization's readiness to conduct successful planning. If it makes sense to go forward, then proceed with forming a planning committee and get ready to succeed!

IDENTIFY OUTCOMES

Organizations considering a strategic planning process face one or more important decisions or choices, such as the following: What do we do about a potential loss in funding? Should we close down a program, change its focus, or explore a collaborative partnership? Should we buy a building or should we lease more space? Sometimes the need for a plan is more vague (we don't really know where we're going), and sometimes it is more concrete (our biggest funder is cutting its support next year). The reasons for planning—and the issues or choices that need to be addressed during the planning process—have a major impact on how to go about planning.

The questions highlighted in Worksheet 1.1 provide a framework for determining planning outcomes and issues. It is okay for the key issues and choices to be somewhat vague and/or overlapping; the planning process is designed to help bring clarity to the questions, as well as to create answers. If, however, the reasons for planning are not important ones, then the process will likely fizzle for lack of commitment. In that case, deciding not to plan, at least for now, is the right decision.

Once these issues and questions are drafted, make sure that strategic planning is the appropriate way to deal with them. A pressing need to address a cash shortfall may be very important, but it is immediate and does not have obvious strategic implications. Therefore, it is necessary to sort the issues into one of two categories. First, there are *strategic issues*, questions that have a longer-range focus (at least one to three years) and are fundamental issues regarding organizational ability to achieve its desired impact. The second category is *operational issues*, the questions that are shorter term (less than one year) in focus.

Why list nonstrategic issues at the beginning of a strategic planning process? The first reason is because some urgent, but operational, issues will be on planning committee members' minds. This provides a place to put these concerns. The second reason is that, when you step back, you may see strategic implications. For example: "Improve follow-through of the board on fundraising goals" is an operational issue, but it begs a larger question, "Is board fundraising a viable long-term revenue strategy for us?"

→ SEE WORKSHEET 1.1 TO ASSIST WITH THIS STEP.

WORKSHEET 1.1	IDENTIFY PLANNING PROCESS ISSUES AND OUTCOMES
How to do this activity?	Use the Planning Process Issues and Outcomes worksheet to: • List your expectations—what success will look like at the completion of the planning process, and what you hope to accomplish • Identify the strategic (longer-term) questions that need to be addressed during the planning process • List any operational issues (shorter-term) • Clarify whether any issues are nonnegotiable
Why do this activity?	• You have to agree on ends (what you wish to accomplish during the planning process) before you can agree on means (how you will go about planning). • The planning process is one of identifying strategic questions and then gathering information to answer those questions. • This worksheet helps to sort out—and make explicit—the issues and outcomes that often are assumed to be clear in everyone's mind.
Who to involve in the process?	Strategic Planning Committee (plus other key board and staff members, if their input would be helpful)

Both strategic issues and operational issues are important and will need to be addressed by the organization. Separating them can help determine whether certain operational issues need to be addressed before serious attention can be paid to the strategic issues or whether they can be handled concurrently. Any crisis situation will have to be brought under control before a strategic planning process is initiated.

Finally, if certain decisions are not up for discussion, then those decisions should be explicitly taken off the table. These nonnegotiable issues may be program-oriented ("We are not going to expand our geographic boundaries") or business-oriented ("Any new program effort must generate revenue"). Articulating nonnegotiable issues up front will help avoid wasting people's time or setting them up for unrealistic expectations about what they can and cannot change.

In Worksheet 1.1, we provide space for potential strategic issues in each of the five core dimensions. Most issues fall under one of these headings, and the worksheet provides a simple way to see whether you have identified all of the key issues you will want to address. The dimensions are as follows:

- *External environment.* What are the most important forces or changes in your environment to which your plan must respond?

- *Theory of change and program portfolio.* How well are you achieving your mission with your programs, and how could you have a greater impact?

- *Business model.* Are your operations financially viable, and how can you ensure the long-term financial stability and sustainability of your organization?

- *Organization capacity.* What would it take to maximize your organizational capabilities in terms of planning, human resources and leadership, organizational culture, and communication, and your technology and facilities infrastructure?

- *Leadership.* How well do your senior staff leaders and the board carry out their respective roles and work together?

CHECK CONDITIONS FOR SUCCESS

In addition to committed leadership, several other important criteria should be considered in determining readiness:

1. Commitment, support, and involvement of top leadership, especially the executive director and board president

2. Commitment to clarifying the roles of all participants in the planning process, including clarity about who will have input into the plan and who will be the decision makers

3. Balanced mix of individuals on the planning committee, from big-picture visionaries to a detail-oriented thinkers group that is committed to full participation and is likely to be able to work well together (including the ability to disagree with each other)

4. Willingness to encourage participation of board, staff, and as appropriate, external stakeholders

5. Commitment of organizational resources to complete the planning process as designed (including time of staff and board members, money for consultants, and needed research)

6. Board and staff who understand the purpose of planning and are clear about the desired process outcomes and issues to be addressed

7. A willingness to question the status quo and look at new ways of doing things, along with a willingness to ask the hard questions and face difficult choices

8. No serious conflict exists between key players within the organization.

9. No high-impact decision (e.g., a major funding or policy decision) is about to be made by an external source that would dramatically change the course of the organization.

10. Organization is not in the middle of merger discussions.

11. Board and top management are willing to articulate constraints and non-negotiable issues up front.

12. Commitment to tying the strategic planning process to the organization's annual planning and budgeting process

These conditions for success are highlighted in Worksheet 1.2 and form the readiness assessment.[1]

→ SEE WORKSHEET 1.2 TO ASSIST WITH THIS STEP.

WORKSHEET 1.2	**SET YOUR PLANNING PROCESS UP FOR SUCCESS**
How to do this activity?	• Before embarking on a strategic planning process, make sure the conditions for successful planning are in place. Check yes or no in the conditions checklist. Explain any negative responses.
	• Decide whether to proceed with planning: go or no go. If significant barriers exist that might impede the process, deal with those barriers before continuing.
Why do this activity?	Helps you decide whether you are ready to embark on a planning process or whether strategic planning is the appropriate management tool to use
Who to involve in the process?	Executive director and board president (plus other key board and staff members, if their input would be helpful)

If some of the conditions for success are missing, then an in-depth strategic planning process may not be appropriate at this time. Even if an organization is halfway through the planning process before realizing that it wasn't ready to plan, it should stop and reassess how to proceed. Consider the following situations:

- "Fall is our busiest time of the year. We should wait until spring." This is easy: Wait.

- "We won't know what is going to happen to our most important funder [or competitor, constituency, customer base] until X happens next year." In this case, program planning for the coming year is appropriate, but a longer-range strategic plan will be difficult to create without serious work on contingency planning.

---

[1] Adapted from George Steiner, *Strategic Planning* (New York: Free Press, 1979), p. 290–293.

- "As a result of some initial planning discussions, we have initiated merger discussions with another organization." Here, the initial strategic planning process has already defined a possible fundamental strategy: merge. The organization should wait until the merger discussions are completed, and then the new entity's board and staff should engage in a joint effort.

If the lack of readiness has to do with a lack of commitment to planning, a lack of commitment to inclusiveness, or a lack of willingness to consider new possibilities, then the situation is more difficult. Sometimes it is possible to influence the strategic planning orientation of the individuals in question. However, sometimes it just doesn't make sense to conduct strategic planning until the players change. An executive director might wait until after the next board election, or a board might have to assess whether an executive director's lack of leadership in this area is enough of a problem to warrant finding a new executive director. In these situations, the readiness assessment is a judgment call, as is the decision about how to respond to a suspected lack of readiness.

If current problems might interfere with the ability of top leadership to focus on the future, then either delay the strategic planning process or abbreviate the planning process to allow some overall strategic thinking to take place that doesn't require in-depth data gathering or discussions at the present time. Alternately, two parallel planning processes could take place—one that addresses the immediate issues and one that focuses on the larger strategic issues. Top leadership must be involved with the strategic issues.

In most cases, though, the assessment serves as a guide to potential problems in the process, so they can be addressed or confirmed. By addressing readiness criteria, the strategic planning committee can focus attention on setting up the planning process to be successful.

PLAN FOR DATA COLLECTION

If strategic planning is to achieve the strategic and organizational benefits we have discussed, then the process must be informed by relevant data—both objective facts as well as opinions from stakeholders. A stakeholder is anyone who cares about the organization, anyone who has an investment, a "stake," in the success of its mission. This encompasses those who must implement the strategic plan, those who benefit from its implementation, and those who could significantly help or hinder its implementation.

Part of the thoughtfulness and creativity of the strategic planning process can lie in identifying individuals and groups who traditionally might not be regarded as stakeholders and involving them in the process. This might include those who can contribute unique and valuable perspectives, as well as those who should be included because of other substantive or political reasons. A truly inclusive process can achieve the following:

- Help build internal and external enthusiasm for and commitment to the organization and its strategies. Those who feel they have contributed to the planning process will feel invested in it and are more likely to take ownership of the organization's goals and efforts.

- Add objectivity to the process. Outsiders can identify jargon or ask critical questions about issues that insiders might assume to be common knowledge or may simply take for granted.

- Develop the foundation for future working relationships

- Establish a continuous exchange of information among staff, management, clients, and other key stakeholders

- Ensure an adequate depth and breadth of data from which to make informed decisions

These internal and external stakeholders will have different levels of participation and various roles in the planning process. It is especially important to be clear about which stakeholders are providing input and which are making decisions. Being asked an opinion is not the same as having a final say in related decisions, but stakeholders sometimes lose sight of that distinction. Leaders need to let participants who provide input know what was done with their information and the rationale for the decisions that were made.

The nature of stakeholders' participation will depend on several factors, such as an organization's size, culture and management style, range of constituents, breadth of services, and so on, but the following are some general understandings of specific stakeholders' roles in the strategic planning process.

Internal stakeholders include the board of directors, executive director and senior staff, other staff and volunteers, and advisory boards.

External stakeholders include people you serve, those with whom you partner, funders, and other people or organizations whose support is required to move the organization's vision forward. Identifying how and when to involve external stakeholders is an important activity when designing your planning process. External stakeholders have perspectives that inform your strategic decisions and can help build a closer relationship between key stakeholders and your organization. Most people are honored to be asked their opinion about your organization's future. Stakeholder Engagement is the focus of Step 2. At this stage of planning Data Collection, your task is simply to anticipate the ways you might involve stakeholders to incorporate what would be required to do so into your work plan.

→ SEE WORKSHEET 1.3 TO ASSIST WITH THIS STEP.

WORKSHEET 1.3	DEVELOP A PRELIMINARY PLAN FOR GATHERING INFORMATION
How to do this activity?	Using the strategic planning outcomes and issues identified in Worksheet 1.1, brainstorm a list of internal and external stakeholders from whom you wish to get input. After identifying all possible stakeholders, clarify what you wish to accomplish by involving each stakeholder group, as well as ideas for how to best involve them.
Why do this activity?	Although you won't actually do most of the information gathering until the Strategic Analysis section, developing an initial plan is important, because it helps define the scope and scale of the data collection process. Understanding the information needs, you are better able to design a successful strategic planning process.
Who to involve in the process?	The strategic planning committee identifies the internal and external stakeholders and suggests processes to get the information that is needed. After the initial brainstormed list of stakeholders is created, additional input into the data-gathering process sometimes is sought from board and staff members who are not on the committee.

ANTICIPATING OTHER NEEDED RESEARCH

Most of the needed research will be conducted later, so a detailed assessment of research is not needed at this point. However, the team should identify whether any extraordinary research or engagement will require additional expense or special arrangements and can be factored into the workplan. Examples of significant efforts that may need advance planning include an extensive market study, an assessment of your fund development function, or a broad-based series of focus groups to gather input from external stakeholder groups.

It is helpful to gather any documents or other information that will provide needed background for the strategic planning committee all in one place. Examples of this type of information include mission-related documents, financial documents, organizational capacity documents, and leadership documents.

Mission-related documents include:

- Mission, vision, values statements
- Your current strategic plan
- Annual plans

- Program descriptions/workplans
- Needs assessments
- Client satisfaction surveys
- Previous evaluation designs and results
- Evidence of the organization's innovation or reputation in the field
- Other data on major developments in the field

Financial documents include:

- Fundraising plans and results
- Budgets
- Audits
- Recent financial reports

Organizational capacity documents include:

- Your organizational chart
- Internal newsletters or other communication vehicles
- Personnel policies
- Previous organizational effectiveness surveys and/or climate surveys (or other formal review of culture and staff satisfaction)
- Volunteer management plans
- Information technology plans

Leadership documents include:

- Information on senior team membership backgrounds
- Details on any existing leadership development activities
- Board development plans
- Board minutes
- Board roster and details on committee structure
- Previous board self-evaluations
- Your board manual

DESIGN YOUR STRATEGIC PLANNING PROCESS

Whether you are working with a planning consultant to design your strategic planning process or are designing the process in-house, you will want to design a planning process that meets your organization's specific needs. Consider previous strategic planning endeavors and what has worked or not worked. Our whole approach is participatory, thus we assume that a strategic planning committee will be formed. In addition to a committee, you should address the following process design choices:

- Who will lead the process?
- Who will be on the strategic planning committee?
- Who makes which decisions? That is, who will decide the strategic direction for the organization, and what degree of input will be sought from the board and staff?
- How intensive will the process be? Will it be abbreviated, moderate, or extensive?
- How will you involve external stakeholders?
- What will be the use and timing of retreats or other large group gatherings?
- Who will be the primary writer of the plan? This may occur with guidance from a consultant if necessary.
- Will you use a consultant? If so, how will you best use the consultant, and what are your expectations with regard to the consultant's role?
- How will board and staff be kept informed about the strategic planning discussions?

Who Will Lead the Process?

Usually, either the board president or the executive director led the strategic planning process, but sometimes a board member may be appointed chair of the planning committee, or a senior staff representative may hold the leadership.

Who Will Be on the Strategic Planning Committee?

An effective committee includes six to eight individuals. The committee can be larger if there is a need to include a broader representation of stakeholders. However, a committee that is too large—comprising more than 12 members—may make it more difficult to coordinate meetings and to have discussions. The committee should combine visionaries (people who see what the organization can be and can rally the organization around that vision) with action-oriented members (people who will ensure that the projected goals and tasks are realistic). It should comprise a diverse group of staff and board members who are committed to a vision for the common good, rather than just advocating for the particular population they represent. As a group, the committee should have informal power and the respect of the entire organization.

Use of Subcommittees and Task Forces

Research and initial analysis will be done outside of the meetings of the strategic planning committee. This work can be assigned to staff, or it can be a board–staff team. Another approach that is very valuable for a few major and complex decisions is to assign a task force to investigate and propose both alternative answers and, if they can, specific recommendations for the full strategic planning committee to consider.

Who Makes Which Decisions?

It is important to determine whether you will have a top-down or a bottom-up process. A top-down process assumes that those with the highest level of responsibility in an organization are in the best position to be big-picture thinkers and to plan what is best for the organization. This approach is more expedient and can be an appropriate exercise of leadership. The main drawback to this approach is that it often results in plans that do not have the understanding and support of line staff (those most directly involved in providing services to clients), and the plan may not prove feasible or in the best interests of the clients. A bottom-up planning process starts with input from individual staff members or departments, thereby addressing the need for staff input and investment. Such a process, however, can produce a patchwork plan that lacks coherence for the organization as a whole and results in an uncoordinated, possibly even wasteful, use of resources.

For most organizations, the best strategy seems to be a hybrid approach, one that strikes a balance between the need for decisive leadership and productive collaboration, featuring the open communication of a bottom-up planning process as well as the clear coordination of a top-down process. The net result is an effective combination of the best of both models of participation. The planning process described in this workbook is such a hybrid.

Regardless of the flow of decision making for the organization, the board in its governance role approves the final planning document.

Will You Hold Retreats and Large Group Gatherings?

Although they are not required, retreats and large group gatherings can play a seminal role in a successful strategic planning process. Retreats with board, staff, or both can be held (1) at the beginning of a process, to gather input and build interest; (2) toward the middle, when proposals have been formed, to discuss and debate emerging proposals; or (3) toward the end, to bring closure and help shift energy toward putting the plan into action. Gatherings that include external stakeholders along with internal stakeholders can be organized in many ways, over one or more days, to spur creative thinking, allow for structured discussion among a wide range of constituencies, and help identify major issues and possible strategies. Because these events take advance planning, decide up front in what ways you will incorporate such events in developing the strategic planning schedule.

Who Will Be the Primary Writer of the Plan?

The primary writer of the plan should be the board or staff person who has the skill and time to do so. In certain circumstances, a consultant might assist in the writing of the plan, although this approach can be problematic if it results in staff and board members feeling that the plan is the consultant's alone and that they do not have ownership of the words and concepts.

Will You Use a Consultant?

Many organizations include an outside consultant in part or all of the planning process. An experienced strategic planning consultant can help you design the process, facilitate many discussions, serve as a project manager, and ensure that the written product meets your needs. On a more limited basis, consultants can facilitate retreats and meetings, serving as a neutral party so that good ideas do not get lost among the emotions or personalities of the participants. Organizations also look to consultants with specific expertise in the organization's field to assist with framing key issues and sometimes conducting necessary research.

When working with consultants, it is important to clearly define the scope of the project, identify the benefits expected for each party, and agree on responsibilities and mechanisms for accountability. The relationship must be one on which you can depend. Different situations allow for different ways to involve consultants.

When hiring consultants, consider the following tips:

- You may choose to use different consultants for different roles. For example, you may hire one consultant to facilitate the planning process and another to do some of the research.

- Interview at least two consultants. You will be able to explore different approaches to the project and may utilize the ideas of more than one consultant.

- For substantial projects, ask for references and a written price bid from each consultant interviewed.

- Agree on one person to whom the consultant will report. The process will get confusing if different people are asking for different things.

- Have a written memorandum of understanding or contract with the consultant, with payments based on the consultant's performance of agreed-upon tasks.

- Throughout the project, give the consultant feedback about his or her work.

- If the organization is working with other consultants, make sure the other consultants and the planning consultant are informed of each other's work and are coordinating efforts.

- Do not expect a consultant to make tough decisions or value-based choices for you. A consultant can help articulate alternative courses of action and the implications of various choices, but the organization's decision makers should make the important decisions.

- Agree in advance on how you will pay the consultant's fees, including any overruns.

How Will Board and Staff Be Kept Informed About Strategic Planning Discussions?

Thought should be put into deciding how the board and staff will be kept informed about discussions and decisions during the planning process. It is not advised to wait until the last minute or to keep everyone in the dark about the strategic decisions that are being made.

The initial leaders of the planning process can use Worksheet 1.4 to consider what the planning process might look like and the expected roles and authority of board, staff, external stakeholders, and consultants.

→ **SEE WORKSHEET 1.4 TO ASSIST WITH THIS STEP.**

WORKSHEET 1.4   CHOICES TO CONSIDER WHEN DEVELOPING A PLANNING WORKPLAN

How to do this activity?	Answer each of the questions on the worksheet, taking into consideration the thinking that went into the previous three worksheets. What planning processes will best help your organization achieve its planning outcomes, ensure a successful planning process, and involve appropriate stakeholders?
Why do this activity?	By designing a process that meets your specific organizational needs, you will be able to develop a plan for planning that can be successfully implemented.
Who to involve in the process?	The strategic planning committee—either on its own or with a consultant—answers the planning process questions. After a workplan is developed, the board of directors should approve it.

Write a Planning Workplan

The planning committee is now ready to finalize an overall workplan to manage the planning effort (this is the plan to plan). The workplan should outline the activities involved over the course of the entire planning process, the processes to be used for all activities (such as interviews and retreats), the people responsible for executing or overseeing those tasks, the desired outcomes, the resources required (e.g., time and money), and time frames. The more clarity you have with regard to what activities are needed, who is involved, who is responsible for overseeing and ensuring that an activity happens, the process you will use, by when it should be completed, and products to deliver, the more your planning process can be managed effectively and efficiently.

In the first appendix we provide sample workplans for three different levels of intensity in a strategic planning process: abbreviated, moderate and extensive. As noted earlier we believe meaningful planning can be done in a wide range of constraints - in these workplans we suggest the most important activities in each time frame.

CREATE AN ORGANIZATION PROFILE

An organization profile establishes the baseline—where you are starting. For members of the strategic planning committee who do not have a grasp of the complete organization, this profile is educational. For others, it provides a brief high-level summary of the outlines of your organization: key dates, top leadership, and important programs.

→ SEE WORKSHEET 1.5 TO ASSIST WITH THIS STEP.

WORKSHEET 1.5	ORGANIZATION PROFILE
Why do this activity?	To provide a snapshot baseline of where your organization is now as you plan for the future
How to do this activity?	Answer each of the questions on the worksheet, providing a thorough high-level summary of history, leadership, program, and funding model.
Who to involve in the process?	Executive director, share with strategic planning committee

CAUTIONS FOR FACILITATORS

Facilitators should be aware of and work to avoid the following pitfalls during the strategic planning process:

Step 1: Set up for Success

Going ahead when not ready. The readiness assessment is a critical step, so take these issues seriously or the likelihood of failure looms ahead.

Taking too little or too much time. Certainly, not giving enough time to planning is a problem, but many people hold an unconscious bias that more time equals more value. Time is not the same thing as attention. Be realistic about the quality of attention required from senior leaders for valuable planning to take place.

Find the right consultant. If you are using a consultant, or if you are the consultant, take care to ensure that there is a good match between the skills and consulting style offered and the organization's needs.

> ### WORKSHEET 1.1   Identify Planning Process Issues and Outcomes
>
> ❏ What would success look like at the completion of the planning process? What does your organization wish to achieve from a planning process?
>
> ❏ What issues or choices do you think need to be addressed during the planning process?
>
> ❏ Are there any nonnegotiables that need to be articulated up front? Any constraints regarding the planning process?

What would success look like at the completion of the planning process? What do we wish to achieve from a planning process?

- *A plan that would enable us to communicate to our current and future supporters as well as to staff and board what we want to accomplish over the next three to five years*

- *Willingness to look at new and different ways of doing things*

- *Staff and board working together more effectively*

- *Greater board engagement*

- *We need a plan that carefully examines not only our programmatic goals but also what infrastructure is needed to be in place to support those goals.*

- *As part of our strategic planning process, we need to figure out how to better define what success is in our programs— moving beyond outputs (numbers of clients given advice or represented in court) to outcomes (either a win in their case, or did we prevent the eviction, or at least keep the family in their home for three extra months). We are facing a lot of pressure from funders (both government and foundations) to define what outcomes our services will result in and how we will predict and then measure whether we achieved the outcomes. Hopefully we can be better at defining outputs as part of our planning process, so that when funders ask about outcomes measurements, we can rely (easily and comfortably) on the strategic plan.*

Many of the strategic issues discussed during a strategic planning process address fall under these five categories:

1. *External Environment.* Are there some important forces or changes in our external environment to which our plan must respond? (Are there political, economic, social, demographic, technological, or legal forces that are significantly impacting our organization?)

2. *Mission.* Are we achieving our mission with our current portfolio of programs, and how could we have a greater impact?

3. *Business Model.* Are our operations financially viable, and how can we ensure the long-term financial stability and sustainability of our organization?

4. *Organizational Capacity.* What would it take to maximize our organizational capabilities in terms of our human resources, information systems, financial reporting, organizational structure, organization culture and communication, PR and marketing, program evaluation, planning, and our technology and facilities infrastructure?

5. *Leadership.* How well do our senior staff leaders and the board carry out their respective roles and work together? Are we paying sufficient attention to building an organization that promotes leadership?

What are the **specific strategic questions or choices** that our organization wants to address during the planning process?

Strategic (longer term) issues to be addressed—framed as a question:
How do we better serve the needs of residents who live in the southern corridor of our county? Currently, our two offices are located in the Northeast and Central regions of the county, which means that people who live in the southern parts of our county have limited help. In addition, we have started to receive requests for our services from individuals in neighboring Valley County. They report that the current legal aid program is not able to provide quality services. What should we do to ensure that residents in both counties receive the legal assistance they need?
What should be our future areas of law to focus on, and who should we serve? Should we only provide services in our current four program areas? Should we continue to offer limited legal assistance in the area of Consumer Issues? Are there other areas that we should focus our energies on, such as disability access, legal issues that face frail elders, helping military families, responding to disasters, immigration issues? Are we offering services in specific areas of law because of historical reasons (our attorneys are comfortable in those areas) or because those are the areas of law where the populations we are serving truly have the greatest need?
In order to achieve our mission, we offer services along a continuum of intensity and depth. At one end (the "light" touch) is the creation of informational materials for laypeople about legal topics that a legal aid program might make available online and in hard copy through the community. At the other end (the most intense services) is impact work—either class action litigation or legislative/policy work to change the laws. How much should we focus on either end of the continuum, and how much on all the work in between? Currently, we cover the full range of: advice and counsel, brief services, limited scope, full-scope representation, and impact work. In particular, how much of an advocacy role do we want CLAS to play, and how do we fund such activities?
How do we maximize the involvement of law firms in supporting us both financially and through the donation of volunteer attorneys to help in providing services to our clients? And, if we are able to access many of the private-sector resources in our community, we need to make sure we have sufficient volunteer management capacity.
Our reserves are slowly dwindling, and we have not been able to keep up with costs. How can we maximize the involvement of our board of directors in raising necessary resources to support our work, and what can we do to bring our costs in line with our resources while meeting increasing need for our services?
What do we do about the fact that our long-term executive director is planning to retire in the next few years?

(continued)

WORKSHEET 1.1 *(continued)*

We have recently experienced a higher degree of attorney and other staff turnover than we have in the past. What can we do in the long term to retain qualified staff? How can we ensure that our staff and board reflect the populations that we serve?
Is our current infrastructure sufficient to provide sufficient support for our program activities? While our programming and budget has dramatically grown over the last few years, we tend to still operate in start-up mode in terms of our investment in core infrastructure—from IT to HR operations, etc.
What is our future revenue model (the mix of grants, private-sector funding, individuals, etc.)? When we started, 85 percent of our budget was from government sources, but now it is less than 40 percent.
Short-term focus: Are there some operational questions that need to be addressed in the near future? If yes, list below: (These issues are not necessarily linked to the longer-term issues above).
We currently have three vacancies on our board. We need to fill those positions. In addition, our board is not very involved these days; perhaps we need to do some training on roles and responsibilities. Also, greater board engagement is a huge issue. We currently don't have term limits but should consider implementing them, and some of our board seem to be disengaged—often attendance at board meetings and even getting quorum can be an issue. And given the revenue shifts over the last 15 years with decreasing government funding, our board needs to be more of a fundraising board, and that may need shifts in expectations, board culture, and skills.
Our Northeast office lease is up at the end of the year, and we need to decide whether to renew or find another location. Staff feels that our current office is too small and are advocating for a larger facility.
Attorneys are spending too much time doing administrative work; we need to hire at least one additional support staff in both offices.
We have had the same auditor doing our audit for the last 10 years, and we have been told that it may be a good idea to change auditors after such a long period. Should we seriously look at hiring another accounting firm?
None of our informational and reference materials are in languages other than English. Given the high percentage of our clients who speak Spanish, shouldn't we get all of our materials translated into Spanish?
We have seen an increase in staff complaints about their supervisors.

Are any issues nonnegotiable (not open for discussion)? Any constraints regarding the planning process that we need to address as part of our preplanning thinking?

A nonnegotiable is that we will not handle criminal cases. Also, we should probably not change our income eligibility levels.

WORKSHEET 1.2 Set Up Your Planning Process for Success

❑ Are the conditions and criteria for successful planning in place at the current time? Can certain pitfalls be avoided?

❑ Is this the appropriate time for our organization to initiate a planning process? Yes or no? If no, where do we go from here?

	The Following Conditions for Successful Planning Are in Place:	Yes	No	Unsure or N/A
1	Commitment, support, and active involvement from top leadership, especially the executive director and board president	x		
2	Commitment to clarifying roles and expectations for all participants in the planning process, including clarifying who will have input into the plan and who will be the final decision makers	x		
3	Balanced mix of board and staff members on the Planning Committee—big-picture visionaries thinkers and detail-oriented thinkers—a group who is committed to participating fully, and is likely to be able to work together well (including the ability to disagree with each other)	x		
4	Willingness to encourage participation of board and staff and, as appropriate, external stakeholders	x		
5	Commitment of organizational resources to complete the planning process as designed, including time of staff and board members, money for consultants and needed research, etc.			*Need to find grant for consultant*
6	Board and staff understand the purpose of planning and have agreement regarding the desired outcomes of the process and the important issues to be addressed.			*Not sure board and staff are on same page*

(continued)

WORKSHEET 1.2 *(continued)*

7	A willingness to question the status quo, to look at new ways of doing things; a willingness to ask the hard questions and face difficult choices			*Some resistance to change*
8	No serious conflict between key players within the organization	x		
9	No high-impact decision (e.g., a major funding or policy change) is about to be made by an external source that would potentially and dramatically change the course of direction of the organization	x		
10	The organization is not in the middle of merger discussions	x		
11	Board and top management are willing to articulate constraints and nonnegotiable issues up front	x		
12	Intention to tie the strategic planning process to the organization's annual planning and budgeting process	x		

Other Issues/Concern That Would Influence the Success of the Planning Process

We have a lot on our plate, so we're concerned about how much time the planning process might take. Also, staff have questions about whether this is solely a board function and what role staff get to play (do they have a say?).

Based on your assessment, is this the appropriate time for our organization to initiate a planning process? Yes or No? If no, what steps need to be put in place to ensure a successful planning process—where do we go from here? Or, should the organization consider doing something other than a formal strategic planning process?

YES, it is the right time for us to do some planning, but we need to address some of the stated concerns.

| WORKSHEET 1.3 | Develop a Preliminary Plan for Gathering Information from Internal and External Sources |

❏ Using the strategic issues you identified in Worksheet 1.1, start to develop a plan for gathering information from both internal and external sources so as to answer those questions and get greater buy-in and support for the planning process and your plan.

Data Collection from Internal Stakeholders—How Might We Engage the Board and Staff and Other Internal Stakeholders?

Internal Stakeholders	Outcome of Contact with Them? (Such as perceptions about the organization, specific answers to strategic questions, greater buy-in and support for SP decisions, etc.	How Best to Involve Them (Such as surveys, discussions at regularly scheduled meetings, retreats, in-depth program evaluation worksheets, etc.)	Timing—What might be the best point in the process to engage this stakeholder group? Any early outreach required?
Staff Do we want to engage: All of the staff Management team Some staff (specific) Volunteer staff Entire department/ program units	Perceptions about the organization—yes Specific answers to strategic questions—yes Greater buy-in and support for strategic plan— definitely director of development and finance director should be on SP Committee. At least one department head should also be on the SP Committee and perhaps a junior attorney who can address some of the generational issues.	Surveys and meetings (small group and large, but not sure whether it's practical for all staff to come to a retreat that we want to hold sometime during the process—need to discuss pros and cons of such a large meeting) Departments need to do some program evaluation.	At our regular staff meeting, we should check in about staff's thoughts on strategic issues. We should start with an online survey about their perceptions of CLAS (SWOT analysis, visioning, etc.). Also, perhaps we should do some type of staff climate survey to find out how staff are feeling about supervision, benefits, organization culture, etc.
Board of directors	Perceptions about the organization—yes	We should start with an online survey about board members' perceptions of	As soon as possible—We need to make sure entire board is fully committed to

(continued)

WORKSHEET 1.3 *(continued)*

	Specific answers to strategic questions—not sure degree of help Greater buy-in and support for strategic plan— definitely	CLAS (SWOT analysis, visioning, etc.).	this process and understand what their expectations are.
Others Do we want to engage others, such as advisory board members, former staff members, former board members, *etc.*?	Definitely should involve advisory board members.	Could they help us better understand community needs? Should we involve them through an advisory board retreat, individual meetings, or phone calls?	

Data Collection from External Stakeholders—How Might We Involve External Stakeholders?

External Stakeholder Group: (List specific names if possible)	Outcome of Contact with Them? Questions to answer? What information do we want to gather from this stakeholder? Is relationship building the primary reason to engage this stakeholder?	How Best to Involve Stakeholders (i.e., questionnaires, interviews [face-to-face or phone], focus groups, meetings, etc.)	Timing—What is the best point in the process to engage this stakeholder group? Any early outreach required?
Constituents/ Clients (current, past)	Clients are our best source of information in terms of quality of work, timely assistance, and how helpful we have been.	Continue to do client satisfaction surveys Perhaps one or two focus groups? Not sure if we should survey past clients—perhaps focus group	Certainly before we set future priorities
Institutional Funders	Relationship building, but also some of the funders	Consultant to do phone calls	Early on in the process

WORKSHEET 1.3 *(continued)*

(foundations, corporations, government agencies)	have unique perceptions in terms of the external environment. Also, would like to know their perceptions of our organization.		
Individual Donors	Relationship building	Have development director identify key large and/or long-term donors and do one-on-one phone interviews. SP Committee members to make phone calls; could we do a focus group?	Once we have a general sense of our future priorities, find out how likely they are to support any future endeavors, especially changes in services or growing our program.
Government Officials	We only have two government grants, but relationship building is always important, and they might be helpful in terms of external environment funding.	Have members of the SP Committee or consultant do the phone interviews.	
Partner Organizations	We have a few projects that we partner with other organizations—it's important that we know how their experience has been working with us.	Hopefully consultant will make calls.	As part of the program evaluation section
Others to Contact	We should contact some of our current pro bono volunteers about their experience working with us. Speak with some other nonprofits in the community who also focus on poverty and serving low-income communities.	Have all current pro bono volunteers fill out a survey, and have our consultant make calls to a few current and past volunteers. Someone from SP Committee to speak with other nonprofits.	As part of the program evaluation section

(continued)

WORKSHEET 1.3 *(continued)*

Which of the Following Documents Would Help Provide Important Background Information and/or Inform Our Strategic Issue Decisions? (*Check appropriate documents to assemble.*)

Program-Related Documents	**Organizational Capacity Documents**
• Mission, vision, values statements ✓ • Current strategic plan; annual plans ✓ • Program descriptions/workplans • Needs assessments ✓ • Client satisfaction surveys ✓ • Previous evaluation designs and results • Evidence of organization's innovation or reputation in the field • Other data on major developments in the field ✓	• Organizational chart ✓ • Internal newsletters or other communication vehicles • Personnel policies ✓ • Previous organizational effectiveness surveys and/or climate surveys (or other formal review of culture and staff satisfaction) ✓ • Volunteer management plan • Information technology plan • Previous strategic plans ✓
Financial-Related Documents	**Leadership Documents**
• Fundraising plans and results ✓ • Budgets ✓ • Audits ✓ • Recent financial reports ✓	• Senior team membership, background ✓ • Succession planning and leadership development documents • Board minutes ✓ • Board roster and committee structure ✓ • Previous board self-evaluations • Board manual

Other Data: Where else should we look outside of our organization for information about trends, competitors, innovative programming, etc.?

• *Foundation Center might have some information about legal aid grant making in our field and area.*

• *Charitynavigator and Guidestar have information on programs and finances of nonprofits, and may be able to shed light on neighboring counties' legal aid programs.*

• *Need to look at Legal Services Corporation's own strategic plan and its reports that document IOLTA (Interest on Lawyers' Trust Accounts) and other funding trends, as well as the range of services that IOLTA-funded programs offer.*

• *Census Bureau for number of people eligible to receive our services*

WORKSHEET 1.3 *(continued)*

- Recently released State Bar reports on (a) impact of economic downturn on hiring of attorneys of color and (b) low-income populations' access to civil legal aid system

- National reports by both NLADA (National Legal Aid and Defenders Association), the American Bar Association (particularly their Center on Pro Bono), and the national Association of Pro Bono Counsel (APBCo) will have information about funding and innovative programming.

SAMPLE WORKSHEET FOR CASE STUDY: COUNTY LEGAL AID SOCIETY (CLAS)

> ## WORKSHEET 1.4   Choices to Consider When Developing a Planning Workplan
>
> ❏ What has been our previous experience with strategic planning?
>
> ❏ What are some of the choices we want to consider when designing our strategic planning process?
>
> ❏ Are there other considerations that need to be factored into the writing of the strategic planning workplan?

What has been our previous experience with strategic planning—what has worked or not worked in the past that might inform the design of our strategic planning process?

Last time we did strategic planning was six years ago; it was the first time we seriously did some planning, but it was facilitated internally and, as such, we didn't make the hard choices that we should have made. Also, because it was facilitated internally, it exacerbated some tensions between the board and staff in terms of who gets to make these hard decisions: the board had some questions about whether program priorities needed to be updated or reexamined, and the staff was reluctant to look at making any real changes. Staff was, and still is, resistant to change—a lot of staff have been here for a long time. This time we really need to hire a consultant who can help us look at our organization in depth and perhaps make the hard choices needed moving forward.

Some of the choices we want to consider when designing our strategic planning process:

- **Who will lead the process?** *Led by a consultant and the executive director and board member who is chair of SP Committee (need to decide how these co-lead roles will play out in real life)*

- **Membership of Strategic Planning Committee?** *Three members of the board (president, chair of SP Committee, and one other board member) and five members of the staff (executive director, finance director, development director, and attorney who has been on staff the longest and heads our Family Law Project, as well as a junior attorney because retention issues are very important)*

- **Who makes what decisions (who decides the strategic direction for the organization, and what degree of input is sought from the board and the staff?)** *Hopefully we can reach consensus (decisions everyone is willing to live with and support) and have broad engagement by board and staff. Board is the final decision maker and approves the plan, but it's important to have the total support and recommendations of senior staff.*

- **How extensive a planning process to have?** *Our workplan needs to ensure that we complete the process within four months.*

- **Will we involve external stakeholders in addition to internal (board and staff) stakeholders?** *Important to include external stakeholders, which is something we didn't do during the last process.*

- **Do we want to hold some retreats or other large group gatherings, and what might be the appropriate timing of these meetings? (Are there special events, preset meetings, or deadlines that we might want to keep in mind?)** *Before we start to write the plan, we need to schedule one all-day board/staff retreat, during which time we will make presentations in terms of priorities and get feedback* *and major discussions. We need to further discuss whether all staff should be invited to the retreat or only management team and program directors.*

- **Who will be the primary writer of the plan (with guidance from a consultant if necessary)?** *Executive director with support of consultant*

- **Are we going to use a consultant and, if yes, how best to use a consultant (what are our expectations regarding the consultant's role)?** *We need major guidance as to how to efficiently do this process, and expect the consultant to both facilitate discussions, make recommendations about processes, and help us ask the hard questions.*

- **How will we keep the board and staff informed about the SP discussions and decisions?** *At monthly board and staff meetings, SP Committee reps should make reports.*

- **Are there other considerations for the SP process that need to be factored in when designing our workplan?** *We need to complete the process in time to fit in with our annual budget process.*

SAMPLE WORKSHEET FOR CASE STUDY: COUNTY LEGAL AID SOCIETY (CLAS)

WORKSHEET 1.5   Create an Organization Profile

❏ Make sure you have an overview of your organization's profile including key programs.

Current Mission Statement:

Promote equal access to justice by providing counseling and legal representation for disenfranchised and low-income people in Central County

Then & Now:

- First Year of Operation (Date, Services and Numbers Served; number of staff): *1977: 35 clients served—housing and family law; 3 staff members*

- Current Operations (Date, Services and Numbers Served): *2014: 3,500 clients served*

Executive Director: *Jane Doe (cofounding executive director) [Jane Doe has been with us since our organization started, and became the sole executive director in 1980.]*

Number of Board Members: *12, but we currently have three vacancies*

Number of Staff (full time, part time, volunteers): *4 leadership/management team (all attorneys), 7 staff attorneys including 2 post-graduate Fellows, 9 other staff members, 11 law school interns, and 105 volunteer lawyers*

Current-Year Budget: *$2,200,000*

Current Programs:

- Housing: *CLAS work in this area includes helping individuals resolve landlord–tenant disputes, assisting renters who are facing eviction, and helping people maintain housing subsidies.*

- Public Benefits: *CLAS assists people to obtain and maintain government assistance, such as TANF (federal benefits for families), food assistance benefits, Social Security, General Assistance (GA), Supplemental Security Income (SSI), etc.*

- Health Care: *CLAS has always been committed to helping individuals access timely, affordable, and quality health care, as well as health coverage through government assistance programs.*

- Family Law/Domestic Violence: *CLAS assists victims of domestic violence by obtaining restraining orders, helping parents obtain and keep custody of their children, and assisting family members in obtaining guardianship for children without parents.*

Overview of Key Programs

Housing

- Short Description of Program: *Helping individuals resolve landlord–tenant disputes, assisting renters who are facing eviction, helping people maintain housing subsidies, and addressing substandard housing (slumlord landlords)*

- Program Budget: *$548,000*

WORKSHEET 1.5 *(continued)*

- How Funded: *Community Foundation grant, County Government funds from federal Housing & Urban Development (HUD), restricted donations from individual donors, portion of IOLTA (State Bar) funding*
- Number Served: *1,016*
- # of Staff: *1 senior attorney, 3 staff attorneys, one paralegal, and 25 percent of the half-time Pro Bono Coordinator*

Public Benefits

- Short Description of Program: *CLAS assists people to obtain and maintain government assistance, such as Social Security, General Assistance (GA), Supplemental Security Income (SSI), etc.*
- Program Budget: *$365,000*
- How Funded: *Contract with the county to provide SSI services, portion of IOLTA (State Bar) funding, allocation of unrestricted donations and event proceeds*
- Number Served: *875*
- # of Staff: *1 senior attorney, one full-time staff attorney, and 50 percent of a staff attorney (shared with the health program), about 25 percent of a paralegal, and 25 percent of the half-time Pro Bono Coordinator*

Health Care

- Short Description of Program: *Help individuals access timely, affordable, and quality health care.*
- Program Budget: *$493,000*
- How Funded: *Foundation grants and some restricted donations from law firms and corportations*
- Number Served: *925*
- # of Staff: *1 senior attorney, one full-time staff attorney, and 50 percent of a staff attorney (shared with the benefits program), one full-time project coordinator, and 25 percent of the half-time Pro Bono Coordinator*

Family Law

- Short Description of Program: *CLAS assists victims of domestic violence by obtaining restraining orders, helping parents obtain and keep custody of their children, and assisting family members in obtaining guardianship for children without parents.*
- Program Budget: *$420,000*
- How Funded: *Federal Violence Against Women Act grant (in collaboration with local social services providers), foundation grants, and an allocation from unrestricted donations*
- Number Served: *731*
- # of Staff: *1 senior attorney, 1 staff attorney, 1 legal secretary, and 25 percent of the half-time Pro Bono Coordinator*

Advocacy

- Short Description of Program: *Working primarily in coalition with other legal aid programs across the state, we advocate to government officials regarding the impact of regulations—or lack of enforcement of—on vulnerable*

(continued)

WORKSHEET 1.5 *(continued)*

populations. Although not a formal program, we advocate for systemic change in how vulnerable populations are treated by governmental agencies.

- Program Budget: *Not a formal program*
- How Funded: *Not funded*
- Number Served: *Unknown*
- # of Staff: *As needed*

Pro Bono

- Short Description of Program: *CLAS works with law firms and the University's Legal Aid Program to provide pro bono assistance to our clients, supplementing the work of our staff attorneys.*
- Program Budget: *Not a separate program; Pro Bono Coordinator position shared between all four program areas.*
- How Funded: *Written into a few of the foundation grants, and the rest is covered through an allocation of unrestricted donations.*
- Number Served: *Works with 105 volunteers each year; places approximately 75 pro bono cases for ongoing representation each year.*
- # of Staff: *1 half-time Pro Bono Coordinator (not an attorney)*

CHAPTER 2

Step 2: Stakeholder Engagement

FIRST STEPS	STRATEGIC ANALYSIS	SET YOUR COURSE
1. Set up for Success	4. Environmental Scan	9. Complete the Strategic Plan
2. Stakeholder Engagement	5. Theory of Change and Program Portfolio	10. Use Your Plan Successfully
3. Mission, Vision, Values	6. Business Model	
	7. Organization Capacity	
	8. Leadership	

ENGAGE INTERNAL STAKEHOLDERS

If your strategic plan is to be used, your staff and board need to understand it and be committed to it. The most important outcome of strategic planning is not the document but the actual decisions made with shared understanding and commitment of board and staff. In this way, some say, *the process is the product.* Thus, it is important to solicit their input early in the process. This can be done in several ways, and it is often helpful to use more than one approach. Involvement may take place at a single retreat, or input may be sought at more than one point in the process.

Many of our clients worry that by soliciting input widely, decision makers will end up beholden to and/or constrained by that input. There are three important things to understand in this regard:

1. *The input of the people who belong to the organization is valuable.* There is knowledge, insight, and diversity of opinion. Understanding what people on the board and staff consider most important, where they believe the problems lie, and what they think might be done to achieve greater success is necessary data for the process.

2. *This step is not about achieving consensus.* Rather, it is about structuring participation that will allow for meaningful leadership. The chances of someone supporting the end product are enormously greater if they have had a chance

to participate meaningfully in the process, and if they feel heard. This is a simple concept, but it requires an honest commitment to listening, which is not the same thing as being in the same room while someone is talking. People need to feel that, through the survey, through small and large meetings, through participation in task forces, or whatever media is employed, they have truly contributed to the strategic planning work.

3. *It is essential that you make clear that you are soliciting stakeholder input, but not committing to a specific course of action.* Very few people have a problem with this approach if you are clear. A problem will arise, however, if people think they are giving you answers and you come back later and tell them, "No, I just wanted your ideas, but we've gone in a different direction." Meaningful participation may be as simple as an e-mail asking for input, or it might be engagement at one or more in-depth discussions. The planning committee needs to assess what is required to make each stakeholder group feel meaningfully involved.

Perspectives various internal stakeholders' can offer include:

• *Board of directors.* The board, in its governance capacity, has the responsibility to think about what is important for the entire community and not just one particular client. The board must make sure that the plan's goals are consistent with resources and that the organization is sustainable.

• *Executive director and senior staff.* The executive director is usually the chief planner and, together with the senior staff, is the chief driver of the plan throughout the entire process. Even if she or he is not managing the planning process, the executive director works closely with the chair of the planning committee and often serves as the prime liaison between the staff and the planning committee.

• *Staff members.* Paid and volunteer staff have programmatic expertise and familiarity with the field and program work, information that is vital to shaping a relevant and workable strategic plan. Their involvement not only builds buy-in for the organizational goals and strategies but also links the plan's vision with the realization of that vision on a day-to-day basis. Staff members can be engaged through helping to collect data (market research) and evaluate programs. Program managers should have significant input on long-term program objectives and should assist in the development and monitoring of operational plans. Ideally, staff members should be represented on the planning committee.

• *Advisory boards.* Strategic planning can be a good time to involve advisory boards. They are an important bridge between your internal and external stakeholders; they are closer to the organization than other outsiders and yet are still likely to be more objective than board or staff members.

Early in the process, a combination of initial meetings and a short survey is relatively easy and effective. In fact, the questions on Worksheet 2.1 can be adapted for a survey. Many of our clients use online software to facilitate the process. Regularly scheduled board and staff meetings are a natural place to go over the strategic planning approach, to reinforce the importance of people's engagement, and to get high-level input on planning process goals and what everyone sees as the key strategic questions. Depending on the time available, you may have more in-depth discussions about what vision people hold for your organization and the potential new strategic directions to consider.

Your plan for internal stakeholder engagement does not need to be elaborate to be sufficient. Set up the process in a way that this participation is part of the workplan, not an extra activity. This can be done in varying levels of intensity.

Analyzing Strengths, Weaknesses, Opportunities, and Threats

One simple evaluation framework is a strengths, weaknesses, opportunities, and threats (SWOT) analysis, which can be done at the level of the whole organization or for each program. This can be done through a survey, in meetings, or at a retreat. The point is to get very broad input. If this is your first outreach to people, use the SWOT framework to help gather and organize input on the organization (strengths and weaknesses) and the environment (opportunities and threats).

Briefly, *strengths* are your organization's internal strengths—what it does well. *Weaknesses* are internal areas in which the organization could improve. *Opportunities* are external occasions to pursue your organization's mission, as well as changes taking place in the external environment that might provide such opportunities. *Threats* are factors or changes in the external environment that might hinder your organization's mission.

Regardless of how detailed the review of SWOT is, successful organizations exploit strengths rather than just focusing on weaknesses. In other words, this process isn't just about fixing the things that are wrong but also about nurturing what goes right. The same should apply to how an organization approaches its opportunities and threats—the external forces that influence the organization. During the strategic planning process, the organization wants to figure out how it can best use its resources to take advantage of strengths and opportunities and to overcome weaknesses and threats.

During the SWOT analysis, planners should look at the interplay of strengths and weaknesses with opportunities and threats. Many times an opportunity can only be taken advantage of if the organization has a corresponding strength. For example, increased demand for services (an opportunity) can only be met effectively if the organization has the necessary infrastructure and staff (the strengths) to provide quality service. Conversely, if an organization is facing a significant shift in the political arena that could adversely affect its ability to get funding (a threat), then the organization will not be able to respond quickly if it has poor relationships with government officials or a small and inactive membership (weaknesses). The planning committee should make note of any of these interplays of SW and OT and refer back to them during the next section: Strategic Analysis, Steps 4 through 8.

Expanded Options for Input

The strategic planning committee can expand the specificity and range of input by adding different questions or by expanding the opportunities for participation in the planning process. For instance, it is a simple matter to add questions about the vision individuals have for your organization and the values they see as most important and to add more expansive surveys on organizational assessment. This doesn't require much extra effort, but it does provide richer data. You can employ the same methodologies (e.g., surveys and group meetings) that were used for the SWOT.

The ways to involve people are nearly as varied as the number of nonprofits. For instance, you might hold specific strategic planning input sessions in person or by phone for each office, each department, or simply at different times of day, if it is not convenient to bring everyone together. You also can ask each department or work unit to do its own initial analysis and to develop recommendations for action. Subcommittees can add members or special meetings on a specific topic, to which other members of the organization may be added. You also may ask staff and board members who are not on the strategic planning committee to help conduct external stakeholder interviews, other research, and so forth.

Organization Self-Assessment

One option is to use an assessment instrument on a wide range of organizational topics from the full board and even the full staff. It is a great way to invite participation and generates a good amount of data. It also becomes possible to see where there are differences in perceptions between board and staff members. Putting an instrument into an online format, such as SurveyMonkey, makes it easy for people to fill out, and easy to tabulate responses.

There are also three other excellent online resources we recommend if the group wants to engage a larger number of people in this process.

- RoadMap Consulting in San Francisco has two online self-assessment instruments. "My Health Organization" focused on individual organizations, and "My Health Alliance" focused on coalitions and networks. Both are offered on a subscription basis and provide data analysis and consulting support if desired. http://roadmapconsulting.org

- TCC Group in New York has an online self-assessment instrument called The Core Capacities Assessment Tool (CCAT). Similar to RoadMap it is available for purchase and they also offer analysis and consulting support if desired. http://www.tcccat.com

- A third resource is free and was produced by the large private sector management consulting company McKinsey and Co. It is a highly detailed instrument produced for nonprofits in partnership with leading national nonprofit organizations. It is more than many organizations need in terms of depth but definitely provides a robust resource. https://www.ocat.mckinseyonsociety.com

However you decide to gather input, you will want to synthesize the data for use by the committee. Worksheet 2.1 asks two sets of questions: (1) a series of questions about one's vision for the organization, and (2) the more familiar SWOT—strengths, weaknesses, opportunities, and threats. This list of questions is a starting point, but strategic planning committees can choose to modify or substitute questions they feel will be most useful. The worksheet provides a sample for how the collected responses can be summarized into major themes.

→ **SEE WORKSHEET 2.1 TO ASSIST WITH THIS STEP.**

WORKSHEET 2.1	INTERNAL STAKEHOLDER ENGAGEMENT—BOARD AND STAFF
How to do this activity?	Use the questions on the worksheet as the basis for organizational interviews or surveys, or adapt the worksheet to match questions your organization has chosen to ask
Why do this activity?	To get valuable input and to provide an early opportunity for participation by the people who will implement the plan
Who to involve in the process?	All board and staff members, or selected subsets of each group

GATHER INPUT FROM EXTERNAL STAKEHOLDERS

External stakeholders may be funders, partner organizations, former board members, experts and academics in your field, media representatives, or elected officials. The number of external stakeholders to contact varies widely, depending on the planning effort. For most moderate planning efforts, 10 to 20 contacts is about right.

Reasons to involve specific external stakeholders include the following:

- *Clients.* The sole reason for most nonprofits' existence is the betterment of society in some way. Directly involving past and present clients (and perhaps potential clients) in the planning process helps ground the strategic discussions in the lived reality of the people for whom you work. If this input is gathered regularly as part of ongoing evaluation, that input may be sufficient.

- *Funders.* Past, current, and potential institutional funders provide another valuable perspective on client needs and how others in the community are either meeting or failing to meet those needs, and they may be willing to share future funding priorities.

- *Government funders and regulators.* Local (and sometimes state and national) officials can have a great influence on the external environment within which an organization operates. Asking for their perspective about your field and your organization can provide valuable input and strengthen relationships.

- *Individual donors.* An individual donor base is one of your most important resources. The strategic planning process is an invitation to get them involved in creating your future, and they will therefore be more invested in supporting that future.

- *Community leaders.* Community leaders, including elected officials, offer a valuable perspective on an organization's strengths and weaknesses, insight into the community's needs, and knowledge about the competition.

- *Competitors and potential collaborators.* Competitors (those who compete for funding as well as those who compete for clients or other resources) may be approached to contribute to an organization's assessment of its environment and its position in the field.

- *Other agencies in parallel or related fields.* When individuals from related fields are involved in an organization's planning process, their knowledge and experience can be leveraged not only for the benefit of the clients being served but also to foster cooperation and decrease unnecessary competition.

- *Previous staff and board members.* Staff members who were previously employed with the organization, or former board members, sometimes are considered unofficial alumni, and they offer a historical perspective that can be helpful in informing the future choices facing the organization.

Gathering input from external stakeholders at the beginning of your process helps stimulate and enrich your understanding of your organization and environment. However, some organizations will decide to postpone this step they talk with stakeholders about some of the questions and issues that are surfacing during strategic analysis. The advantage of waiting is that "live" proposals can be floated for feedback and/or interest from potential partners. Either way, the basic purpose and process are the same.

There are two reasons to involve external stakeholders in the strategic planning process. First, they have an outside perspective and information that will help you make better strategic decisions. A stakeholder may have insights into the opportunities or threats that affect the organization—something like new data revealing that 60 percent of all nonprofit organizations in the city are facing serious rent hikes. Likewise, if an external stakeholder has heard about the organization—or has had some contact with the organization—then his or her perceptions of the organization's strengths and weaknesses can be compared to perceptions of internal stakeholders.

For instance, perhaps staff and board members think that the organization has a positive reputation in the community, but stakeholders have heard there is a long waiting list and people are going elsewhere. A stakeholder's expectations also can inform an organization about unmet or growing needs in the community. Perhaps a community leader will reveal an expectation or hope, not previously considered internally, that the organization expand its services to a neighboring community or to add a different type of program. All of this is valuable input that external stakeholders are uniquely positioned to provide.

Gathering input from external stakeholders always improves the quality of a strategic planning process. Even if internal stakeholders are 90 percent correct about their assessment of the organization's situation, getting input from outsiders will provide either much-needed confirmation or new perspectives that will contribute to the development of sound plans.

A second reason to involve external stakeholders in the strategic planning process is that it offers the opportunity to build relationships. Your organization should work to maintain, improve, or build a better relationship with these people. If a stakeholder does not know much about the organization, then the interview represents an opportunity to explain what services are offered and how the organization is making a difference in the community. If the organization has a good relationship with the interviewee, the conversation can be the vehicle to affirm that partnership and to find out how to expand that relationship. If the organization has a problematic relationship or no relationship with the person being interviewed, then the interview can be a vehicle to rebuild or build such a relationship.

Although it is useful to have a preset and agreed-upon protocol for each stakeholder group, the actual discussion should be somewhat free-flowing, and the interviewer should be willing to ask follow-up questions about comments he or she hears. Those questions might deviate somewhat from the preset questions. Typically, these interviews are not a scientific study but rather a listening, outreach effort. The questions are there to guide the discussion.

SYNTHESIZE STAKEHOLDER INPUT

After receiving stakeholder input, you will assign a committee member or consultant to synthesize this input. This is important for use by the strategic planning committee, but it is also frequently valuable to share this synthesis with the stakeholder constituencies. Everyone likes to read about themselves, and stake-holders want to know that you actually heard them, rather than just providing an opportunity for them to vent. It also is helpful to look at the parallels and differences in feedback from external stakeholders compared with input from staff and board members. Feedback from external stakeholders is typically not shared with them in detail but in the form of a few themes that might be cited in the eventual plan.

→ SEE WORKSHEET 2.2 TO ASSIST WITH THIS STEP.

WORKSHEET 2.2	**THE EXTERNAL ENVIRONMENT: PERCEPTIONS OF OUR ORGANIZATION BY KEY EXTERNAL STAKEHOLDERS**
How to do this activity?	Use the questions on the worksheet as the basis for organizational interviews or surveys, or adapt the worksheet to match questions your organization has chosen to ask
Why do this activity?	To get valuable input and to provide an early opportunity for participation by the people who will implement the plan
Who to involve in the process?	All board and staff members, or selected subsets of each group

INCORPORATE EXTERNAL INPUT INTO YOUR SWOT ANALYSIS TO UPDATE CRITICAL ISSUES AND QUESTIONS

Now that you have gathered input from external stakeholders to add to what you heard from your board and staff, update the Strengths, Weaknesses, Opportunities and Threats. Incorporating additional perspectives will provide a richer under-standing of where your organization stands. In order to refine your understanding of key questions, issues, and especially opportunities use the SWOT Analysis Grid to work with the information in the four dimensions.

SWOT Analysis Grid

The "SWOT Analysis Grid" is an additional exercise to use in thinking about new opportunities for your program portfolio (see Table 2.1). A SWOT analysis grid is a way of looking at the broader implications of the SWOT analysis work done in Step 2, Stakeholder Engagement. The grid can help make visible some important dynamics that influence an organization's strategic choices (i.e., the intersection of strengths, weaknesses, opportunities, and threats), and can offer suggestions about actions the organization should consider undertaking. In effect, this grid asks a

TABLE 2.1   SWOT ANALYSIS GRID

	Opportunities	Threats
Strengths	INVEST Clear matches of strengths and opportunities lead to competitive advantage	DEFEND Areas of threat matched by areas of strength indicate a need to mobilize resources either alone or with others
Weaknesses	DECIDE Areas of opportunity matched by areas of weakness require a judgment call: invest or divest; collaborate	DAMAGE CONTROL/DIVEST Areas of threat matched by areas of weakness indicate need for damage control

Source: Adapted from Kevin P. Kearns, "Comparative Advantage to Damage Control: Clarifying Strategic Issues Using SWOT Analysis." *Nonprofit Management and Leadership* 3, no. 1 (Fall 1992): 3–22. All rights reserved.

planner to consider the interplay of core competencies with the key forces in the organization's environment.

In an article titled "From Comparative Advantage to Damage Control: Clarifying Strategic Issues Using SWOT Analysis," Professor Kevin Kearns states that if an organization simply brainstorms strengths, weaknesses, opportunities, and threats:

> SWOT analysis can degenerate into a superficial list-generating exercise that produces four unconnected lists: strengths, weaknesses, opportunities, and threats. Without a systematic effort to relate the lists to each other, they are of limited utility, especially in clarifying fundamental policy choices facing the agency . . . SWOT analysis requires nonlinear and iterative thinking, which assumes that goals and strategies emerge from the juxtaposition of opportunities and threats in the external environment and strengths and weaknesses in the internal environment. Dimensions of a critical issue and related responses may emerge that otherwise might not surface. For example, one small community-based counseling center faced two significant threats: a major loss of public support as a result of rumors of embezzlement and increasing demands from funders for more complex financial reporting. These threats intersected with weaknesses in financial management in the "damage control/divest" cell of the SWOT analysis grid. Because the organization believed that its programs were valuable, the initial response was to quell the rumors and build financial management capacity. However, the grid highlighted the fact that these threats were compounded by organizational weaknesses. Thus, instead the organization developed a new strategy that was, in effect, to divest its financial management function by collaborating with a larger organization as its fiscal agent.[1]

---

[1] Kevin P. Kearns, "Comparative Advantage to Damage Control: Clarifying Strategic Issues Using SWOT Analysis," *Nonprofit Management and Leadership* 3, no. 1 (Fall 1992): 3–22. The SWOT analysis grid is a widely used approach. Modifications of the grid have been attributed to R. Christensen et al., *Business Policy: Text and Cases* (Homewood, IL: Irwin, 1983); and J. Freedman and K. Van Ham, "Strategic Planning in Philips," in B. Taylor and D. Hussey (eds.), *The Realities of Planning* (Elmsford, NY: Pergamon Press, 1982).

In discussing the interplay of strengths, opportunities, weaknesses, and threats, the planning committee may find a much more advantageous way to frame the question. For example, during the mid-1990s, the Public Broadcasting Service (PBS) increasingly needed to look at its loss of government funding, which was a major threat to its survival. PBS's strength was a loyal and relatively affluent audience. A recognized strength from the past (and a lesson from its history) was the use of innovative programming (e.g., *Sesame Street*). Rather than simply asking, "How can we replace our government funding?" the question was reframed as, "How can PBS leverage or mobilize its strengths to avert or respond to the loss of government funds?" This led to redoubling efforts to provide greater visibility to funders who were willing to sponsor specific programming, with great success.

CAUTIONS FOR FACILITATORS

Facilitators should be aware of and work to avoid the following pitfalls during the strategic planning process:

Step 2: Stakeholder Engagement

Perceptions are not THE truth. During this step you are engaging internal and external stakeholders by asking for their perceptions of the organization. Remind organizational planners, that perceptions are exactly that, perceptions. They need to be understood in the context of other data.

Don't assume need for confidentiality. External stakeholders often do not require confidentiality and knowing the source of comments provides additional meaning. Ask the stakeholders their preference.

Take advantage of tech. Use the technology that is available to make gathering perceptions from internal stakeholders easier to collect—well crafted, online surveys can help to gather perceptions more efficient. On line surveys are not a very effective process for engaging external stakeholders, with the possible exception of on-line client evaluations.

SAMPLE WORKSHEET FOR CASE STUDY: COUNTY LEGAL AID SOCIETY (CLAS)

> **WORKSHEET 2.1 Internal Stakeholder Engagement—Board and Staff**
>
> ❑ What is your vision for the future for our organization?
>
> ❑ What are the major changes we may need to consider undertaking to achieve your vision?
>
> ❑ What are our organization's key opportunities and threats—the political, economic, social, technological, demographic, and/or legal trends that may impact our organization's ability to achieve its mission?
>
> ❑ What are our major internal strengths and weaknesses?

SUMMARY OF STAFF SURVEY RESULTS

1. In order to best achieve our mission, **what is your vision for our organization within the next five to ten years?**

   A. **Programmatic Vision** (What specific things would you like to say we have accomplished within the next five to ten years in terms of programs/mission accomplishment?)

      - *Continued provision of excellent legal services*

      - *Greater education and training so that clients can be able to better help themselves*

      - *Increased advocacy efforts and higher levels of services for individuals (beyond legal advice and some brief assistance)*

      - *Able to say that we are able to meet the needs of the entire county (greater reach to underserved areas in our county)*

      - *Greater use of private-sector volunteer resources to truly expand the service available to our client communities*

      - *Should we expand into neighboring Valley County?*

   B. **Business Model Vision** (How should we be financing our programmatic vision for our organization?)

      - *Proactively reduce our reliance on government funding through increased support by law firms, individual attorneys, and corporate (in-house) legal departments in terms of pro bono hours and financial contributions*

      - *Increased financial support by board members*

      - *Increased financial support by local corporations*

      - *Continued/increased support of organization by current funders, especially Community Foundation and State Bar*

      - *We are a financially healthy and solid organization with sufficient resources to fund current programs and expansion.*

      - *Ensure that we add to our reserves annually by running a surplus budget (what is our ideal profitability level?).*

(continued)

WORKSHEET 2.1 *(continued)*

- Perhaps explore an earned-income possibility—where we would charge higher-income clients a sliding scale for some nonurgent services. There are some barriers to this: The State Bar funding complicates and restricts our ability to do this, but some other legal organizations are already doing this in some immigration and family law cases.

C. **Organizational Capacity Vision** (What is your vision for what we would need to be doing in the future in terms of the organizational capacity needed to support your vision? Organizational capacity includes planning, human resources, organization culture and communication, technology and facilities infrastructure, and governance.)

- Longer retention of staff attorneys
- Better pay
- Improved benefits and total compensation packages (including retirement, etc.)
- Improved supervision and mentoring supports for newer attorneys; explicit professional development plans for all staff
- Increased pro bono lawyers and increased pro bono hours (greater number of lawyers contributing more pro bono hours)
- Increased media attention that highlights the needs of vulnerable populations as well as showing the excellent work that we are doing to help clients in need
- New offices
- Updated technology (equipment and software to support timely and accurate data collection; explore whether our current case management system is adequate to meet our needs, particularly for foundation reporting)
- Increased support staff
- Continued improved working relationship between board and staff
- Staff should reflect the populations we serve.

D. **Leadership Vision** (What is your vision in terms of the organization's leadership? What should be the future governance and support roles and makeup of the board, expectations for senior management, as well as leadership development for the organization?)

- We have increased the number of board members from 15 to 18.
- We are able to fill board vacancies in a timely manner and have a multiyear plan for new board member recruitment (so we aren't just recruiting friends of current board members).
- Board members are all trained in their roles and responsibilities and there is greater commitment to members fulfilling their governance and support responsibilities; board members understand the board governance and fundraising best practices recommended by the American Bar Association's standards for civil legal aid providers.
- We have successfully transitioned to a new executive director.
- We have a written succession plan for all key positions, and an Emergency Succession Plan is in place.

WORKSHEET 2.1 *(continued)*

- *All staff attorneys who are in management positions are trained in effective supervision.*

- *Our leadership makes sure we are proactively dealing with the generational issues that comes from having attorneys from three different generations (Boomers, Generation X, and Millennials) with differing expectations about work structures, leadership opportunities, etc.*

2. Given your vision for the future (as stated in the first question), what—from a programmatic perspective—do we specifically need to do more of, less of, differently, or start to do in order to make progress toward achieving the results articulated above?

   - *More Spanish-speaking staff and materials in Spanish*

   - *Increased advocacy efforts (in collaboration with additional partners)*

   - *Decide how to best meet needs of entire county (including exploring the use of technology to better reach some areas)*

   - *Increased outreach to underserved populations*

   - *Increased capacity to work with non-English-speaking clients (Asian Pacific Islander populations)*

   - *Incorporate pro bono as a structural component of our programs, rather than an add-on afterthought, and bring law firm full-time pro bono directors to the table in planning how to do that.*

3. Given your vision for the future (as stated in the first question), what—from a resource development, organizational capacity, and/or senior management and board leadership and governance perspective—do we specifically need to do more of, less of, differently, or start to do in order to make progress toward achieving the results articulated above?

   - *Need the board to be much more knowledgeable about what we do and committed to assisting in raising additional money*

   - *Identify new generation of donors and determine how to approach volunteers about also becoming donors. We don't do a great job of approaching our volunteers about also being donors, which is a loss!*

   - *Greater community outreach to make sure we are reaching the constituencies who most need our services*

   - *More private-sector donors to offset a decrease in government funding*

   - *More pro bono attorneys*

   - *Be more willing to look at new and different ways of doing things (an organizational culture that is less resistant to change)*

   - *Increased physical presence in areas that are not currently served*

   - *Explore whether the use of technology can help us reach some difficult-to-reach areas and groups (could we imagine providing some services virtually—through online video-chatting or videoconferencing?)*

   - *Increased leadership development and leadership opportunities for newer attorney staff, so that they can develop and grow within our organization, rather than feeling that they have to leave to continue to develop*

   - *Higher board engagement*

   - *Improved technology (systems and tools) to support our operations, case management, and delivery of services*

(continued)

WORKSHEET 2.1 *(continued)*

4. What three things do you want to make sure DO NOT CHANGE as we move forward?

   - *Excellence in our work*

   - *Excellent staff (committed and knowledgeable staff attorneys and other staff)*

   - *Passion and loyalty to the organization and to the clients we serve*

5. What should be the **primary measures of our organization's success**? In other words, how should we know we are achieving our mission impact?

   - *Positive outcome of our cases (Did we help our clients, have the positive impact we wanted to have, prevent or alter the outcome that would have occurred if the client had not had our assistance?) and effective ways of demonstrating and communicating those outcomes to external stakeholders including funders*

   - *Number of clients helped*

   - *Client satisfaction*

   - *Decrease in staff turnover*

6. What do you see are the **major external opportunities facing our organization** in the next three to five years, and how might we respond as an organization? What do you think are the **significant external challenges/threats** that might have an impact on our success over the next three to five years, and how do you think we should respond? (Includes political, economic, social, technological, environmental, and legal trends that will either have a negative or positive influence on our organization's future success.)

   Opportunities

   - *Economy has improved, and so time is right to expand our fundraising efforts to corporations and individuals.*

   - *Affordable Care Act supports individuals getting the health care that they need, but many are not enrolled.*

   - *Increased demand for services from neighboring Valley County = need to decide whether we should expand into that county or work with current Valley County Legal Services to improve the quality of their work.*

   - *Use of technology: Some legal aid programs in our state are creating virtual assistance programs and using technology to serve clients in other areas in their service areas, as well as conducting intakes through e-mail or online, and conducting appointments through confidential, secure video-chat tools. Our IT infrastructure is also a deficit: How can we build up our own IT to possibly be able to do something similar, and how does it fit within our service delivery structure?*

   Both Opportunity and Threat

   - *Greater influx of non-English-speaking populations—bring on staff who can communicate with clients in native language*

   - *Larger demographic shifts in the low-income population in our service region*

   - *Shifts in the requirements for law schools mean that law school clinical programs may start offering services that are similar to ours (possible competition?), and on the flip side more law students may need volunteer hours during their law school experience: How might we capitalize on the availability of law student volunteers or coordinate with the local law school to avoid duplication of services?*

WORKSHEET 2.1 *(continued)*

Threats

- *Continuing reductions in government funding sources at the federal, state, and local levels; increased competition in our county from new nonprofits for foundation grants*

- *Shift in the way large law firms structure their services and work: Is that going to have any impact on availability of pro bono attorneys and resources? Law school debt loads: As new attorneys graduate with unprecedented amounts of law school debt, are we going to be able to continue to recruit quality attorneys with our salary scale?*

7. What are the **major strengths of our organization**, and how can we take advantage of those strengths?

- *Strong commitment by staff to helping vulnerable populations receive legal assistance they need = need better benefits and salary to retain talented and committed staff*

- *Longevity of staff with depth of knowledge in their fields of practice = better benefits and salary*

- *Commitment to involving staff in decision making that impacts their work*

- *Excellent reputation in the community*

8. What are our **major weaknesses**, and how can we overcome those weaknesses?

- *Poor salaries and benefits = improved salaries and benefits*

- *Lack of sufficient support staff = hiring plan for bringing on additional staff*

- *Weak grants management = hire grants administrator so staff attorneys who manage programs can have more time doing legal work and less grants management*

- *Lack of consistent and effective supervision of staff = training of supervisors*

- *Communication among programs is poor = develop and implement improved communication and collaboration systems*

- *Inability to track cases and case data = put in place a new client tracking system that is able to generate reports needed for internal and external purposes*

- *Lack of an effective partnership between the board and staff = training on roles; increased opportunities for board and staff to interact with each other*

- *Leadership (board and staff) who have been at the organization for a very long time*

- *Facilities are too small to comfortably accommodate the number of staff we have.*

- *We don't reach the entire county.*

> **WORKSHEET 2.2**   **The External Environment: Perceptions of Our
> Organization by Key External Stakeholders**
>
> ❏ Summary of external stakeholder interviews.

External Stakeholders Interviewed: (name and position)

- *Charles S., CEO, Community Foundation*

- *Maria B., Executive Director, Community Services Agency*

- *Henry C., Valley Legal Aid*

- *Susan M., Director, Central County Health and Human Services*

- *Linda H., Executive Director, State Bar Association*

- *Larry O., Executive Director, Senior Services Inc.*

- *Joanne B., Executive Director, Migrant Worker Services*

- *Amy W., retired judge, Superior Court*

- *William C., Managing Partner, law firm of Smith & Smith LLP (long-term funder and provider of pro bono lawyers*

- *Janice D., CEO, International Products Group (long-term funder)*

- *Judith L., Executive Director, Disability Action*

1. **"What has been your primary experience in terms of your connection with our programs and services, as well as your interaction with our staff?"**

   - *All individuals interviewed spoke about a high degree of professionalism and helpfulness of staff.*

   - *Words that came up over and over in terms of interaction with staff: innovative, collaborative, knowledgeable, dedicated, integrity, passionate*

   - *Some said that they were concerned that staff seemed to be overextended and sometimes were delayed in returning phone calls and e-mails.*

2. **"What are our organization's primary strengths?"**

   - *Dedicated and experienced staff committed to the organization's mission*

   - *Longevity*

   - *Respected in the community*

   - *Fills an important niche in the county*

   - *Works collaboratively with partners*

   - *Willing to share expertise*

   - *Innovative programming—proactive in identifying needs in the community and trying to fill them*

WORKSHEET 2.2 *(continued)*

3. **"What are our organization's primary weaknesses?"**

- *Seems to be understaffed*
- *Pro bono program could be better organized.*
- *Does not get the respect and recognition it deserves—not a lot of media attention.*
- *Not enough bilingual staff*
- *Depressing office space*
- *Not able to sufficiently serve entire county.*
- *Have not been able to put together a board of advisors.*
- *Board of directors is not very visible in the community (as compared to other nonprofits).*

4. **What do you think are the greatest challenges facing our organization?**

- *Cuts in legal aid funding*
- *Board of directors not very visible in the community—where are the ambassadors for the organization?*
- *Sometimes it seems like the organization is already overextended, so how will it be able to respond to new issues or crises, like new relief in the area of immigration or opportunities like the Affordable Health Care Act, or changes to local government policies or programs that impact low-income residents in our county?*
- *Ensure that the organization is accessible to all populations in our county, including those who cannot necessarily travel to the legal aid office in-person or those for whom English is not their primary language.*
- *Can legal aid strengthen its relationship with our county's bar association? It seems that there might be missed opportunities for collaboration there.*
- *From the perspective of a law firm partner, our own firms are undergoing shifts in how we structure our services to clients. This could mean some changes in how we structure our approach to pro bono—legal aid will need to be ready to respond to any such changes.*

5. **Are there particular trends and developments in our field of service that we need to consider when setting priorities for the future?**

- *Use of technology: How can legal aid leverage the developments in technology and incorporate it into the delivery of services to clients? And what does the development of for-profit companies providing legal services online mean for legal aid? Are they potential collaborators or competitors?*
- *Changes in how large law firms structure their own business model and services*
- *Changes in law schools: As some law schools reduce their class sizes and begin to modify the law school curriculum to focus on graduating "practice-ready" attorneys, how can legal aid be involved in helping with that? Benefiting from it? And how does legal aid continue to recruit new attorneys as they graduate with steadily increasing (and staggering) loan debt?*
- *IOLTA (state) funding (tied to federal interest rates) continues to be cut each year on top of many years of reductions.*
- *Exciting new developments in some areas of law, such as health care and immigration, mean clients need entirely new services in those areas.*

(continued)

██ **WORKSHEET 2.2** *(continued)*

- Cuts in funding for the courts and county agencies—legal aid's clients have to access the courts, which have reduced their service and closed courtrooms as a result of their own funding reductions. Low-income residents of our county are also impacted by the reduction in funding to key county safety net programs, particularly those for young children. These impacts on legal aid's client populations make their services even more needed (and complicate the delivery of those services).

6. **If additional future resources were available, what would you like us to consider in the future: Are there things we should be doing more of, less of, or differently so as to better serve the needs of the community?**

   - Greater systems change/advocacy efforts
   - More self-help educational programs
   - Immigration reform and immigration rights work
   - Increased collaboration with senior centers to provide help to seniors
   - Increased collaboration with the local courts—perhaps on-site clinics or other similar services
   - Better pro bono programs to engage private-sector attorneys in giving back

7. **What do you think distinguishes us from organizations that are doing similar work?**

   - Longevity
   - Breadth and depth of experience
   - History of collaborating with nonlegal nonprofits and organizations
   - Working in areas of law most needed by low-income and underserved groups—provide a broad range of services

8. **What can we do to increase the awareness of our work and programs by the community?**

   - More outreach at social services (safety net) nonprofits
   - Coordination with the local bar association (like perhaps a regular column in their newsletter?)
   - Some improvements to the organization's website (sometimes hard to navigate)
   - Board of directors could be more effective ambassadors (perhaps could speak at law firms and other organizations?)
   - Perhaps engage past clients in helping to spread the word about the services

9. **Are there ways that you think your organization and our organization could work together (more effectively) in the future?**

   - A more organized pro bono program will allow more of our attorneys to get involved.
   - Perhaps our staff and your staff could have some joint brainstorming meetings.
   - Talk together before community-based advocacy meetings and plan a joint advocacy strategy.
   - Create a one-page cheat sheet on which attorneys at other community-based organizations should contact about specific questions or areas of law.
   - Recruit board members from our organization.

10. **Is there anything else you would like us to consider during this strategic process?**

    - People appreciate being involved and want to see the final plan.

CHAPTER 3

Step 3: Mission, Vision, Values

FIRST STEPS	STRATEGIC ANALYSIS	SET YOUR COURSE
1. Set up for Success	4. Environmental Scan	9. Complete the Strategic Plan
2. Stakeholder Engagement	5. Theory of Change and Program Portfolio	10. Use Your Plan Successfully
3. Mission, Vision, Values	6. Business Model	
	7. Organization Capacity	
	8. Leadership	

A primary reason to undertake a strategic planning process is to establish or reaffirm within the organization a shared understanding of why an organization exists and its aspirations for the future. The most succinct reflections of this shared understanding lie in the organization's mission, vision, and values statements. A mission statement is a statement of purpose, a vision statement is a vivid image of the future you seek to create, and a values statement outlines your organization's guiding concepts, beliefs, or principles.

Similarly, anyone coming into contact with your organization wants to know what your purpose is and why your organization exists. This is the question a mission statement should answer. People also want to know what you are trying to achieve. What does success look like for you—what is your vision? And they want to know what beliefs and values guide you—what you stand for.

There are other important questions. Whom do you serve? How do you bring about change—what is your program work? Where do you do your work? These are all important questions, but nonprofits tend to confuse rather than clarify when they try to put too much detail in the mission statement. In order to provide additional information, many organizations provide brief mission and vision statements, with a paragraph or two providing more detail on the nature of programs, who is served, and where. Similarly, values are sometimes simply listed, although often organizations will add another paragraph or, for example, highlight in a sidebar on their website a brief discussion of their values and how they guide the organization's work.

REVISIT YOUR MISSION STATEMENT

The most compelling mission statements we see now are one memorable sentence. Consider the Monterey Bay Aquarium's mission statement: "The mission of the nonprofit Monterey Bay Aquarium is to inspire conservation of the oceans."

That's it! There is much more that can be said about the Monterey Bay Aquarium. It does a great deal of research and education, is engaged in policy advocacy, provides job training for young people, rescues and rehabilitates wildlife, and more. But in this mission statement, the aquarium makes it clear that its *primary* purpose is not entertainment or education but environmental conservation focusing on the ocean. Those 15 words say a lot.

It is difficult to sift through all of the important ideas informing and inspiring an organization, but it is worth the effort. The aquarium's mission statement answers only one question, related to its purpose. And purpose is always to create change. So the mission statement has a verb ("to inspire") and an object ("conservation of the oceans").

In its strategic planning process, a food bank boiled down a longer and less direct version of its mission statement to this: "Alameda County Community Food Bank passionately pursues a hunger-free community."

A second approach that is frequently used is to include in the mission statement both purpose (an ends statement) and program (how the purpose is accomplished—a means statement). For instance, "Lambda Legal is a national organization committed to achieving full recognition of the civil rights of lesbians, gay men, bisexuals, transgender people, and those with HIV, through impact litigation, education, and public policy work." By adding the words "through impact litigation, education, and public policy work" to its mission statement, Lambda Legal tells you what it *does* to serve its mission. This approach sharpens a reader's understanding of what Lambda Legal is about.

Another example of this second approach is used by the American Cancer Society: "The American Cancer Society is the nationwide, community-based, voluntary health organization dedicated to eliminating cancer as a major health problem *by preventing cancer, saving lives, and diminishing suffering from cancer, through research, education, advocacy, and service*." [Italics added]

Each of these mission statements helps internal and external stakeholders quickly understand both what these organizations do and why they do it. A mission statement should also help an organization decide what *not* to do. The American Cancer Society may very well consider a new education program aimed at reducing smoking among young women, for instance, but it would not consider a request to fund a major research project on promoting adult literacy. Both Lambda Legal and the American Cancer Society provide more information, but this approach comes with two costs: (1) the statement is longer and likely more difficult to remember, and (2) it is also more complex because there are two different ideas: why and how.

In sum, a mission statement should include at least one and possibly two elements. First, it should include a *purpose sentence* that describes the ultimate result an organization is trying to achieve. This answers the question about why the organization exists and focuses on an end result. The *business statement* describes what the organization does—the primary methods, programs, or services used by the organization to achieve its purpose. Your programs and services are a means to an end. The statement of what the organization does often also includes a description of for whom the service is provided.

Create a Purpose Sentence by Identifying the Focus Problem

To draft a purpose statement, it may be sufficient to simply ask the question, Why do we exist? However, this direct approach to defining an organization's purpose can be surprisingly difficult. To define or clarify an organization's purpose, especially when a variety of programs can be seen to be contributing to different types of change, the group may need to step back from the day-to-day activities to look at purpose from the outside in. Start with the most important change you seek, the focus problem your organization is trying to solve.

For example, based on information in their website the focus problem for Big Brothers Big Sisters of Metropolitan Chicago could be articulated as "many of our children are 'getting into trouble': underperforming in school, getting involved with the juvenile justice system, and not achieving employment upon becoming adults." The ideal future impact, if the problem were solved, is articulated in their vision: "All children achieve success in life." Their purpose, described in their mission statement, which also includes its primary program approach, is to "Empower our next generation through life-changing, high-impact one-to-one mentoring."

The Importance of Clarifying Purpose

Failure to state and communicate clearly an organization's purpose (in ends terminology) can lead an organization to inadvertently restrict its effectiveness. One program whose stated purpose was "to provide counseling to youth ages 13 to 18" (a narrow, *means* statement) inadvertently shut off any hope of innovation by too narrowly restricting the scope of its programs and vision. Because its focus was only on counseling, the staff and board were limiting the impact of the organization's work. They rewrote their purpose to reflect an *ends* statement: "to increase the mental health of youth in our county." Given a broader focus, the organization expanded its vision to include new programs, such as a crisis hotline, after-school programs, and workshops on coping with stress.

A too broadly defined purpose can also leave an organization unable to prioritize program activities. One local community organization had long owned a building, within which it provided several small programs, and which included a much-used large meeting room. By renting out the meeting room to other community groups, the organization received a small but steady income. As long as the organization's purpose statement was vaguely defined as "meeting the needs of the community," renting out the room took priority over new activities because it generated revenue. Following a strategic planning process, the organization sharpened its focus on meeting the *cultural* needs of the local *South Asian* community. As a result, many new uses were found for the meeting space, including use for youth groups, senior citizen cultural activities, and programs celebrating South Asian culture and targeted at the general public. Because of the importance of these activities to the organization's purpose, new funding was acquired to offset the loss of the rental income, and in the process the organization made more strategic use of one of its primary assets: its building.

Clarifying purpose is also important, because different understandings of purpose within an organization can lead to confusion and conflict. A shelter for battered women was asked by a funder to develop a program for men who were batterers. The organization's board and staff were deeply divided on this issue; some wanted the new program and some did not. A consultant who was brought in to facilitate conflict resolution asked the group to tell her the purpose of the organization, which revealed some stark differences in understanding. Some people felt that the shelter's purpose was to provide shelter to battered women and their children, whereas others stated that the organization's purpose was to eliminate the cycle of violence in the family. Not surprisingly, those who most felt that the new program fit within the organization's purpose were the ones who stated that the end result of their work was prevention—the elimination of violence in the family—and that it made sense to provide services to men who were batterers. Neither of these constructions was "right," but they were different, and they led people to different conclusions about how to respond to a new opportunity.

After much discussion, the shelter for battered women rewrote its purpose sentence to include both closely related ends. It read, "Our purpose is to reduce—and work toward the elimination of—violence in the family." This meant that the new program idea to work with men *was* agreed to be a reasonable option to evaluate. Interestingly, the group chose not to develop and implement this program, but only because they did not feel they had a core competence in that area. They did, however, identify a men's organization that they assisted in developing a violence prevention program for men who had been convicted of domestic violence.

Finally, an organization may not realize when it is time to go out of business or change its purpose. Perhaps the most famous example of this is the March of Dimes. As many people know, the initial purpose of the organization that came to be called the March of Dimes, founded by President Franklin Roosevelt in 1938, was to eliminate polio. Because the purpose statement was clear, however, within three years of the creation of the Salk vaccine in 1955, the organization had to choose whether to go out of business or to refocus its mission. The board of directors decided that it had achieved significant capacity to bring about change and chose to broaden its purpose to eliminate birth defects and combat infant mortality.

THE EXAMPLE OF ALICE

Lewis Carroll's *Alice's Adventures in Wonderland* speaks indirectly to the importance of mission statements. In discussion with the Cheshire Cat, Alice asks, "Would you tell me, please, which way I ought to go from here?"

"That depends a good deal on where you want to get to," said the Cat.

"I don't much care where—" said Alice.

"Then it doesn't matter which way you go," said the Cat.

"—so long as I get somewhere," Alice added as an explanation.

"Oh, you're sure to do that," said the Cat, "if you only walk long enough."

Source: Lewis Carroll, *Alice's Adventures in Wonderland* (London: Heinemann, 1907), pp. 75–76).

Write a Purpose Sentence

A purpose sentence includes two elements. First, it includes an infinitive verb that indicates a change in status, such as "to increase," "to decrease," "to eliminate," or "to prevent." Second, it includes an identification of the problem to be addressed or the condition to be changed, such as conservation of the seas, full recognition of civil rights, cancer, or cultural assets in the community. Together, these might form a purpose sentence such as "to decrease [infinitive verb] infant mortality rates in our city [problem]." The purpose essentially becomes the mission statement. For example:

> The mission of the Boys and Girls Clubs of America is **to enable** all young people, especially those who need us most, **to reach their full potential** as productive, caring responsible citizens.

Note that this example focuses on an outcome more than on methods. They describe how the world is going to be different—what the organization intends to change. Thus, the purpose of an agency serving the homeless should not be described in terms of its method, which might be "to provide shelter for homeless individuals." Instead, the purpose should be described in terms of a broader end result, such as "to eliminate the condition of homelessness in our region."

FROM FOCUS PROBLEM TO IDEAL FUTURE TO PURPOSE STATEMENT

Identify the focus problem. For instance, youth who are involved in the juvenile justice system, are homeless, live in the inner city, are poor, or are otherwise at risk have special needs for their physical and emotional well-being. Among the issues these youth face in their environment are violence, racism, sexism, poverty, lack of education, and substance abuse. These factors often represent obstacles to accessing and utilizing services effectively, and contribute to their higher rates of morbidity and mortality.

Articulate ideal future impact if the problem were to be solved. For example, in concert with the constellation of service providers who work with these youth, it is necessary to have quality comprehensive health care designed to meet their special needs.

Draft the purpose sentence. A relevant purpose sentence might be, "Improve the health of at-risk youth."

Summarize Your "Business"

What business are we in? The word "business" is a slightly more global way of thinking about your program portfolio. Where the purpose sentence is an ends statement, the business statement or statement of program methods is a summary statement about means. Program statements often include the verbs "to provide," "by," or "through."

For example, if the purpose of an agency serving youths is "to improve the health of at-risk youth," then the organization would define the methods used to pursue that purpose, such as "by providing direct medical services, counseling, and health education to youth at Juvenile Hall." Similarly, an organization whose purpose is to eliminate homelessness might choose one or more of the following methods: constructing housing for homeless individuals, advocating for changes in public policy, and/or providing counseling and job training to homeless individuals.

Try the exercise in Worksheet 3.1 to help your organization determine the difference between ends and means. Examine the statements in the table. Which are statements of purpose (ends) and which are statements of programs (means)?

WORKSHEET 3.1	DISTINGUISHING BETWEEN PURPOSE (ENDS) AND PROGRAM (MEANS)

Statement	Ends	Means
1. Eliminate the causes of birth defects		
2. Provide counseling and support to victims of crime		
3. Make a profit and/or increase shareholder wealth		
4. Assure that comprehensive, culturally acceptable personal and public health services are available and accessible to Native American and Alaska Native people		
5. Conduct biomedical research		
6. Heal the wounds of crime		
7. Increase the mental health of our clients		
8. Provide leadership training and legal assistance to migrant workers		
9. Decrease the problems of single-parent children		
10. Provide food and shelter to the homeless		

If you identified statements 1, 3, 4, 6, 7, and 9 as purpose statements, you understand the difference between purpose (ends) and programs or services (means).

Logically, it makes sense to define your purpose before you define your program. However, sometimes it is easier for people to relate to what the organization does, because that is more visible. So, if your business is building houses, then you might define your ends, or the purpose of your business as, "We build housing in order to decrease homelessness." Likewise, if your organization puts on art shows featuring the work of artists with developmental disabilities, you might decide that "our mission is to increase the visibility of artists with developmental disabilities."

If it helps to talk about what you do and then why you do it, as a way to clarify your mission statement, then by all means do what works best for your group!

Putting the Mission Statement Together

The mission statement, when completed, should be a simple yet powerful and inspiring statement that communicates to both internal and external stakeholders what the organization is all about. Use Worksheet 3.1 to help you complete this step. Keep in mind that the briefer the statement, the easier it is for board and staff members to remember it.

It can be surprisingly challenging to agree on a mission statement. The book *Reinventing Government* states that

> the experience of hashing out the fundamental purpose of an organization—debating all the different assumptions and views held by its members and agreeing on one basic mission—can be a powerful one. When it is done right, a mission statement can drive an entire organization from top to bottom. It can help people at all levels decide what they should do and what they should stop doing.[1]

WRITE YOUR VISION STATEMENT

A vision is a guiding image for success. (Think "vision" as in "to see with your eyes.") In architectural terms, the vision is the artist's rendering of the creation of the building and suggestion about the impact it will have. Whereas a mission statement answers the questions about why the organization exists, a vision statement answers the question, "What will success look like?" The pursuit of this shared image of success motivates people to work together.

The vision of the Hawai'i Community Foundation is: "We want to live in a Hawai'i where people care about each other, our natural resources, and diverse island cultures—a place where people's ideas, initiatives, and generosity support thriving, responsible communities." To work toward this vision, they define their mission as: "The Hawai'i Community Foundation helps people make a difference by inspiring the spirit of giving and by investing in people and solutions to benefit every island community."

Vision statements can and should be inspirational. Martin Luther King Jr. said, "I have a dream," and then he offered a vision that changed a nation. He did not say, "I have a plan." That famous speech is a dramatic example of the power that can be generated by a person who communicates a compelling vision of the future. Although John F. Kennedy did not live to see his vision for NASA come to fruition, he set it in motion when he said, "I believe that this nation should commit itself to achieving the goal, before this decade is out, of landing a man on the moon and returning him safely to Earth." When it came time to appropriate the enormous funds necessary to accomplish this vision, Congress did not hesitate, because this vision spoke powerfully to values the American people held dear—the view of America as a pioneer and a world leader.

An organizational vision statement might not put a man on the moon, but it should be compelling in the same way that Kennedy's and King's visions were. It should challenge and inspire the group to stretch its capabilities and achieve its

---

[1] David Osbourne and Ted Gaebler, *Reinventing Government* (Reading, MA: Addison-Wesley, 1992), pp. 130–131.

purpose. The organizational vision statement focuses on how the world will be improved if the organization achieves its purpose.

The first focus of an effective external vision statement should therefore be the client to be served or the constituency whose lives are to be affected by the organization. Good examples of vision statements are as follows:

- "Children, adults and seniors of Alameda County do not worry about where their next meal is coming from." (Alameda County Community Food Bank)

- "The Julia Morgan Center for the Arts seeks to change people's lives by making art a common experience of everyday life and learning."

- "We envision a barrier-free, inclusive, diverse world that values each individual and their voice. In this world, all people with disabilities enjoy the power of equal rights and opportunities, dignity, choice, independence and freedom from abuse, neglect and discrimination." (Disability Rights California)

- "The vision of the National Association for the Advancement of Colored People is to ensure a society in which all individuals have equal rights without discrimination based on race." (National Association for the Advancement of Colored People)

Whereas the primary vision, which is externally oriented, defines how the organization plans to change the world, an internal vision may be helpful to highlight a particular change or operational goal. Examples of internal vision statements are as follows:

- "We will have a 100,000-square-foot gallery that has all the great neon artworks of the twentieth century on display." (Museum of Neon Art)

- "Our vision is an America in which all seniors live a nourished life with independence and dignity." (Meals on Wheels)

- "We will achieve a diversified funding base, which will adequately support all of our programs." (Every nonprofit organization the authors have ever worked with!)

Drafting a Vision Statement

As with the mission statement, the drafting of a vision statement begins with intuition and ideas, evolves through discussion, and results in a shared sense of direction and motivation. All board and staff members should be involved in initial brainstorming and some subsequent discussion, and the planning committee should more fully engage in the process. As with any such process, differing ideas don't have to be a problem. People can spur each other on to more daring and valuable ideas—dreams of changing the world that they are willing to work hard for, encouraging each other to dream the impossible. And as was true in crafting the mission statement, the organization will probably refer back to its vision statement throughout the planning process and may modify it as it becomes clearer where the organization can and should be in the future.

VISIONING EXERCISE: HEADLINE NEWS

A powerful exercise is to pick a time five or ten years in the future and imagine that your organization has been wildly successful. What would a story about your success in the *New York Times* or another news outlet include? Ask individuals to write a headline that describes their vision of success for the future. Examples of headlines include:

- "Curb Cuts Happen: Local Disability Organization Successfully Advocates for the City to Make it Easier for People in Wheelchairs to Negotiate City Streets"
- "Supreme Court Upholds Right of Same-Sex Couples to Marry"
- "Dropout Rate Decreases to All-Time Low"
- "Audubon California Celebrates Opening of Twentieth New Nature Education Center"

Begin by asking each participant at a planning retreat to undertake the following:

It's five years (or ten years) from now and our organization has just been written up in a major publication.

1. What would the headline be saying about our organization?
2. What would be a featured quote about the organization, and who would be saying it?
3. Provide two or three bullets that would serve as the outline for a sidebar story about our organization.
4. Draw a picture, chart, or other graphic that would appear in the publication (include a caption).

The challenge is to create a vision that is grand enough to inspire people but is also grounded in sufficient reality that people can start to believe that it can and will happen. No Olympic athlete ever got to the Olympics by accident; a compelling vision of his or her stellar performance helped surmount all of the sweat and frustrations for many years. Sometimes organizations far surpass their initial visions; as progress happens, what is possible expands. Nonetheless, the picture we carry around to remind us of why we are working so hard continues to inspire this success.

Visioning During the Strategic Planning Process

The creation of a vision statement and the process of visioning helps inspire board and staff and can begin to suggest criteria for setting priorities. The visioning exercise is helpful early on in the process to stretch the team's thinking. It can also be used in

Step 5: Theory of Change and Program Portfolios to inform the ideal scope and scale of services and products. Visioning can help an organization to better answer questions such as:

- What services and products should we be offering now and in the future that would best enable us to achieve our external vision of the future?

- Should we make changes in the services or products we are currently offering, or how we go about doing our business, to be better able to achieve our preferred future?

While the vision statement is focused externally, a similar thought process can be used internally to clarify what the organization will need to do from a management and operations perspective to ensure that infrastructure is in place to support the effective and efficient provision of goods and services to meet the needs of clients and customers. This is sometimes called an internal vision. Such an exercise can be used during Steps 7 and 8, focused on organization capacity and leadership.

ARTICULATE YOUR FUNDAMENTAL VALUES

Nonprofit organizations are known for being values-driven. Spelling out the values the organization supports helps tap the passion of individuals and aligns the heart with the head. Values usually focus on service, quality, people, and work norms. For example, an organization's values might be "Integrity, quality, and excellence in service provision must always be maintained," "Individuals should be empowered to make educated decisions about their health choices," or even something as simple as "We are client-centered." Values might also include related beliefs, such as a vegetarian association's assertion that "Eating vegetables is more economically efficient and ecologically responsible than eating beef."

Other examples of values, beliefs, assumptions, and guiding principles include the following:

- "Self-confidence is not taught or learned; it is earned by surpassing your own self-set limitations." (Outward Bound)

- "Understanding the world geographically as a youth is a prerequisite to acting with global responsibility as an adult." (National Geographic Association)

- "The vitality of life depends on the continued addition of new perspectives, new beliefs, and new wisdom." (Yerba Buena Center for the Arts)

Examples of Values Statements

The Exporatorium is a museum of science, art, and human perception located in San Francisco, California. We believe that following your curiosity and asking questions can lead to amazing moments of discovery, learning, and awareness and can increase your confidence in your ability to understand how the world works. We also believe that being playful and having fun is an important part of the process for people of all ages.

Planned Parenthood Federation of America believes in the fundamental right of each individual, throughout the world, to manage his or her fertility, regardless of the individual's income, marital status, race, ethnicity, sexual orientation, age, national origin, or residence. We believe that respect and value for diversity in all aspects of our organization are essential to our well-being. We believe that reproductive self-determination must be voluntary and preserve the individual's right to privacy. We further believe that such self-determination will contribute to an enhancement of the quality of life, strong family relationships, and population stability.[2]

Glide Memorial Church: Our Core Values emerge from GLIDE as a spiritual movement. They are rooted in empowerment, recovery, and personal transformation. Our values inspire and guide our behaviors. They are the ground we stand on.

- *Radically Inclusive:* We welcome everyone. We value our differences. We respect everyone.

- *Truth Telling:* We each tell our story. We each speak our truth. We listen.

- *Loving and Hopeful:* We are all in recovery. We are a healing community. We love unconditionally.

- *For the People:* We break through barriers. We serve each other. We change the world.

- *Celebration:* We sing. We dance. We laugh together. We celebrate life.

The Importance of Values and Principles

Whether they are spoken or not, all organizations have core values. Most successful organizations make these explicit, debate them, and update them from time to time. Ideally, the personal values of staff, external constituents, and supporters will align with the values of the organization. When developing a written statement of the organization's values, stakeholders can contribute to the articulation of these values and evaluate how well their personal values and motivations match those of the organization. This process will help build stakeholder commitment to the organization and strengthen alignment between individuals and institutions. Explicit values also help in recruiting and selecting staff and board members who share the organization's values.

---

[2] www.plannedparenthood.org/about-us/who-we-are/mission

One exercise to undertake during this step is to perform a gap analysis that compares an organization's currently modeled values with the core values that an organization wishes to personify.[3] This is especially important if an organization's staff is operating with a different set of values than they wish to exemplify in the future. The strategic plan then becomes the vehicle to bridge the gap between what is and what an organization wishes to be.

The board and staff of Support for Families of Children with Disabilities wanted to practice what they believe in, so they put in writing the practices that would put their values into action. One of their six principles and behaviors is Diversity.

Diversity. Disabilities cut across all ethnic, linguistic, and socioeconomic groups. We will endeavor to bring together the different groups with the understanding that, working together, we can make systems change.

Practical Impact: What We Commit to Doing in Everyday Practice

- Reflect diversity, not only in the people we serve but also in our staff, our volunteers, and our board.
- Actively seek involvement from diverse groups in all of our activities.
- Provide information, education, and parent-to-parent services that are linguistically and culturally responsive.
- Consistently provide written materials in the languages of the families we serve.
- Consistently provide presentations and trainings in the languages of the families we serve.
- Consistently provide interpreters at trainings, clinics, and so on.

PUTTING NEW VALUES INTO PRACTICE

Hope, an organization whose purpose is "to enhance the quality of life of individuals with disabilities and their families," articulated within its strategic plan such values as "empowering clients to be the best they can be," "valuing family," and "placing high value on honesty, ethics, integrity, respect, equality, and commitment."

To bring into relief how these aspirational values were different from current, unspoken mental models, their planning consultant suggested that board and staff members articulate old mental models, mindsets, and assumptions they would like to discard. The process elicited some humor as different beliefs were put on the board:

- We'll do what we need to do to get by.
- We focus on disabilities rather than abilities.
- The government should give Hope money because we run good programs.
- The staff knows what is best and makes decisions for clients.

---

[3] Karl Albrecht, *The Northbound Train: Finding the Purpose, Setting the Direction, Shaping the Destiny of Your Organization* (New York: American Management Association, 1994), p. 159.

The process allowed participants to think clearly about how their behavior would need to change to match their stated values, and in the process poke fun at themselves in order to let go of the old mental models. The participants identified the following new mental models, among others:

- Hope Rehabilitation Services is driven by a "quality first" mentality with regard to internal and external customers.
- We focus on abilities rather than disabilities.
- Hope is more independent and self-reliant—it operates as a business.
- Clients are involved and make their own decisions.

Write Your Organization's Values, Beliefs, and Guiding Principles

It is always more difficult the first time around for a board and staff to define—and agree on—the values, beliefs, and guiding principles that often have been implied. A strategic planning process is an excellent opportunity to make explicit those implied values, or to reaffirm the values, beliefs, and guiding principles that were previously developed in past strategic planning efforts. Worksheet 3.1 provides a framework for defining values, beliefs, and guiding principles, as well as the behaviors that support the practice of those guiding principles.

Be prepared to have some heartfelt debates during the discussion of the organization's values and beliefs. This activity evokes strong feelings and emotions, because most people are not neutral about their beliefs. People feel strongly about their core values, and this is not really about an organization's beliefs but about individuals' beliefs. Take your time, clarify where there is agreement and where there is disagreement, and strive to reach agreement on your core values and beliefs. It is important to reach consensus on these guiding principles, because they are the foundation of your work.

→ SEE WORKSHEET 3.1 TO ASSIST WITH THIS STEP.

WORKSHEET 3.1	**CREATE MISSION, VISION, AND VALUES STATEMENTS**
How to do this activity?	Assign one or two designated writers from the planning committee to review the current mission statement, vision, and values statements (if the organization has them), redraft them as necessary, and present them first to the planning committee, then to board and staff for feedback.
Why do this activity?	Clarity about these statements is vital. You need to know where you are going before you can figure out how to get there. Expect to go through a few drafts before getting one that everyone likes.
Who to involve in the process?	Input from board and staff (and possibly other key stakeholders); one or two people write the draft(s). Formal approval of the mission statement by the board of directors.

CAUTIONS FOR FACILITATORS

Facilitators should be aware of and work to avoid the following pitfalls during the strategic planning process:

Step 3: Mission, Vision, Values

Words matter, ideas are most important. Mission, vision, and values discussions can stir as many debates about the way to say something as about the ideas themselves. Get clear on the important ideas and concepts—groups can do this. Then go to writing—groups can't do this!

Come back to it. Take the opportunity to get a "working draft" that can evolve through the process. It is almost impossible to get a great mission statement in one pass.

Keep it real. Lofty inspiration is important. So is the ability to easily see how a vision or mission is being *directly and meaningfully* addressed by an organization's work.

| WORKSHEET 3.1 | Create Mission, Vision, and Values Statements |

❏ What is a compelling mission statement for our organization?

❏ What is our organization's realistic yet challenging and guiding vision of success? (How can we dare to dream the possible?)

❏ What are some of the values, beliefs, and/or guiding principles that do (or should) guide our board and staff's interactions with each other and with our constituencies? What behaviors should we commit to doing in everyday practice to support our values and beliefs?

Statement

What is the *focus problem(s)* that our organization exists to solve?

(In considering the focus problem or need, address the following questions: What need or opportunity does our organization exist to resolve? Who is affected by the problem? How are they affected?)

- *Low income and other disenfranchised people face legal barriers to basic life necessities, things like safe and stable housing, medical care, education, jobs, economic security, and freedom from violence. These groups simply do not have the resources to access the legal help they need, and our legal system cannot ensure equal access to justice. As a result, poor people often suffer needlessly from solvable legal problems.*

- *For the legal system to truly operate fairly, vulnerable populations need representation by attorneys.*

- *The current legal system and regulations have barriers to truly support one of the important foundational values of our country: "equal access."*

What are the *assumptions* upon which our organization does its work?

- *Clients deserve to be treated at all times with respect, dignity, compassion, and fairness.*

- *By providing legal assistance to low-income and other disenfranchised people, we can help ensure that all people, regardless of their economic or social situation, can have equal justice under the law. We believe legal help can change lives.*

- *We can have a greater impact if, in addition to providing legal services, we challenge policies and laws that are detrimental to people who are poor or disenfranchised.*

- *It is important for vulnerable populations to have their fundamental rights protected, including access to basic necessities such as housing and access to health services.*

- *We assume that we can better achieve our mission by seeking opportunities to empower our clients to advocate for themselves.*

- *One of the underlying causes of poverty is a lack of equal access to basic necessities (food, shelter, freedom from violence, access to quality education).*

Components of Mission Statement:

Mandatory Component: What is the *purpose* of our organization?

(A purpose statement answers the question of why an organization exists; it does not describe *what* an organization does. The sentence should be a short, succinct statement that describes the ultimate result an organization is hoping to achieve.)

To promote equal access to justice

Optional Component: *How* do we go about serving our purpose; what are our primary services or activities?

(Add to the purpose statement a short summary of the methods that our organization uses to accomplish its purpose.)

Provision of counseling and legal representation

Our compelling mission statement:

County Legal Aid Society's (CLAS) mission is to promote equal access to justice by providing counseling and legal representation for disenfranchised and low-income people in Central County.

What should be our tag line or slogan?

Making Justice for All a Reality

Vision Statements

External vision: How would the world be improved if our organization was successful in achieving its purpose? (Write the vision in a way that we will be able to answer the question: "Have we made progress toward our vision?" at the end of the implementation of our strategic plan.)

- *Our clients have the skills and resources necessary to advocate for access to basic human necessities of housing, quality health care, and freedom from violence.*
- *Low-income and other disenfranchised people in Central County have equal access to legal representation in civil courts.*
- *As a result of our advocacy work, there would be fewer barriers to human needs such as housing, health care, food and freedom from violence.*
- *All individuals, regardless of their social or economic status, are treated fairly by the civil justice system.*
- *Government agencies serving low-income communities in our service region will adhere to the laws and regulations governing their behavior and will fairly serve low-income residents.*

Internal vision: *Envisioning our organization's future over the next five years*

Programs and Services Scope and Scale:

- **Advocacy:** *Within the next two years, we will have established a formal program or structure that supports us being able to challenge federal, state, and/or local policies and practices that are detrimental to low-income people.*

(continued)

- **Housing:** *We have increased the number of self-help classes that we offer; at least maintain existing level of services.*

- **Public Benefits:** *We have at least doubled the number of self-help classes we offer so that any individual who needs government assistance can understand how to access those benefits.*

- **Health Care:** *All individuals who qualify for health care are able to access quality care through the Affordable Care Act.*

- **Family Law:** *In partnership with Central County Safe House for Women and Children, we have the capacity—through the establishment of regularly scheduled self-help workshops, counseling and referral services, and/or representation—to help any victim of domestic violence obtain restraining orders and keep custody or obtain guardianship of their children.*

- *We have established a formal* **Consumer Issues** *program so that we are able to, through representation and classes, assist elderly and other vulnerable groups from being victimized by unscrupulous lenders, helping people file for bankruptcy when appropriate, and helping people manage their debts.*

- **Pro Bono** *is not a service program, it is a "staffing capacity" strategy—still, our vision is that every project has a strategic way to involve pro bono volunteer resources where it leverages staff attorney time and expertise and leverages strong relationships with the private sector.*

Business Model (How will we support our programmatic vision?):

- *Law firms continue to partner with us through generous donations of pro bono services and financial contributions; volunteer lawyers give generously.*

- *We will have doubled the number of local, nonlegal businesses that support us.*

- *We will have increased by at least 25 percent the amount of money that individual donors give.*

- *We will maintain the existing level of state money we receive from the State Bar.*

Organizational Capacity (What do we need in terms of human resources and systems and structures that would support our programmatic vision?):

- *We will have implemented a matrix management approach so that we are able to coordinate across departments individuals' access to our services (for example, appoint a staff person to be the "matrix manager" for seniors, one for people with disabilities, and another for Spanish-speaking individuals).*

- *Our data information system uses the most up-to-date technology, and we are able to easily, accurately, and effectively document the work that we are doing. This will enable us to both track impact of our work and easily document levels of service: both internally and externally our improved data system allows us to better document our successes.*

- *Departments work well by themselves, but there is not as much collaboration within the organization as we have with those outside of the organization.*

- *We have increased the salary scale ranges for both staff attorneys and other staff, and our health and other benefits are viewed as generous and help us to maintain staff.*

- *We have implemented a student loan reimbursement program (loan repayment assistance program, LRAP) for staff attorneys, based on tenure.*

WORKSHEET 3.1 *(continued)*

- All staff have money budgeted for professional development.
- We have sufficient staff to meet the community's needs, and that staff reflects the populations we serve.

Leadership (Board and senior management: What do we need in terms of board governance and support—and senior management's leadership and effectiveness—in order to support our programmatic vision?):

- Successful executive transition of long-term executive director
- Increased the number of board members actively involved in governance and support work of our agency: All members make a financial contribution that is considered generous by their peers; board members make legal aid one of their top two charitable priorities; board meetings are every other month rather than monthly and are well attended; and board members participate fully in discussions as opposed to simply listening to presentations.
- We have an Emergency Succession Planning document that ensures that if our executive director takes an unplanned leave of absence, there is documentation as to who does what, when, accountability, limited constraints on authority, etc.
- The board has a multiyear plan for ongoing board recruitment, so we are always assured a rotation of new board members with the specific skill sets needed to meet the opportunities and challenges facing the organization.

Organizational Values, Beliefs, and/or Guiding Principles

What are our organization's values, beliefs, and/or guiding principles?	Practical impact: How do we put our values, beliefs, and guiding principles into practice?
Collaboration	Our work can be more effective if, as opportunities arise, we work in collaboration with other agencies so as not to duplicate existing services.
Diversity	We aim to have our staff and board reflect the diversity of our community, including language expertise.
	When working with populations whose primary language is other than English, ensure that collateral material is available in the language of that population.
	We will maintain a welcoming environment at all times.
Teamwork	We not only collaborate with our clients but also seek out opportunities to collaborate with our fellow staff and are willing to learn from others and work together for justice for all.
	Go the extra mile; put the team first!
Professionalism	We are committed to excellence in our work with clients, including timely communication; we are up to date in our field; and at all times we are respectful in how we treat our clients, colleagues, and community justice partners.

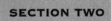

Strategic Analysis

In Steps 4–8, we look individually at the five core content dimensions of strategic planning: environmental scan, theory of change and program portfolio, business model, organization capacity, and leadership. In addition to conducting the analysis in each of these dimensions, one of the central roles of the strategic planning committee is to connect the dots among these different dimensions as the work unfolds.

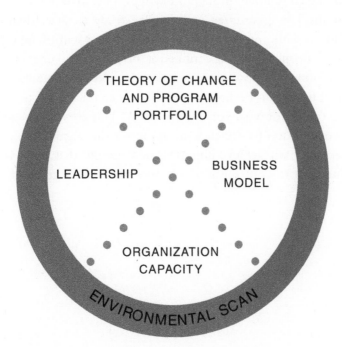

The strategic planning committee as a group is responsible for getting these five steps completed. In practice, a significant amount of work is required outside of the regular strategic planning committee meetings. Another option that works well is to assign each of the five dimensions to one or two members of the strategic planning committee. The point person or people for each dimension are encouraged to enlist the support of staff and/or board members who are not on the committee. For instance, you might tap the chief financial officer or the board treasurer for the money discussion, if one or the other is not on the strategic planning committee. This adds capacity for the task and helps involve other key leaders.

Step 5: Theory of Change and Program Portfolio theory of change and program portfolio requires the greatest amount of work followed by Step 6: Business Model. The level of work required is typically much less for each of the other three dimensions, although how much less will depend on individual circumstances. The planning workplan needs to allow sufficient time for this work to be completed.

One tension in this section is that although all five dimensions are interconnected; it is often more efficient to begin the work of all steps at the same time. If the strategic planning committee is willing to take a little more time, it is certainly possible to take each step in order.

When subcommittees or teams are tasked with looking into one area, by bringing findings and recommendations back to discussions of the strategic planning committee, the dots can be connected, and each member of the committee has an opportunity to engage with each of the dimensions of the plan. The work of the strategic planning committee through these steps is iterative, with many back-and-forth discussions. The committee will then be ready to share draft findings and recommendations with a wider audience of board and staff members.

WARNING: People often feel confused at this point. This uneasiness is actually a good sign! Exploring new possibilities brings with it lots of uncertainty and questions that are difficult to answer. Feeling confused or uncertain at some point is a sign that you are going outside of what you already know. This growth is required for your work to be creative and to stretch your vision for the organization. Embrace the uncertainty and you will achieve important new insights that allow your organization to devote itself to your mission even more fully with greater focus.

CHAPTER 4

Step 4: Environmental Scan

FIRST STEPS	STRATEGIC ANALYSIS	SET YOUR COURSE
1. Set up for Success	4. Environmental Scan	9. Complete the Strategic Plan
2. Stakeholder Engagement	5. Theory of Change and Program Portfolio	10. Use Your Plan Successfully
3. Mission, Vision, Values	6. Business Model	
	7. Organization Capacity	
	8. Leadership	

The first thing to keep in mind when considering the external environment is that although you want to be expansive in considering possible trends and issues, you ultimately want to focus on just a few critical issues. The challenge is to discern the few issues that are or may become significant—those to which your organization must respond or be prepared to respond—whether these are helpful or are obstacles to be overcome.

Second, the purpose of scanning the environment is to ground your strategic plan in the realities of the world around you. The environment is relevant to each of the other four dimensions of your strategic analysis. For instance, these realities clearly affect your strategy and business model. Likewise, in terms of organizational capacity, the prevailing wages in your market affect how competitive your compensation is, and new hardware and software technologies change options about how to upgrade. Current events and trends in your field will also affect both the requirements of leadership and the individuals who are available to serve your organization.

You may appoint an environment subcommittee, or one or two people to take responsibility for the summarizing the big picture and for supporting the work of colleagues who are working on other dimensions, by getting input on specific questions they need to investigate. However, it will make more sense for some of the research to be done by the relevant subcommittees. Ultimately the full Strategic Planning Committee needs to agree on what the critical external issues are for your work.

Some of the environment issues related to strategy and program include:

- General trends in the broader environment, including political, economic, social, demographic, legal, and technology trends, and the built and natural environment
- Trends in the needs of the population or community
- Trends and developments in your field of service
- Changes in competition

Environment issues related to business model include:

- General trends in funding sources, whether from foundations, online giving, or other sources
- Any specific trends that have affected your organization's funding
- Innovative examples of business models that may be relevant, such as partnerships on back office functions

Issues related to organization capacity include:

- Trends in human resources, including compensation policy or changes in prevailing health benefits practice
- Relevant conditions and developments in each of the other elements of capacity: technology, facilities, information technology, and so on.

Some of the environment issues related to leadership include:

- Trends in the field, such as executive transition management, leadership development programs
- Trends and developments in effective governance, such as a new board recruitment service offered by the local volunteer center or locally offered board training services

External stakeholder input can be especially valuable in this step. Whether this input was gathered in a general way early in the process or you have decided to focus your outreach to external stakeholders on specific questions facing your organization, the full strategic planning committee needs to agree on information you seek from external stakeholder engagement.

WHEN IS SCENARIO PLANNING HELPFUL?

There is a whole body of work on the concept of scenario planning that can be highly involved and complex. Major trends and forces that are identified in the external environment step provide context for organizational and program planning. The world is changing all the time, but many of the most significant changes do not occur overnight. Government policy changes can be anticipated. New technology, or funder expectations, and even competitive moves by other players are rarely, if ever, developed *and implemented* in less than a period of a few years.

Scenario planning helps planners prepare for trends or developments that would be game changing, and *might* happen, but for which the outcome won't be known for some time. Will our drought in California end in the next few years? Will an election cycle two or four years away lead toward a significant change in public policy? [Remember it often takes years after an election for policy changes to actually affect your organization.]

The point of scenario planning is to increase *readiness*. For our purposes, we offer two alternative ways to take advantage of scenario planning.

1. Identify a small number (one to three) critical future developments that are possible but not certain and develop contingency plans for these possibilities. For example, a major funder may be in their own strategic planning process; if they change their priorities, how will you respond? Or you've heard that another organization may expand its work into your sphere; again, if that happens, how will you respond? Ideally, the strategies you choose for your organization and programs will prepare you to be ready to pivot if necessary to make the needed changes.

2. When there are two primary uncertainties, a two-by-two matrix can be helpful, as shown in Figure 4.1. Each axis of the matrix is a continuum from 0% likelihood of the event happening to 100% certainty of its happening. For example major funder is considering greatly increasing their support in a particular field. The money won't flow for at least a year or more. At the same time, a well known organization significantly may expand its services in competition with you. How will you respond in each of the four possible

FIGURE 4.1   TWO-BY-TWO MATRIX

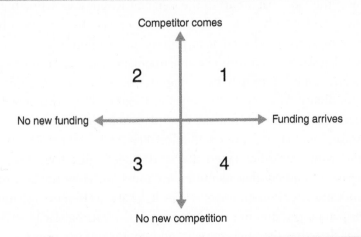

scenarios? Quadrant 4 would be easiest—new money and no new competition. Quadrant 2 would be most difficult—no new money combined with new competition. Are there strategies that will position you well *regardless* of which scenario comes to pass? Strategies that will make your organization stronger and more resilient? For example, building program evaluation infrastructure, or expanding your continuum of services, strengthening your membership engagement or even exploring preemptive discussions about collaboration. Even if some of these ideas are not new, this analysis may change the priority and sequencing of strategy implementation. Developing a more robust program evaluation infrastructure might have been on your agenda for years; this may provide the incentive to make it happen.

ORGANIZE YOUR RESEARCH, SUMMARIZE FINDINGS

Start with information and expertise already at hand. Staff members, and frequently board members, are often in close touch with the changing environment and trends affecting the field. Remember that the knowledge of staff and board members may be valid data in itself! Building from the knowledge on the team, identify areas for further exploration. Are there relevant published reports? Did feedback from external stakeholders suggest areas for further research? Do any of the issues that the team is already familiar with require more investigation to determine what the implications are?

First, based on your research identify and prioritize what changes and trends are taking place. You may identify 10 or more significant changes. Some changes may not have an obvious impact on your strategy, so you will want to identify the handful of the most important changes and trends.

Second, spell out the implications of these changes and trends for your organization. This is the "so what?" part of the step and where you define the *meaning* of these changes and trends. The first level of implication may be obvious—for instance, if a majority of elected state representatives hostile to your agenda has won the state legislature, you won't be able to pursue state legislation successfully. In other cases, the implications may be ambiguous or unknown. Regardless, it is this team's responsibility to bring both prioritized external environmental issues and their implications back to the full strategic planning committee.

At this stage, you may need to do additional research—just make sure to do it in coordination with any other external research needs that have been identified. Finally prepare a summary that identifies key issues and their implications for your organization's strategy. This summary will be helpful as a reference document for the full strategic planning committee and will provide the starting place for the section of the plan that describes the environment, and context of the plan.

CAUTIONS FOR FACILITATORS

Facilitators should be aware of and work to avoid the following pitfalls during the strategic planning process:

Step 4: Environmental Scan

Just do it. Staff may be reluctant to put much time into doing an environmental scan, with the belief that it's either not very important or that they already know the important information. This step should not be skipped, an facilitators of the planning process should negotiate with staff the level of effort to invest; at the very least have staff articulate their assumptions collectively.

Educate all planners Staff may in fact be more in tune to what is happening in the external environment or have recently done similar research. In that case facilitators might suggest that a summary of the staff's environmental scan be presented to the board members of a planning committee.

> **WORKSHEET 4.1**   The External Environment: Summary of Trends and
> External Forces
>
> ❏ Here is a summary of trends in our field and a summary of the external forces/
> opportunities and threats that may have an influence on our organization.

Summary of the External Environment

Theory of Change and Program Portfolio

- **What are the three to five primary forces in our organization's environment (political, economic, social values, demographics, legal, technological, the built and natural environment) that are either supporting our being able to better achieve our mission (external opportunities) or forces that are working against our being able to better achieve our mission (external threats)? What are the implications of these trends in the environment for our organization?**

  o *Shifting Demographics and Increased Poverty: After the recession, there are simply more residents of our county who are living at or below the poverty line. The census data also show new pockets of high density of poverty in our county, as well as demographic shifts in the makeup of our county's low-income and other underserved populations. Our understanding of the communities who are eligible for and in need of our services may be based more on history at this point than the current reality. Our board and staff should look together at these data to be able to understand the shifts in population and how our programs and services should perhaps shift as a result (for example, there is an increased need for our materials and resources to be available in languages other than English and Spanish). We should also use some mapping tools to compare the location of poverty throughout our county against the clients we are serving (comparing census data to our case management system, comparing by zip code) to see if we are actually providing services in the neediest areas of our county and whether there are any locations in our county that we are not reaching. With this kind of data analysis, we think that the demographic shifts might be an opportunity to engage new funders or expand existing funding because of the new and increased needs for our services.*

  o *Economic Shifts in Law Firms and Law Schools: Both law firms and law schools are key partners in our programs and delivery of services. We rely on law firm attorneys to participate as volunteers in our pro bono programs and law students as interns during the academic year and summers, as well as potential recruits as staff attorneys upon graduation. Law firms may be experiencing shifts in how they deliver their services as the corporate clients change expectations. This may (or may not) impact how some law firms structure their pro bono programs; we need to monitor this area and be ready to shift our own pro bono projects to respond as needed. In addition, some of the law schools in our local area are reducing the size of their incoming classes to respond to the current high employment rate of their graduates. At the same time, some law schools are shifting their curriculum away from the traditional law school content to classes that emphasize hands-on experience and opportunities that help students be more "practice ready" as they graduate. These law school shifts may present opportunities for us to partner even more with local law schools and create a new pipeline of both staff attorneys and also future volunteers.*

  o *Technology: There have been many advances in technology in the delivery of legal services in both the nonprofit and for-profit sectors. This includes everything from improved case management database systems for*

WORKSHEET 4.1 *(continued)*

legal aid programs, making the ongoing management of cases more efficient and effective, to outreach to clients through online tools and even texting, to providing direct services to clients through virtual tools (e.g., web-based video or videoconferencing). Our current IT systems do not support growth in this area, and we need to examine the developments in the area of technology, distill lessons learned and best practices, seek out projects that would make sense for us to replicate (or even pilot), and then determine what IT infrastructure we need to be successful.

- **What are the major trends and developments in our field of service that we need to consider when setting priorities for our future?**

  o *Developments in the Law: There have been exciting new developments in many areas of law in which we provide services, including immigration and health care access, among others. We need to consider how we are able to respond quickly and effectively to ensure implementation of these types of changes in our county and how that might impact our staffing and other internal infrastructure needs. We need to have a way of responding when the changes are within our existing program priorities and a way of assessing whether we add new services to respond to changes in the law for which we do not have existing programs (including considering the costs of new projects and exit barriers to discontinuing those services in the future).*

  o *Mergers of Other Legal Aid Organizations: Several legal aid organizations in the northern area of our state merged into one, multicounty large legal services nonprofit. Funders have talked very positively about this development and encouraged others to consider whether merger might be appropriate. It is not clear yet whether this is the beginning of a trend, but as other smaller legal services nonprofits have also closed their doors in the same time period, we should be monitoring developments in this area and considering whether merger (for example, with the much smaller legal aid nonprofit in neighboring Valley County) might be an option in the future.*

- **Who are our major competitors and what distinguishes us from the competition? Has the competitive environment changed and, if yes, how has it changed and what are the implications for how we respond to competition in the future?**

  o *There is currently an all-volunteer legal aid program operating out of Central City's Senior Services, as well as a program at the Disability Access Project that provides legal services to their clients. Unlike these two programs that provide legal assistance for specific populations, CLAS offers a broad range of assistance to vulnerable populations. One of our collaborations is with Central County Safe House for Women and Children; this collaboration allows us to partner with them and use our knowledge of the legal system with their extensive knowledge of domestic violence prevention.*

  o *Although we do assist seniors and people with disabilities, we do not have specialized expertise in these areas. Since our last strategic planning process, two legal aid programs in the cities of Applewood and Warm Springs have folded. In addition, while they are not competitors in terms of clients, the legal aid program in Valley County continues to receive funding from government agencies, although we have gotten feedback from their clients that they are not providing quality and timely services and do not cover the areas of law most needed by low-income residents of that county.*

(continued)

WORKSHEET 4.1 *(continued)*

Business Model

- **What are the general trends in terms of funding from foundations, individuals, online giving, etc., that are or will have an impact on our current business model?**

  o *Continued Reduction in Government Funding: Our state and local county government funding sources were reduced every year for the last five years, and we do not envision a quick recovery in this area. Historically our revenue model has relied heavily on government funding, but that has been increasingly volatile over the last 5 to 10 years and no longer seems to be a viable strategy. We must reduce our reliance on government funding and reexamine our overall revenue model.*

  o *Postrecession Recovery by Law Firms: In contrast, although law firm charitable giving decreased during the recession (as their business decreased), all signs are that law firms are recovering nicely from the recession and may be able to increase their charitable giving again in years to come. At the same time, many firms now connect their charitable giving to the firm's involvement in pro bono relationships with the legal services nonprofits. We need to examine whether our pro bono and fund development programs are structured appropriately to be able to build strong donor and pro bono relationships with firms and benefit from their economic recovery.*

  o *Charitable Giving from Individuals: Studies show that all generations indicate they will make higher charitable contributions in the coming year than they did last year; this is the second year in a row showing higher donor giving expectations. In addition, data show that the newest generation of donors (those around 35 years of age) have high inclinations toward philanthropy and may be a very generous and engaged population in years to come. At the same time, national studies show that nonprofits are failing at retaining current donors, with as high as a 70 percent lapse rate year to year. We need to reexamine our overall donor stewardship structures, make sure we have a plan to reduce our own lapse rate, and think about how we are working to engage the newest generation of donors now as a long-term strategy.*

- **What are general external economic factors that have affected—or may impact—our organization's ability to support our programs in the future?**

  o *IOLTA (Interest on Lawyer Trust Account) Funding: As long as federal interest rates remain low, IOLTA funding (which is tied to the federal interest rate) will also remain at historically low levels (after having been reduced each year for the last five years). This funding used to be the most stable component of our grants portfolio, and this may never be the same again.*

  o *Increased Poverty: Low-income communities in our state were hit hard by the recession and have not recovered. Census data show an increase in poverty density in some areas of our county, and an overall increased number of county residents living at or below the poverty line. We simply have more people in our county who are eligible for our services, and the demand for our assistance already outstripped existing resources before this increased need.*

  o *Reduced State Funding for the Local Courts and County Safety Net Programs: Reduced government funding has not only impacted our organization; it has also resulted in reduced funding for the local courts and county agency's safety net programs that also serve our clients. The courts have reduced the hours that their clerk windows are open and have closed down some courtrooms in areas that directly impact our clients, including probate court for guardianships of children and the courts handling evictions. Our clients now need to travel much further distances to either file or respond to cases in these areas of law.*

WORKSHEET 4.1 *(continued)*

- **Are there innovative examples of business models that may be relevant for us to consider during our planning process (e.g., partnerships on back-office functions, collaborative efforts)?**

   o *Collaborations on Outsourcing: Some legal aid nonprofits in our state have started talking about sharing an accountant contractor. This might very well reduce our costs and would ensure that our accountant was well versed in the state and other grants common to legal aid nonprofits.*

   o *Collaborations on Funding: Several nonprofits in the southern part of our state have created a new collaborative project to serve immigrants in each of their respective service regions and have received large foundation grants for this work. We should explore whether other legal aid nonprofits in the counties near us would be interested in collaborating in this way in areas where we work in the same areas of law or serving similar client populations.*

Organizational Capacity

- **Are there trends in human resources, including compensation policy (e.g., changes in prevailing practice around health benefits), staff retention strategies, etc., that we should pay attention to during our planning discussions?**

   o *Retirement Benefits: Our organization does not provide any matching retirement benefits for our employees; we only make a 403(b) plan available to them. We are hearing from an increasing number of legal aid nonprofits in our state that they are providing employer-matching in retirement benefits. We must consider whether we need to do this in order to be able to continue to recruit quality new and midlevel attorneys.*

   o *Loan Repayment Assistance Programs: Although the federal government has created a system to help new attorneys defer some debt and have access to some loan repayment assistance after they work for a period of time in legal aid, other legal aid nonprofits in our state also provide their own loan repayment assistance to their attorney staff. We do not have this program, and we need to reconsider this and determine the cost of providing such assistance.*

   o *Professional and Leadership Development Planning: Other legal aid nonprofits have invested in providing training and professional development in supervision by senior staff attorneys and ways to provide leadership development opportunities to newer staff. We need to have a system for ensuring annual professional development plans for all staff and a proactive way of developing leadership skills to ensure a pipeline of diverse and highly engaged leaders in our organization.*

- **Are there relevant developments in technology, management information systems, planning and evaluation, etc., that we should factor in when agreeing on structures and systems priorities that support our organizational capacity to sustain quality services and, if needed, growth?**

   o *Better Case Management Programs: There continue to be developments and improvements (even in the system we currently have) that we are not taking advantage of. Having a better internal IT structure will help us be more efficient in managing our cases, support internal data reports to evaluate our programs and services, and help us report more effectively to external stakeholders, including funders.*

   o *Increased Focus on Outcomes Measurements by Funders: County agency funding, our state IOLTA funding program, and even national funders like the Legal Services Corporation are all exploring requiring different types of measurements of outcomes in legal services cases. We need to study these developments and implement change in our own systems, so that we are staying in front of this trend and prepared to lead, rather than just respond.*

(continued)

WORKSHEET 4.1 *(continued)*

o *Virtual Legal Services: Some legal aid nonprofits in our state are exploring the provision of assistance through virtual or other web-based video and other tools. This is an exciting opportunity and one that we should determine whether we can incorporate components or lessons learned in our own programs—and use online video-chat or videoconferencing to expand the geographic reach of our services without requiring new brick-and-mortar presence in different areas of our service region.*

Leadership: Senior Team and Governance

- **What trends in the field, such as executive transition management, leadership development programs, etc., will influence sustaining a "leaderful organization"?**

  o *More emphasis is being placed on ensuring that sound emergency succession plans are in place and implementing programs to develop leadership and management skills for midlevel managers. In addition, our local nonprofit consulting firm that provides consulting and training services to nonprofit organizations currently provides workshops on executive transition management and assists organizations to do executive searches.*

- **What trends and developments are there regarding board governance that we should look at in terms of setting short-term and long-term board priorities (e.g., a new board recruitment service offered by the local Volunteer Center, board training services offered locally, a trend towards smaller boards, etc.)?**

  o *Better use of advisory boards, including clarity as to their function and a clear structure in terms of terms, recruitment, etc.*

  o *Many organizations are creating a multiyear strategy for board recruitment.*

  o *Boards are moving toward some type of regular self-assessments of their own work.*

  o *Many boards are striving for 100 percent of the board making financial contributions and every board member helping with fundraising. This is in keeping with the fact that the local community foundation has new expectations in this area and now asks for an explicit description of board gifts and solicitations and the total dollar amounts raised by the board in their grant forms.*

Highest Priority Issues from Environmental Scan

1. *Growth in needs and changes in demographics of service population and their access to service—demands organization-wide responses.*

2. *Technology advances provide many opportunities to increase efficiency and provide better service—we are behind the curve on taking advantage of this potential.*

3. *Opportunity is present to energetically go after increased support from law firms and individuals—we cannot afford to wait; the opportunity will not last forever.*

Many other important issues have been identified and are worth attending to at the department level.

CHAPTER 5

Step 5: Theory of Change and Program Portfolio

FIRST STEPS	STRATEGIC ANALYSIS	SET YOUR COURSE
1. Set up for Success	4. Environmental Scan	9. Complete the Strategic Plan
2. Stakeholder Engagement	5. Theory of Change and Program Portfolio	10. Use Your Plan Successfully
3. Mission, Vision, Values	6. Business Model	
	7. Organization Capacity	
	8. Leadership	

Your theory of change and program portfolio are the heart of your strategic plan. Everything else (e.g., money, staff, buildings, technology, and board) is designed to carry out your organization's program work. Your mission statement is your broadest definition of your ends; the theory of change provides the rationale underlying the means. Your theory of change is your organizational program strategy as seen from the 30,000-foot perspective. It is a summary statement that makes clear the ways your programs work together; in other words, the theory of change is an overarching answer to the question, "How are we going to accomplish our mission?"

Your program portfolio is the collection of programs through which you carry out your strategy. Just as an artist's portfolio is a collection of her artistic work and is intended to represent the artist's talents and accomplishments, or an investment portfolio is a collection of investments that together are selected to accomplish your investment objectives, your program portfolio is a collection of programs that are designed to work together to achieve your mission. Each element in your program portfolio must make a critical, necessary contribution to the organization's overall theory of change. Individual, disconnected programs do not create a whole that is greater than the sum of its parts.

We begin this step by looking at the big picture and what you are currently doing in order to articulate your theory of change. We finish by asking how you want to grow your impact through adding, changing your programs, or sometimes actually updating your theory of change itself.

Begin this step by reviewing your updated mission statement, vision, and values, as well as the questions and issues raised at the outset of the strategic planning process (see your previously completed Worksheet 1.1: Identify Planning Process Issues and Outcomes, and Worksheet 3.1: Mission, Vision, Values). Developing proposals for how your organization can increase its impact includes substeps:

- *Needs assessment.* Identify the nature and dimensions of the problem you are working to solve. Addressing the problem successfully is what funders consider the social impact. In addition, think about the relevant clients/constituencies considered to be of value—this is the "value proposition" you offer.

- *Program portfolio assessment.* Describe your current program portfolio and assess its effectiveness.

- *Competitive analysis.* Assess how well your organization is currently doing its job, relative to others.

- *Define your current and future theory of change.* This then is foundation for your overarching program strategy. By understanding how you can increase your impact, you will be in a position to propose a sound future business model.

At this point in the strategic planning process, the work becomes more iterative: each of the next four dimensions of the model (program portfolio and theory of change, business model, organization capacity, and leadership) is interrelated, and analysis of one dimension may lead you to have to revisit some of the tentative decisions you will reach during the next steps in the process. Therefore, once you have looked at all five dimensions (after step 8) you will need to come back to these integrating questions:

- Are you responding appropriately to major environmental forces?

- How well is your current business model supporting this program portfolio?

- How well are current programs resourced in terms of organization capacity and leadership? Have you identified gaps, or opportunities to change, drop, or add programs?

- What are the implications for your future theory of change and program portfolio?

- Based on all of the above, what should be your core future strategies (see Step 9)?

NEEDS ASSESSMENT AND VALUE PROPOSITION

A for-profit sector needs to understand what the unique value their product or service is for their consumers. So too nonprofit organizations need to understand what needs their constituencies have (including clients as well as donors) and what value these constituencies place on the organization's services.

In order to think about how to increase your progress toward your mission, you must be able to describe the nature (scale, scope, dimensions, etc.) of the problem you are trying to solve. This tends to be easier in the area of human services, which deals with questions such as how many homeless people there are in your city, region, or state, or how many children with special needs live in your service area. For other issues—such as water quality, the status of immigrant rights, or a community's need for arts and culture—it can be more difficult, and perhaps for this reason is every bit as important.

The mission of one organization we worked with is "to engage vulnerable children and youth, enrich their connection with family and community, and empower them to lead healthy, rewarding lives." Clearly, there are several dimensions to the system this organization wants to impact. Still, it is possible to identify an estimate of the number of youth, at different age groups, in the regions they are serving and some description of the nature and extent of the needs to which they want to respond.

One place to begin to define the boundaries of the needs you are addressing is to go back to your focus problem from the mission statement exercise. If you clearly articulated your focus problem, this will be a good starting place.

After you have clearly defined the focus problem, your needs assessment should answer the following questions:

- *Scope*: What is the current scope of the problem?

- *What populations are impacted by this problem*: What important populations are relevant to your programming? If more than one, is one or more populations a higher priority than others? Are there segments that are not served, and if so, why?

- *Trends in Needs*: What are the trends in the scope of the problem? How is it changing? Is it growing or declining; for example, is there a change in demographics of a service population, or trends in public opinion that factor in policy advocacy work? Are there positive or negative trends in related systems, competition, or understanding of the problem/need?

- *What do your current and future populations consider of value?*

- *What are the implications for what programs and services you should be offering in the future?*

The Environmental Scan will have gathered some of this information. Fill out your understanding of the needs you want to meet, the problem you want to solve as thoroughly as possible within your constraints. Summarize the needs assessment to share with the full strategic planning committee.

→ SEE WORKSHEET 5.1 TO ASSIST WITH THIS STEP.

WORKSHEET 5.1   NEEDS ASSESSMENT

How to do this activity?	This step can involve a lot of research, or be the product of an internal discussion. The extent of needs assessment desired will drive the process for this step.
Why do this activity?	All organizations exist to respond to community needs. This is the starting place for creating strategy.
Who to involve in this activity?	Planning Committee or Task Force/Subcommittee

PROGRAM EFFECTIVENESS

Beyond the general input collected from internal and external stakeholders, the planning committee needs to assess the quality and effectiveness of current programs in some detail. Questions to answer include the following:

- How well are your programs responding to the problem you have defined?
- What is the cost, and cost effectiveness, of your programs?
- In general, how able has your organization been to gather the necessary resources (funding, staffing expertise, technology, partnerships, etc.) that are necessary to support each of your programs adequately? (Funding specifically will also be looked at comprehensively in Step 6.)

Program planning looks both to the past (to learn to what degree your programs have had the impact you want) and to the future (to assess future needs, funding opportunities, and emerging opportunities to meet the needs).

Ideally, program evaluation is an ongoing process for an organization. Client feedback mechanisms should be built into programs, so that client satisfaction and progress are monitored continuously. These data are often required by funders, and the broader public is demanding greater visibility into the effectiveness of nonprofits. Regular formal evaluations should be performed by outside evaluators or by staff or volunteers to help an agency consider how to improve a program, the degree to which a program is making a difference, and whether the program is cost effective. If this is a current practice at your organization, planners will be able to use current program evaluation information.

For many organizations without well-developed program evaluation systems, the strategic planning process provides an opportunity to comprehensively look at program effectiveness. For some organizations, one of the most important decisions about programs in the strategic plan is to prioritize a more formal approach to evaluation in the future.

CLARE DISCOVERS THE DIFFICULTY OF WORKING AT THE NATIONAL ORGANIZATION OF CLONED PEOPLE.

Program assessments should list the program name and purpose, its revenue and expenses, the scope of services (numbers served, nature of services), and relevant evaluation data, such as data on program effectiveness or benchmarking comparisons. Program evaluations may use both subjective and objective information, as well as quantitative and qualitative data. Objective data consist of fact-based information, such as a review of records, descriptive statistics, and the like. Such data are more easily collected and less easily disputed, because they translate experience into quantifiable data that can be counted, compared, measured, and manipulated statistically. Subjective, qualitative data consist of what people say about the programs in interviews, focus groups, or other meetings; direct or field observation; reviews of written materials; informal feedback; satisfaction surveys; and questionnaires. Qualitative data are also highly valuable, but they can be more difficult to use as proof of effectiveness.

→ **SEE WORKSHEET 5.2 TO ASSIST WITH THIS STEP.**

WORKSHEET 5.2	EVALUATE CURRENT PROGRAMS
How to do this activity?	Have each program's staff meet and discuss the questions on the Program Assessment. The program manager should summarize the discussions and complete Worksheet 5.2.
Why do this activity?	Information about the needs and perceived effectiveness of your programs is necessary, and program staff are some of the most informed about client needs and how their programs actually operate. If there is a need to reallocate resources or cut costs for particular programs, it is particularly helpful to involve staff in imagining new and different ways of doing things and in making suggestions for the future.
Who to involve in this activity?	Appropriate program staff; summary of findings will be presented to planning committee.

COMPETITIVE ANALYSIS

How well are you doing your job, *relative to others*? This step may include a great deal of detail or may be done in summary fashion. Looking at your programs in the context of the environment and of other players in your field is central to creating sound strategy and a sustainable business model. A competitive analysis should consider the following factors:

- *Competitors and/or collaborators.* Who are the other significant players in your field, whether overlapping or adjacent to your program work?

- *Performance.* How does your performance compare with others in your region or with broader performance benchmarks from similar regional or national programs?

- *Competitive advantage.* What does your organization do well that distinguishes it and that would be difficult to replicate?

Traditionally, nonprofits did not think of themselves as competitively oriented, and many nonprofits remain highly collaborative, frequently putting the accomplishment of mission ahead of their organizational interests. Nonetheless, the competitive environment has changed. Expectations of the public and funders are increasing and, especially for large individual and institutional funders, they are more willing to shift their support to another organization or strategy they find more compelling. In addition, nonprofits must compete on a day-to-day basis, not only for funding, but also for staff, influence, and media attention.

TABLE 5.1   COMPETITIVE STRATEGIES MATRIX

		High Program Attractiveness "Easy" Program		Low Program Attractiveness "Difficult" Program	
		Alternative Coverage: HIGH	Alternative Coverage: LOW	Alternative Coverage: HIGH	Alternative Coverage: LOW
GOOD Fit with Mission and Abilities	STRONG Competitive Position	1. Compete aggressively	2. Grow aggressively	5. Support the best competitor	6. "Soul of the agency"
	WEAK Competitive Position	3. Divest aggressively	4. Decide: Build strength or get out	7. Divest systematically	8. Work collaboratively
POOR Fit		9. Divest aggressively		10. Divest systematically	

Source: Adapted from I. C. MacMillan, "Competitive Strategies for Not-for-Profit Agencies," *Advances in Strategic Management 1* (London: JAI Press Inc., 1983), pp. 61-82.

As part of the process of deciding what programs to maintain, eliminate, expand, or start, an organization should ask some of the following pragmatic questions:

- What is the current and future demand for this service?

- Is your organization the most capable to provide this service? Why? What makes you the (or one of the) best?

- By offering this service, are you meeting a need that is not being effectively met by anyone else?

- Could your clients be better served and resources used more effectively if you were to work with another agency in delivering some services?

One venerable and still highly useful tool in looking at competitive position is the Competitive Strategies Matrix shown in Table 5.1. In 1983, Professor Ian C. MacMillan, then at Columbia University and now at the University of Pennsylvania, wrote one of the first articles to specifically address the issue of competition in the nonprofit sector. In "Competitive Strategies for Not-for-Profit Agencies," MacMillan developed a matrix to help nonprofits assess their programs within the context of a nonmarket economy, and within the reality of decreasing funds to support client needs.[1] The matrix was based on the assumption that duplication of existing comparable services among nonprofit organizations (unnecessary competition) can fragment limited resources and leave all providers too weak to increase the quality and cost effectiveness of client services. The matrix also assumed that trying to be all things

---

[1] I. C. MacMillan, "Competitive Strategies for Not-for-Profit Agencies," *Advances in Strategic Management 1* (London, JAI Press Inc., 1983), pp. 61–82.

to all people could result in mediocre or low-quality service and that nonprofits should focus on delivering higher-quality service in a more focused and perhaps more limited way.

MacMillan assessed each current or prospective program according to four criteria: (1) fit with mission, (2) potential to attract resources, (3) alternative coverage, and (4) competitive strength. If a program is not a good fit with the mission, then it needs to be dropped or changed. The intersection of the other three criteria creates an eight-cell matrix, and in each cell a recommended strategic response is suggested.[2]

- *Fit with mission.* Criteria for good fit include congruence with the purpose and mission of the organization, the ability to draw on and share skills, and resources in the organization.

- *Potential to attract resources.* Criteria to rate "high" in attractiveness include good funding possibilities, attractiveness to volunteers, breadth of support from your constituents or supporters, and ability to demonstrate effectiveness.

  - Stable funding, possibilities for attracting new revenue

  - Complements or enhances existing programs

  - Enjoys market demand from a large client base

  - Appeals to volunteers

  - Includes measurable, reportable program results

- *Alternative coverage.* This is the extent to which other organizations are doing similar work.

- *Competitive position.* This dimension assesses an organization's strength in delivering a program relative to other providers. No program should be classified as being in a strong competitive position unless it has some clear basis for declaring superiority over all competitors in that program category. Criteria for a strong competitive position include:

  - Good location and logistical delivery system

  - Superior track record of service delivery

  - Serves large share of the target clientele currently

  - Better-quality service and/or service delivery than competitors

  - Superior organizational, management, and technical skills needed for the program

  - Most cost-effective delivery of service

---

[2] This matrix is an adaptation of MacMillan's matrix. In addition to reframing the growth strategies, we have renamed one of MacMillan's variables, Program Attractiveness, to Potential to Attract Resources.

The indicators of a strong competitive position are "competitive advantages." The competitive strategies matrix can be used to assess existing and potential new programs in relation to each of the four criteria. Each cell in the matrix contains a suggested growth strategy.

Perhaps one of the most important concepts contained within the matrix—soul of the agency—is defined by MacMillan as a program that is unable to attract sufficient resources to pay for itself, and has low alternative coverage, but that makes a special and important contribution to society. Clients who depend on soul-of-the-agency programs have no other place to turn to for help, and they are therefore relying on the organization to continue to provide that service. The challenge for organizations that provide soul-of-the-agency services is either to use their scarce, unrestricted resources to subsidize the services or to subsidize them from other programs. All nonprofit managers will recognize that many of the most-needed services delivered by nonprofits are in this cell of the matrix. Nearly all organizations need to find a mix of programs with strong funding support along with other funding streams to be able to support critical soul-of-the-agency programs. The competitive strategies matrix offers guidance on which programs an organization should keep and grow in addition to any that are soul-of-the-agency programs.

For example, a private art school, acting on numerous parent requests, was considering offering classes for elementary school children. Although the new service was ascertained to be a good fit, it was deemed unable to attract sufficient resources to pay for itself or to enhance existing services. The school was in a strong competitive position because it was well respected as the place to get formal art training in the county, but it was also aware that many other agencies in the city catered to elementary school children. The children's art classes were assessed as fitting into cell 5, where the suggested growth strategy is to build up the best competitor. The art school worked with a small children's museum in a nearby city to offer art classes at the museum, taught by art school faculty, with the assistance of the children's museum's education director.

→ USE WORKSHEET 5.3 TO DO A COMPETITIVE ANALYSIS OF ALL CURRENT PROGRAMS.

WORKSHEET 5.3   COMPETITIVE ANALYSIS

How to do this activity?	Program directors can complete the assessment or engage their staff in a discussion and then summarize the discussions and complete Worksheet 5.3.
Why do this activity?	Competitive analysis is a fundamental dimension of strategy development.
Who to involve in this activity?	Program director and potentially program staff

SHOULD WE CONTINUE TO SUPPORT THE CHILDREN'S THEATER PROGRAM?

In its strategic planning process, the small but successful City Theater Company had an important strategic decision to make about its new multicultural children's theater program. As a pilot program, it was well received by communities of color. The foundation that funded the pilot stipulated that in the second year, the funding should be matched. The new program was also partially competitive with a long-established and extremely popular children's theater, located in the same city but not targeting a multicultural approach. There were intense positive and negative feelings about the program from both board and staff members. Continuing the funding of the children's program could potentially drain resources from the theater's other programs. The strengths, weaknesses, opportunities, and threats (SWOT) analysis proceeded as follows:

Strengths: Successful first-year pilot with staffing established; actors from adult theater programming intricately involved in the multicultural children's theater program; and good reviews in the local paper.

Weaknesses: Funding not readily available; would need to fund second year with funds from adult theater, creating a moderate risk to an agreed-on expansion; and revenues from ticket sales not sufficient to cover direct costs.

Opportunities: Well received by communities of color, and increased demand for arts programs in these communities; remote possibility of funding from a private foundation interested in using the program as a national model.

Threats: Competitive relationship with established children's theater; decreased funding for the arts on both a national and state level.

In the SWOT grid the group did for themselves, the multicultural children's program fell into two boxes. First, if the strengths of the successful first year were juxtaposed with the opportunities of client demand and loyalty, and the possibility of alternative funding, then the suggested strategy was to invest resources. If, however, the weakness of the lack of confirmed resources was judged to be more significant than the perceived strength and was juxtaposed with the same opportunities, then the suggested strategy was Decide: Build strength or divest. The board and staff were split on the invest/divest decision.

By using the competitive strategies matrix, the proposed solution became clearer. Although the children's program was successful, it did not seem like it was going to be able to attract resources to cover its costs. The children's theater was clearly in the stronger competitive position, even though it did not have a multicultural focus.

The planning committee made a recommendation to the board of directors that the children's theater be approached as a collaborative partner in the continued development and expansion of multicultural programming for children. The children's theater accepted the proposal. This decision helped the board to look at increased partnership as a core strategy in its strategic plan.

THEORY OF CHANGE

After Steps 5.2 and 5.3, the planning group should have a good overview of the current program activity and the general competitive strength of the mix of programs. With your mission statement (and consideration of focus problem), you have identified the broad impact you seek to achieve. At this point, we want to get much more specific about exactly what impact you will hold your organization accountable to. A theory of change articulates how your organization's programs will achieve the desired impact. It is called a theory because you are expected to have research, experience, or other evidence that supports the linkages between the program work you do and the results you expect to see.

Although a visual map of a theory of change can look simple and obvious, a meaningful theory of change requires a great deal of clarity about *causal* links between programs and the outcomes desired. (*If* we do this activity, *then* this outcome will result.) Many organizations have a graphic representation that fits on one page, although we have also seen highly detailed versions that stretch to 20 pages detailing the role of each program! However, even at a summary level articulating a theory of change is powerful because it bridges the focus on what you do (means) to what you want to accomplish (ends). As an exercise, it also helps strategic planners test the logic of their programs, which often has not been clearly articulated before. (Just because the logic has not been made explicit does not mean that it is flawed, but it does make it difficult to assess.)

A theory of change has three fundamental components. The first is the *inputs*. Think of this as the fuel your organization runs on—that fuel includes both concrete resources (staff, expertise, funds, equipment, etc.) and assumptions (about circumstances or about logical connections). Second is the *processes*—the actual activity your organization produces in the course of running programs. The program process has a design (for instance, deliver educational classes) and produces outputs (for instance, 25 students attended 10 training sessions). The third and critical component is *results*, or outcomes. Your organization is in business to deliver change—changed lives, changed public policy, cleaner oceans, and so on. The theory of change claims that if you have the necessary inputs (resources) and use them to conduct certain processes (program activity with certain observable outputs based on certain assumptions), then the desired change will take place.

The description and illustration of the theory of change created by the Center for Employment Opportunity in New York City provides an easy-to-understand summary of its approach to accomplishing its mission (the long-term impact it seeks): helping people with criminal convictions successfully transition back into society after incarceration. According to the Center for Employment Opportunity's website,

> [The] CEO's theory of change posits that if the employment needs of persons
> with criminal convictions are addressed at their most vulnerable point when they

FIGURE 5.1   **CENTER FOR EMPLOYMENT OPPORTUNITY'S THEORY OF CHANGE MODEL**

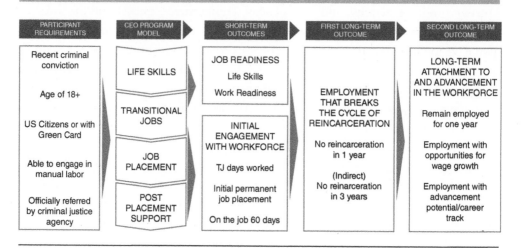

Source: http://ceoworks.org/about/what-we-do/ceo-model-3

are first released from incarceration or soon after conviction [inputs: access to the right clients including partnership with the justice system and referring agencies, and the right timing: soon after release—implied inputs include all necessary funding and resources]—by providing life skills education, short-term paid transitional employment, full-time job placement, and post–placement services [process: program activity/outputs], they will be develop job skills [short-term outcomes] less likely to become reincarcerated [mid-term outcome] and more likely to build a foundation for a stable, productive life for themselves and their families [long-term impact]."[3]

When diagrammed, the theory of change looks like Figure 5.1.

→ USE WORKSHEET 5.4 TO DRAFT YOUR THEORY OF CHANGE.

An alternative to this worksheet is an online resource. The Center for Theory of Change is an online resource that provides step-by-step templates and guidance for creating a theory of change (www.theoryofchange.org). They provide tutorials and many different examples. Their models vary, but a common example from their website looks like Figure 5.2.

Once you fill in the worksheet, the group needs to step back and see if there are any leaps of logic that just don't stand up to scrutiny. Sometimes, the reason is that there is more than one step between programs and outcomes. Then you want to put it into words, so that you can hear whether it makes sense and accurately captures your approach and the impact you seek.

---

[3] Center for Employment Opportunities, CEO Theory of Change, http://ceoworks.org/about/what-we-do/ceo-model-3/

FIGURE 5.2   THE HUNGER PROJECT

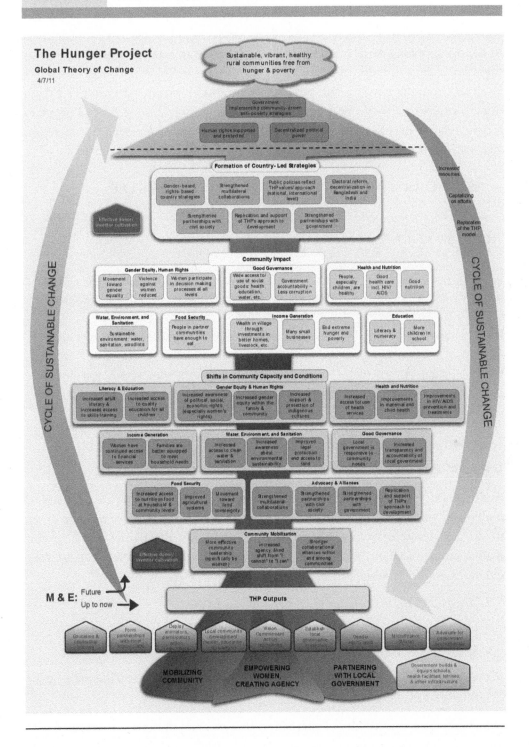

Reflecting on the draft theory of change, a planning group may realize that if additional programs were added, the collective impact would be greater. Or it might realize that not all of its programs are making a meaningful or necessary contribution to the primary long-term impact. Finally, an organization might realize that for its theory of change to work, an assumption is that there are other resources or services available (from the government, other organizations, or private companies). Taking steps to ensure these other resources are in sufficient supply may be another program activity that is necessary to succeed. Often this becomes the seed for increased advocacy work.

→ **SEE WORKSHEET 5.4 TO ASSIST WITH THIS STEP.**

WORKSHEET 5.4   THEORY OF CHANGE

How to do this activity?	This worksheet will most likely need to be revisited several times during the planning process by staff and the Strategic Planning Committee.
Why do this activity?	It is essential to understand how your program work will lead to the impact you seek.
Who to involve in this activity?	Program and management staff, board leaders, and the Strategic Planning Committee

DRAFT FUTURE PROGRAM PORTFOLIO

At this point, you have collected a lot of information and have done a lot of work to understand your current programs. Seek to pull together the work of this step to see the bigger picture of your program portfolio. Three final activities will help you draft a future program portfolio. The first thing to do is to reflect on the four questions you have addressed so far.

- What did you learn from your needs assessment?
- How effective are your current programs individually and as a group?
- What is the competitive position of your various programs?
- What is your theory of change? Do you need to make any changes to your theory of change?

Second, assess the viability of alternative new program options. An excellent tool for prioritizing programs and/or opportunities (for which a program might be established) is something we call a Priority Criteria Matrix.

Using a Priority Criteria Matrix to Select New Programs and Opportunities

Essentially the planning committee might prioritize programs by comparing them against some list of criteria that they have established.

Some of the criteria might include (but would certainly not be limited to):

- Congruence with purpose (fits within our mission)
- Program self-sufficiency (program can pay for itself either through fees for service or contributions or grants)
- Documented need (current and future demands for product or service)
- Increases organization's visibility (improves its public image)
- Increases networking potential (supports collaborative efforts with other organizations)
- Enhances existing programs (complements current programs)
- Fills a need not being met in the community (not duplicating services that are effectively being done by others; we can do it better than others)
- Proven track record (credible service, demonstrated results)
- Supports or is part of a core strategy
- Produces a profit—surplus revenue to support other programs (after paying its share of indirect costs)
- Benefits outweigh or at the very least equal costs (cost-benefit analysis)

The planning committee may choose to assign a weighted number to each of the agreed upon criteria and then rate each program using that criteria. In Worksheet 5.5, given the scores, possible new Programs A and B would be likely programs to consider for the future.

→ SEE WORKSHEET 5.5 TO ASSIST WITH THIS STEP.

WORKSHEET 5.5   EVALUATION OF FOUR POSSIBLE NEW PROGRAMS USING A CRITERIA MIX

Criteria	Weight	Program A	Program B	Program C	Program D
Congruence with purpose (fits within our mission)	Required	✓	✓	NO	✓
Leverages strengths to capitalize on an opportunity, mobilizes strengths to avert a perceived threat, prevents a weakness from compounding a threat, or supports the ability of the organization to take advantage of an opportunity that it couldn't do if it continued to demonstrate a specific weakness	20 points	✓	✓		
Program self-sufficiency (program can pay for itself either through fees for service or contributions or grants)	20 points	✓	✓		
Documented need (current and future demands for product or service)	20 points	✓	✓	✓	
Increases organization's visibility (improves its public image)	15 points		✓	✓	✓
Increases networking potential (supports collaborative efforts with other organizations)	5 points	✓	✓		✓
Produces a profit—surplus revenue to support other programs (after paying its share of indirect costs)	20 points	✓			✓
TOTAL SCORE	100		80	Does not fit within mission	40

Third and finally, agree on proposals for what your complete set of programs will look like in the future, based primarily on how your organization can increase its impact, using Worksheet 5.6. In Step 9, as you are coming to final conclusions, the Strategic Planning Committee must ensure there is a good fit between your desired future program portfolio and needed funding, and you have the organizational capacity and leadership to support your programmatic vision. Once you have finished this analysis, it will be possible to finalize and develop additional detail on core strategies in each dimension along with goals and objectives.

→ USE WORKSHEET 5.6, CREATE YOUR FUTURE PROGRAM PORTFOLIO

WORKSHEET 5.6   **FUTURE PROGRAM PORTFOLIO**

How to do this activity?	This worksheet is a summary of the step and can be completed by a few staff and board members for review by the full Strategic Planning Committee.
Why do this activity?	It is essential to understand how your program work will lead to the impact you seek.
Who to involve in this activity?	Program and management staff, board leaders, and the Strategic Planning Committee

CAUTIONS FOR FACILITATORS

Facilitators should be aware of and work to avoid the following pitfalls during the strategic planning process:

Step 5: Program Portfolio and Theory of Change

Don't let this get personal. In this step people may start to get defensive: they are being asked to define client needs, look realistically at their competitors, and take a hard look at whether their current mix of programs is the right mix for the future. This step requires strong facilitation skills to help people genuinely investigate the situation and to keep discussion from becoming personal.

Don't collude with over-reaching. Be careful not to have the organization choose to take on too many "souls of the agency." Many an organization doing good work has gone downhill or closed down because of was trying to do it all.

Get help if needed. Many nonprofit organizations have limited program evaluation capacity. In this case facilitators may need to provide some basic training and/or encourage the organization to get assistance from a consultant who specializes in program evaluation.

SAMPLE WORKSHEET FOR CASE STUDY: COUNTY LEGAL AID SOCIETY (CLAS)

WORKSHEET 5.1 Needs Assessment

❑ What is the nature of the problem your organization seeks to solve?

❑ What are the scope, the scale, and specific characteristics of this problem?

❑ How have things changed and what broad trends are you aware of?

What is the nature of the problem your organization seeks to solve?

- *Many low-income, elderly, disabled, and otherwise vulnerable people in our county do not have access to legal assistance they need, in many areas of the law. As a result they fall victim to predatory landlords, do not receive all public benefits to which they are entitled, and many other situations that greatly diminish their quality of life.*

What is the scope, the scale, and specific characteristics of this problem?

- *This is a broad-based need that impacts many different aspects of an individual's life from housing, to income to education to health care, etc.*

- *This problem affects close to 20 percent of the population in our county—some 30,000 people.*

- *Several characteristics of this population's needs are relevant to our programming:*

  ○ *This population has widely diverse demographics in age, ethnicity, language spoken, physical and mental abilities, level of physical health—it presents many, varied specific situations that need to be addressed.*

  ○ *There is a low level of awareness about legal rights and how to access legal assistance.*

  ○ *Many people are reluctant to seek assistance either because of their legal status, fear of retaliation, or general fear of the government.*

Segments in Needs:

- *Our priority is low-income people.*

- *What is important for us to understand is that while the various subgroups or segments may have similar needs in terms of legal representation—what it takes to serve them well can be different (e.g., what people from different cultures see as respectful and appropriate relationship can be different—it is not enough to simply speak the same language in words).*

- *The growing income inequality is exacerbating already difficult circumstances.*

Trends in Needs:

- *The number of people is increasing.*

- *The growing income inequality is exacerbating already difficult circumstances.*

- *Various public services have been reduced, forcing people into the private market where they are often poorly served, taken advantage of, or not served at all—many of these situations do not have a legal remedy.*

Context:

- *Our environmental scan identified other important issues that relate to how we provide services, and how we must adapt including technology changes and reduced services in neighboring communities.*

WORKSHEET 5.1 *(continued)*

Value:

- *Our funders value numbers—people served and problems solved. They don't necessarily want to understand all the associated difficulties. It is important for us to both respond to their "needs" and to try to educate them to the realities of meeting the needs of the community at the same time.*

- *As noted above in "Segments": What is important for us to understand is that while the various subgroups or segments may have similar needs in terms of legal representation—what it takes to serve them well can be different (e.g., what people from different cultures see as respectful and appropriate relationship can be different—it is not enough to simply speak the same language in words).*

SAMPLE WORKSHEET FOR CASE STUDY: COUNTY LEGAL AID SOCIETY (CLAS)

WORKSHEET 5.2   Evaluate Current Programs

❏ Evaluate each program along the following dimensions: Scale, Effectiveness, Potential for Growth, Quality, Cost-effectiveness, Overall

Note: this worksheet is filled out for one program as an illustration of its use.

Program/Service Name: *Housing*

Name of Person(s) Filling Out This Assessment: *Charles Yee, Senior Attorney and Housing Director* **Date:** *October 1, 2014*

Description
Description of program service (what is service or activity?)

Helping individuals resolve landlord–tenant disputes, assisting renters facing eviction, and helping people maintain housing subsidies

What is the need in the community that this program exists to meet?

Disenfranchised and low-income people traditionally have faced major challenges in meeting their basic need for safe and affordable housing. This population has increased during the recent recession and now numbers over 30,000 living in in some 6,000 units throughout the county.

Scale
Quantity: Units of service, number of clients served, campaigns waged, etc. *1,016 clients in 2013*

Scale of Operations: Total Annual Program Expenses: *$548,000*

Annual Program Revenue: *$527,000*

Effectiveness
Outcomes: What impact does this program currently have, or intend to have, on addressing the need articulated above?

- *Fewer evictions*
- *Individuals' increased knowledge about rights and processes they can use for self-help*
- *Laws enforced*
- *Safe housing helps create safe and livable neighborhoods.*
- *Cities where there are housing opportunities for all without discrimination*

Current measures of success: What evidence do we have to show this program is having the impact we want it to have—how do we know we are being successful?

- *Number of closed cases*
- *Fewer evictions*
- *Number of landlord–tenant mediations resulting in fewer legal actions*

WORKSHEET 5.2 *(continued)*

How should we measure success? Are there other indicators of success we should use in measuring success? How should we measure results/impact/outcomes of this program in improving the quality of constituents' lives/making a difference in the world?

- *Decreased waitlists for clients*

- *New (and enforced) laws that protect tenants from evictions and ensure safe housing*

- *Stopping drug dealers from using houses for distribution of narcotics*

- *Known as the defender/represent community interests at zoning hearings*

- *Ensuring all tenants needing legal assistance are represented (though this would be difficult to measure, and is something that can only happen through the work of many organizations and agencies).*

Potential for Growth?

Are there additional dimensions of need that this program could address if resources were available?

- *Increased advocacy efforts so we can be more proactive in preventing housing discrimination*

- *More clinics/self-help opportunities—to prevent unnecessary escalation of conflicts*

- *Greater involvement by law school students in helping our clients*

If we were to reinvent this program, what changes would we make to achieve greater impact?

- *Greater collaboration among government and nonprofits regarding issues of increased availability of housing—so we could function as part of a coordinated network delivering legal assistance*

- *Enhanced efforts in confronting chronic slumlords*

Potential to Improve Quality/Delivery?

- *Increased community education and outreach—and related collateral material—to the community so clients can learn how to protect their legal rights*

- *We really are understaffed to have the impact we want to have—increasing our capacity would likely improve quality as we would be able to give some more attention to individual cases.*

Are there other ways we might increase quality? (Value proposition describes value from the customer's perspective.) How might we enhance the *value proposition* we deliver to our clients (whether they are individuals, the broader community, funders, or some combination)?

For all of our clients, what they most value is dignity and sensitivity in how we conduct our program work. In this regard, we do our work well.

(continued)

WORKSHEET 5.2 *(continued)*

Client Group	Value Proposition *What does this client most value/expect from us?*	How could we improve the quality/impact of this program *from the perspective of our "customers"?*
Seniors	*Access to safe and affordable residential care and nursing homes*	*Increased collaboration with Senior Center, Department of Aging; develop and implement a Residential and Nursing Home Right Program*
English as Second Language Community (Hispanic, Vietnamese are predominant)	*Our ability to communicate with them in Spanish if needed*	*Need greater language capacity—in particular an additional Spanish speaking attorney; all training material translated into Spanish*
Section 8 Housing	*Access to SAFE housing*	*Work with Housing Authority*
Disabled Citizens	*Accessible housing*	*Partner with local disability rights organization; increase our knowledge of accessible and "visitability" housing*
All of our clients	*Freedom from predatory lending practices*	*Work with the banking community?*

Overall Assessment

What are the greatest STRENGTHS of this program?

- *Track record of success*
- *Long-term staff*
- *Good working relationships with existing community partners*
- *Lead agency in coalition for Housing Policies and Law Reform Initiatve*

What are the greatest WEAKNESSES of this program?

- *Lack of staff who reflect the populations we serve*
- *Insufficient staff to meet needs, resulting in waiting lists and unclosed cases*

What are the most important trends in the external environment that are or will be impacting this program in the future (trends either potentially moving the program forward (OPPORTUNITIES) or holding it back (THREATS))?

- *Fewer but still significant foreclosures*
- *Predatory investors coming in to flip houses*
- *Improved economy = higher housing costs*
- *New mayor with verbal commitment to increasing supply of affordable housing*

> **WORKSHEET 5.3** Competitive Analysis
>
> ❏ Use this worksheet for each program in your program portfolio.
> ❏ Create a summary table with all programs.

Competitive Analysis of Individual Program, using MacMillan Matrix:

Program Name: *Advocacy/Public Policy*

Program "Fit": How well does this program fit with our mission, overall strategy, and other programs?

Good Fit_____x_____

Poor Fit_____

Helps us better achieve our mission by focusing efforts on systemic change rather than simply providing assistance to individuals. We do so by advocating on behalf of our low income clients in legislative and administrative forums and improve state laws and rules that affect disenfranchised communities and individuals.

We are able to utilize the experience and specialized technical skills of our attorneys—across various programs—and focus those skills in favor of changing laws and rules that adversely affect our clients.

Program Attractiveness: How "easy" or "difficult" is it to attract the resources necessary to support and sustain this program?

High Program Attractiveness_____

Low Program Attractiveness _____x_____

We have had little luck in fundraising for our Advocacy/Public Policy efforts. And while public policy efforts have the capacity to enhance—at least indirectly, our existing programs, it's very difficult to fund.

Alternative Coverage: are there relatively many or few other organizations doing this work in your area?

High _____

Low _____x_____

While many groups engage in public policy/advocacy efforts for their specific community, they do not have the staff to do much advocacy work, and certainly not just for low-income individuals. We have the expertise to do advocacy/public policy work, but are not experts in serving many different populations. Thus we do not feel there are many organizations actually doing the work that is needed.

(continued)

███ **WORKSHEET 5.3** *(continued)*

Competitive Strength:

_____Yes, strong competitive position

_____*x*_____No, do not have a strong competitive position

Why or Why Not? What is your program's competitive advantage? (What distinguishes your program in comparison to the competition?)

This is tricky. We bring highly specialized technical skills to bear at all stages of the policy-making process, but we do not have the current experience/technical skills to provide services to specific populations. On the other hand, we do not feel that other organizations are much stronger—so we could rate our Competitive Position as strong. And our level of commitment to this work is similar to that of a program identified as "Soul of the Agency."

Cell # on Macmillan Matrix

1. Grow or Maintain

2. Aggressive Growth

3. Collaborate or Exit

4. Exit

5. Build up best competitor

6. Soul of the Agency

7. Divest systematically

8. Work collaboratively

Based on Macmillan Analysis, and taking other considerations into account, what is your Recommended Growth Strategy?

Suggested Future Growth Strategy for this Program:

Increase _____*x*____Maintain_____   Decrease_____   Eliminate_____

By increasing our policy efforts and harnessing the experience and expertise of other organizations, we can have a greater impact in protecting the rights of disenfranchised individuals.

We would be limiting our ability to achieve our mission if we don't, because our resources will be primarily focused on individuals' problems rather than the root causes of the problem.

WORKSHEET 5.3 *(continued)*

Alternative Organizations in This Program Area

Service/Program: Advocacy/Public Policy

Name of organization	Capacity to provide service	Quality of service	Why did you rate ability to provide service the way you did? Why did you give the rating on quality of service?
Competitor: **Disability Rights**	4 3 [2] 1 Excellent Good **Fair** Poor	4 [3] 2 1 Excellent Good Fair Poor	*Not enough staff. Excellent reputation in the community.*
Competitor: **Senior Advocacy Project**	[4] 3 2 1 Excellent Good Fair Poor	[4] 3 2 1 Excellent Good Fair Poor	*Large volunteer pool able to get seniors to advocate on their behalf. Able to push through favorable legislation.*
Competitor: **Hispanic Community Center**	4 3 [2] 1 Excellent Good Fair Poor	4 [3] 2 1 Excellent Good Fair Poor	*Limited staff are overtaxed and unable to focus on policy work. Was able to recently work to get an important piece of legislation passed.*
Competitor: **AIDS Project**	4 3 [2] 1 Excellent Good Fair Poor	4 3 [2] 1 Excellent Good Fair Poor	*Policy work is valued very strongly at AIDS Project. However, they have gone through some hard times and have not actually been doing very much proactive policy work.*
Competitor: **Asian American Health Service**	4 3 2 1 Excellent Good Fair Poor	4 3 2 1 Excellent Good Fair Poor	*Unknown*

Other Competitors Not Assessed: *None.*

(continued)

WORKSHEET 5.3 *(continued)*

SUMMARY MAP OF CLAS PROGRAMS ON MACMILLAN MATRIX

		High Program Attractiveness "Easy" Program		Low Program Attractiveness "Difficult" Program	
		Alternative Coverage: HIGH	Alternative Coverage: LOW	Alternative Coverage: HIGH	Alternative Coverage: LOW
GOOD Fit with Mission and Abilities	STRONG Competitive Position	1. Compete aggressively PUBLIC BENEFITS	2. Grow aggressively HOUSING	5. Support the best competitor	6. "Soul of the agency" FAMILY LAW DOMESTIC VIOLENCE
	WEAK Competitive Position	3. Divest aggressively	4. Decide: Build strength or get out HEALTH CARE	7. Divest systematically	8. Work collaboratively ADVOCACY
POOR Fit		9. Divest aggressively		10. Divest systematically	

Source: Adapted from I.C. MacMillan, "Competitive Strategies for Not-for-Profit Agencies," *Advances in Strategic Management 1* (London: JAI Press Inc., 1983), pp. 61-82.

SAMPLE WORKSHEET FOR CASE STUDY: COUNTY LEGAL AID SOCIETY (CLAS)

WORKSHEET 5.4 Theory of Change

❏ What is the ultimate impact your organization seeks to achieve?

❏ What are the intermediate outcomes on the path to this impact?

❏ What is the set of programs, the activity, your organization will deliver to bring about these outcomes?

❏ What are the inputs, the resources and assumptions necessary to deliver your programs effectively?

What is the ultimate impact your organization seeks to achieve?

Removing the legal barriers that low-income residents face to life necessities and ensure they have access to advice and representation from attorneys when they experience legal problems.

What are the intermediate outcomes on the path to this impact?

- *This is a broad-based need that impacts many different aspects of an individual's life from housing, to income to education to health care, etc.*

- *This problem affects close to 20 percent of the population in our county—some 30,000 people.*

- *Several characteristics of this population's needs are relevant to our programming:*

  o *This population has widely diverse demographics in age, ethnicity, language spoken, physical and mental abilities, level of physical health—it presents many, varied specific situations that need to be addressed.*

  o *There is a low level of awareness about legal rights and how to access legal assistance.*

  o *Many people are reluctant to seek assistance either because of their legal status, fear of retaliation, or general fear of the government.*

What is the set of programs, the activity, your organization will deliver to bring about these outcomes?

- *Legal education, advice, and counseling on legal issues*

- *Full representation in court and administrative hearings*

- *Policy work on behalf of the community*

- *Pro bono legal services provided by volunteers to expand the capacity of the organization to serve more people*

(continued)

WORKSHEET 5.4 *(continued)*

What are the inputs, resources, and assumptions necessary to deliver your programs effectively?

INPUTS	PROCESSES (Strategies)		RESULTS	
Resources and Assumptions	Program Activities	Outputs	Outcomes	Ultimate Impact
Talented and dedicated attorneys	Deliver direct legal assistance	Cases are managed to conclusion # of cases # completion rate # of successful cases	Successful outcomes win positive changes for clients	
Communications staff and resources				Our clients have equal access to justice under the law.
Requisite funding	Education of prospective clients and referring agencies	# clients contacted # agencies contacted # volume of education, materials, hours	Clients more effective at self-advocacy; agencies more responsive	As a result, our clients are healthier, less stressed, have more options, and are able to lead more fulfilling lives.
Assumption: most clients have legitimate legal claims				
Assumption: Information is a source of power	Advocacy	# of issues addressed # impact of advocacy (new laws, policy changes) effectiveness in building coalitions	Broader systems in which our clients live are made more just, more accessible, more efficient, and more helpful	

WORKSHEET 5.5   Summarize Your Future Program Portfolio

Develop a detailed program portfolio.

For each of your proposed future programs or services:

- What is the program's current level of activity? (This question, of course, applies only to existing programs. New programs will not yet have a current level of activity.)
- What is its proposed growth strategy (expand, maintain, decrease, eliminate, start new program, modify existing program)?
- What is the program's projected future level of activity?

Program or service	What is the program's current level of activity? (This info is in Organization Profile)	What is its proposed growth strategy (expand, maintain, decrease, eliminate, start new program, modify existing program)?	What is the program's projected future level of activity?
Housing	$548,000 # Served = 1,016 # of Staff = 5.25 FTE	Expand— "Grow Aggressively" from MacMillan Matrix Only modification is scale	By end of Year 3: $750,000 Increases from multiple sources # Served: 1,500 # Staff: 7.5
Public Benefits	$365,000 # Served: 875 # Staff: 3.0 FTE	Expand— "Compete Aggressively" from MacMillan Matrix—we need to be better than other providers— most opportunity in So. County	By end of Year 3: $600,000 # Served: 1,600 # Staff: 5.5
Health Care	$493,000 # Served 925 # Staff: 3.25 FTE	Maintain (for now): "Build Strength or Get Out" from MacMillan Matrix—while opportunities are increasing from ACA—we are still not in great competitive position	$500,000 # Served: 1,000 # Staff: 3.5
Family Law	$420,000 # Served: 731 # Staff: 3.25 FTE	Maintain (grow if possible) "Soul of the Agency" from MacMillan Matrix	$450,000 # Served 750 # Staff 3.5

(continued)

WORKSHEET 5.5 *(continued)*

| Advocacy | Not a currently funded program, though we are doing some work in this area | Grow—add a "Director of Advocacy" though not a formal, independent program
"Work Collaboratively" from MacMillan Matrix—we hope to get dedicated funding from individual contributions | $150,000 for director and some administrative support

Service: 6–8 issues per year as areas of focus for advocacy
Staff: 1.0 |

CHAPTER 6

Step 6: Business Model

In this step, we look at how the organization is supported financially. This business model step takes into consideration the financing of the organization as a whole and builds on the program analysis and theory of change work done in Step 5. Here we are doing some basic financial analysis on individual programs as well as assessing the ability of the organization to fund the proposed future program portfolio we created in the last step.

FIRST STEPS	STRATEGIC ANALYSIS	SET YOUR COURSE
1. Set up for Success	4. Environmental Scan	9. Complete the Strategic Plan
2. Stakeholder Engagement	5. Theory of Change and Program Portfolio	10. Use Your Plan Successfully
3. Mission, Vision, Values	6. Business Model	
	7. Organization Capacity	
	8. Leadership	

SUMMARIZE REVENUE AND EXPENSES

If you are unable to produce the data necessary to generate the following three summaries, your financial management systems are most likely inadequate to the needs of a nonprofit today. Without financial data it will be difficult—if not impossible to create a sound future business model with confidence, since your ability to make effective strategic decisions depends on the quality of the information you have available. Thus, financial management is not just the province of financial controls or other oversight functions; it provides the critical information necessary for true strategic thinking and ongoing strategic management.

HISTORICAL SUMMARY AND KEY QUESTIONS

To begin with, prepare an organization-level summary of how revenue, expenses, and net assets have changed over the past few years (Table 6.1). Revenue includes

TABLE 6.1   **REVENUE, EXPENSE, NET REVENUE EXPENSES, AND NET ASSETS**

	2010	2011	2012	2013	2014
Revenue					
Government					
Foundations					
Earned revenue					
Major donors					
All other individual contributions					
Events					
Total					
Expenses					
Personnel					
Operations					
Total					
Net revenue					
Net Assets					
Total					
Operating Reserve					

FIGURE 6.1   **OPERATING REVENUE, EXPENSES, NET**

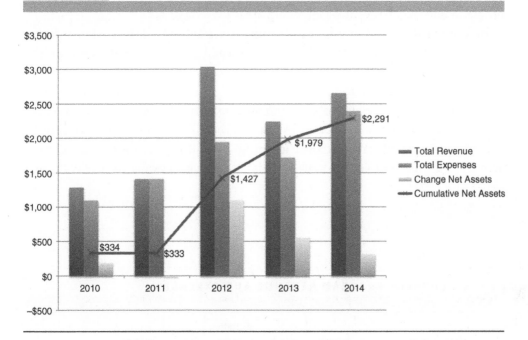

individual revenue sources, by major category, such as foundations, the government, earned revenue, major donors, events, or your annual appeal. Expenses include overall expenses, by major line-item groups. Net assets include total and operating reserves—any unrestricted net assets available to support operations—excluding board-restricted funds, such as those for endowment. Preparing charts with a spreadsheet program will make patterns easy for committee members to grasp.

There are several key questions to ask here, such as:

- What have been the major changes, and what is the story behind these changes in revenue, expenses, or net assets?

- Have you generally run a balanced budget? And if you've run a deficit, was it intentional, such as to invest in a one-time capital upgrade?

- What implications or questions are raised through this review?

You will end up with a graph like the one in Figure 6.1.

CURRENT PROGRAM REVENUE AND EXPENSES

This review helps in analysis of the situation with regard to program operations. Where are you spending the most money? Where are you bringing in the most revenue? This review will include all major lines of business, including both programs and major revenue-generating areas (see Table 6.2).

In looking at the revenue for each program, we are only interested in *dedicated revenue*—revenue you were awarded or earned that is directly tied to the program. This does not include general operating funds (either from grants or from fundraising activities) that are spent on the program if needed to cover the rest of the expenses. However, the analysis of *total expenses* should include both direct and indirect expenses—the overhead/administrative and general expenses that are allocated across each program and major revenue-generating activity. This methodology is called "fully loaded" as opposed to simply "direct expenses."

TABLE 6.2 CURRENT PROGRAM REVENUE AND EXPENSES

	Environmental Education	Nursery	Resource Library	Direct Mail	Solicitation Of Major Donors	Annual Event	Common Costs	Administration	Totals
Contributions				220,000	170,000	135,000			525,000
Restricted foundation grants	14,000	120,000							134,000
Government contracts	900,000								900,000
Fees									
Total revenue	914,000	120,000		220,000	170,000	135,000			1,559,000

	Environmental Education	Nursery	Resource Library	Direct Mail	Solicitation Of Major Donors	Annual Event	Common Costs	Administration	Totals
Direct expenses	746,300	184,300	12,900	147,500	59,000	66,300	160,000	162,200	1,538,500
Allocation of common costs	63,700	15,700	1,100	12,600	5,000	5,700	(160,000)	13,800	(42,400)
Total before administration	810,000	200,000	14,000	160,000	64,000	72,000	—	176,000	1,496,000
Allocation of administration	80,00	20,000	1,000	15,000	6,000	3,000	—	(176,000)	(131,000)
Full costs	890,000	220,000	15,000	175,000	70,000	75,000	—	—	1,445,000
Net	24,000	(100,000)	(15,000)	45,000	100,000	60,000	—	—	114,000

ARTICULATE YOUR BUSINESS MODEL

Once you have the necessary historical data on the revenue and costs of your organization, you are ready to articulate your business model. We define a nonprofit business model very simply as the work you do and mix of revenue sources with which it is funded. This summary and supporting data, is helpful to enable you to see the big picture, to test the sustainability of the model, and to look for opportunities to refine its balance. The first step is to articulate your current business model.

Identify five elements:

1. Who do you serve?

2. Where do you do your work?

3. What programs/services do you provide?

4. How is this work primarily financially supported?

5. What does it cost you to do your work?

For example, an organization might say, "We help students with emotional or behavioral problems, from kindergarten to high school, to succeed by providing specialized services in a variety of settings, including schools, the community, and the home. We work in Broadview County and our work is supported primarily through government contracts supplemented by support from foundations and individuals."

BUSINESS MODEL ANALYSIS

Nonprofits often have developed their program plans and fundraising plans in parallel, as opposed to jointly. Increasingly, as nonprofits generate multiple funding streams and different program activities have different—and changing—potential for revenue generation, it is important to develop program and funding strategies in concert with one another.

Just as businesses surviving in the for-profit sector must strive for sustainable business models, nonprofit organizations succeed when they adopt an orientation toward sustainability.

When you examined your program portfolio in Step 5, you investigated various ways to increase impact and/or add new service offerings from a mission perspective. In this step, you are concerned with determining the sustainability of that future scale of programs by bringing in the financial perspective. Fundamentally, this is a set of questions about growth, and there are only three choices: What programs do you want to (1) grow (or begin), (2) maintain at their current level, or (3) reduce/ eliminate? The decision about growth must be informed by both the potential for advancing your mission and the potential for financial sustainability.

The matrix map offers a representation of an organization's business model and how both mission-specific programs and fund development programs work together to create impact and financial viability.

Matrix Map[1]

When choosing priorities for programs and services, nonprofits can find themselves caught between two critical concerns. Which programs have the most mission impact vs which programs are the most attractive financially?

Adapted from the Growth-Share Matrix developed by the Boston Consulting Group, the matrix map (see Figure 6.2) is a tool to help nonprofits balance these two concerns. Mission impact refers to the importance of a mission-specific or fund development program to the organization's mission-related goals.

FIGURE 6.2   MATRIX MAP

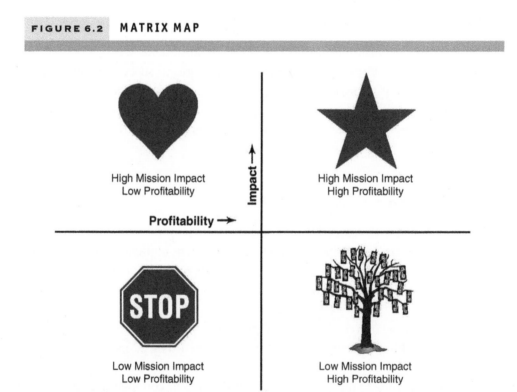

High Mission Impact
Low Profitability

High Mission Impact
High Profitability

Impact →

Profitability →

Low Mission Impact
Low Profitability

Low Mission Impact
High Profitability

[1] The Matrix Map was presented in the 2nd Edition of this book as the CompassPoint Dual Bottom-line Matrix. The concept and supporting materials have been greatly enhanced by three authors associated with CompassPoint: Jeanne Bell, Jan Masaoka, and Steve Zimmerman. Their book, *Nonprofit Sustainability: Making Strategic Decisions for Financial Viability*, was published by Jossey-Bass in 2010. They have a new book *The Sustainability Mindset: Using the Matrix Map to Make Strategic Decisions*, Jossey-Bass, 2014. This section is used with permission and we are grateful for support in adapting the model for our book we received from Steve Zimmerman.

Mission impact can vary in part because of scale: a larger program usually has greater mission impact than a smaller program, but mission impact can also vary by intensity. A tutor-mentor program with middle school students may be viewed by an organization as having higher mission impact than a program in the same school that invites parents for training sessions.

"Profitability" is defined as a program that at a minimum attracts enough financial support to cover its fully loaded costs. In using this matrix we include all activities that attract and use money—thus in addition to traditional programs, we include fundraising efforts, special events, and so on. A program may be well funded and paying for its own direct costs as well as helping with organizational overhead and shared costs. An annual fundraising dinner should be highly profitable—it should pay for its direct costs and contribute to the support of other programs. However, soul-of-the-agency programs are characterized by being highly important and yet not bringing in enough in dedicated revenue to cover all their costs.

A viable business model strategy for an organization combines a set of mission-specific and fund development programs that result in its long-term financial viability as well as high mission impact. As noted in the previous step, we call this a portfolio of programs.

How to Use the Matrix Map

Some of the characteristics of programs with high mission impact are (1) tangible results, (2) visible progress toward the achievement of the organization's mission, and (3) high leverage potential—synergy with other programs.

Some of the characteristics of high financial viability are, at the very least, the program (1) covers all costs (both direct and indirect), (2) generates a surplus of revenue (profit), and (3) is projected to have financial sustainability for the future.

Recommended Strategy for Each Quadrant

Star = High Mission Impact + High Financial Viability
Business Strategy—Invest and Grow

A Star program is one we want to keep and grow. To do so, we should invest in it—invest time, attention, and money. Some of the ways to invest include the following:

- Ensure that the staff on this program is top-notch.

- Develop and institutionalize relationships with the federal agency.

- Recruit board members who have the ability to advise the program and/or strengthen relationships with the funding agency.

- Write an article for publication about a special aspect of the program.

Some of the key strategic questions we ask of programs here are:

- Do we understand the needs and motivations of stakeholders who make the Star program possible?

- Are there opportunities (e.g., new geography, new populations, complementary programming) to expand the program's impact and revenue?

The opposite of a Star program is one that has low impact and low viability:

Stop Sign = Low Mission Impact + Low Financial Viability
Business Strategy—Discontinue or Give Away

If a program falls within this quadrant, the organization must make a decision: Can this program be changed to have a greater mission impact and/or greater financial viability, or should the program be discontinued or given away?

The recommended strategy for a Stop Sign program is to discontinue the program or give it to an organization that can make better use of it. There may not be another organization interested in the program, however, so it may be best to simply let it run out its current funding and then stop.

If the decision is made not to close the program, the key strategic questions to ask yourself for a Stop Sign program are:

- Can we innovate this program to move it out of this quadrant?

- How long will we give ourselves to move the stop sign?

- Is that the best use of resources?

Money Tree = Low Mission Impact + High Financial Viability
Business Strategy—Enhance Impact and/or Maximize Profits

Some programs or activities bring in money that supports the organization but do not do much else to further the organization's mission. These are often special fund development programs, whose primary purpose is to raise money.

The recommended strategy for a Money Tree is to enhance mission impact and maintain profitability. For example, for a special event, an organization might make sure there is an educational component to the event that helps the community of supporters better understand what the organization does. At the very least, any Money Tree programs should be carefully evaluated to see if their profits are maximized so as to support the program's ability to have a higher mission impact.

The key strategic questions to be asked for Money Tree programs are:

- Can the net surplus be increased, and if so, what investment will that growth require?

- Are there means to reducing the program's cost and improve the margin?

- Are there ways to achieve greater impact by making the program stronger?
- Is it aligned with our brand?

Heart = High Mission Impact + Low Financial Viability
Business Strategy—Contain Costs

(Note that programs in this quadrant are analogous to soul-of-the-agency programs in the MacMillan Matrix used in Step 5.)

Most organizations have at least one program that has high impact, is deeply associated with the organization, and is underfunded or cannot generate a surplus because of the constituency it serves or lack of attractiveness for institutional funding. Perhaps it costs more to deliver than the government funding received for it, or perhaps it is an essential service for low-income people that doesn't attract much community support. Such a program is too important—in mission impact and in organizational identity—to close down, but at the same time, it's a drain on the organization's unrestricted assets that often cannot be maintained. The strategy for a Heart program is to keep it, but to contain the costs or see if there is any way of increasing revenues (e.g., by charging a sliding scale).

The key strategic questions to ask for a Heart program are:

- Can we envision this program achieving the same impact—or very close to it—with a different cost structure?
- Is there a different revenue strategy to consider?

Using the Model

Let's look at how the matrix map might be used in assessing an organization's program portfolio. Let's say a community center is looking at four programs and business activities:

1. Renting the building to community groups, such as Alchoholics Anonymous (AA), Girl Scouts, basketball league, and others
2. Home ownership loan and renovation program funded by the federal government
3. Stop smoking program funded by a health foundation
4. Annual fundraising dinner and auction

Choose which quadrant is appropriate for each of the programs and business activities.

Building Rentals   High mission impact ("This is what we're in business to do, to provide space for community efforts."); low financial viability ("These groups can't afford much, and the security, janitorial, and repair costs can get pretty high.").

FIGURE 6.3   **USING THE MATRIX MAP**

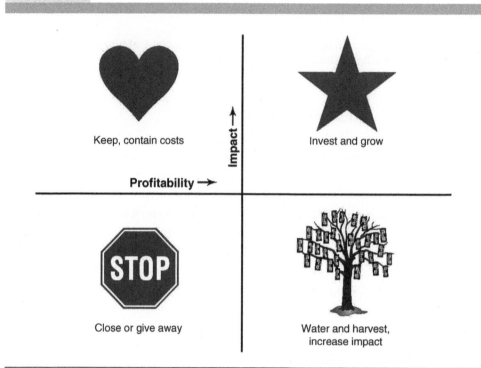

At the community center making space available for community use is part of the center's mission and identity, but the fees are kept low to make it possible for these groups to rent the space. In order to limit the program's drain on the organization's unrestricted funds, the community center could do better financially by raising fees or by leasing rooms for commercial offices. To continue providing this important service without going broke doing so, the center must find a way to limit the net costs of the program. Perhaps the community center can be rented five nights per week, instead of seven. Perhaps one room—not all—can be leased to a commercial entity.

Loan and Renovation Program   High mission impact ("We help people buy and maintain their homes!"); high financial viability ("It pays for two people on staff and its share of the rent, accounting, and other overhead.").

As a Star program, the community center should invest resources so that the program has sufficient resources to operate at a maximum potential and at a level of excellence.

Stop Smoking Program   Low mission impact ("We have a hard time filling seats."); low financial viability ("These foundation grants hardly pay for themselves, given how much time it takes to get them and report on them.").

This program is a Stop Sign. It neither helps many people nor brings in significant funding. It takes up physical and mental space. Almost no one really loves the stop smoking program. The organization must make a decision: Can this program be changed to have a greater impact and/or greater financial viability? If neither can be done quickly, the program should be discontinued or given away.

Fundraising Dinner and Auction   Low mission impact ("The wealthier people in the neighborhood bring their wealthy friends and they socialize with each other."); high financial viability ("We make a lot of money on the event.").

The community center might include a short poetry slam at its dinner that would help its wealthier, older donors become more familiar with and sympathetic to the younger people in the community.

The matrix map is one way of analyzing an organization's current—and potentially new—program portfolio. The matrix provides suggested business strategies regarding the future scope and scale of particular programs.

To represent the full program portfolio graphically using the matrix map, a chart can be generated using the data on each program, as shown in Figure 6.4. One can easily see how the matrix map provokes strategic questions by bringing in the funding perspective.

FIGURE 6.4   MATRIX MAP

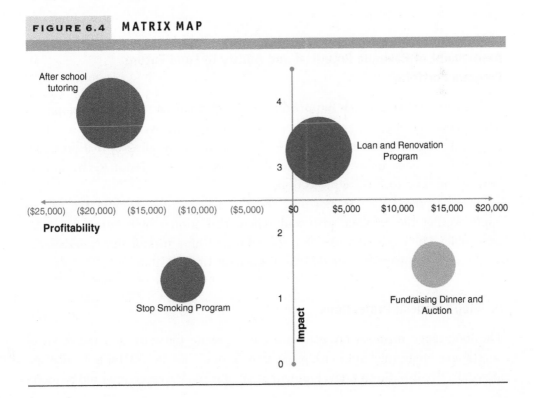

FIGURE 6.5   PROGRAM-LEVEL STRATEGIC QUESTIONS

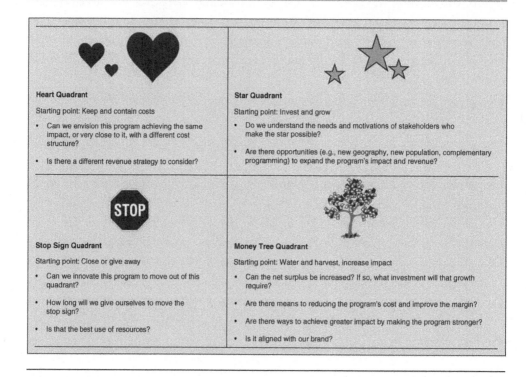

Heart Quadrant

Starting point: Keep and contain costs

- Can we envision this program achieving the same impact, or very close to it, with a different cost structure?

- Is there a different revenue strategy to consider?

Star Quadrant

Starting point: Invest and grow

- Do we understand the needs and motivations of stakeholders who make the star possible?

- Are there opportunities (e.g., new geography, new population, complementary programming) to expand the program's impact and revenue?

Stop Sign Quadrant

Starting point: Close or give away

- Can we innovate this program to move out of this quadrant?

- How long will we give ourselves to move the stop sign?

- Is that the best use of resources?

Money Tree Quadrant

Starting point: Water and harvest, increase impact

- Can the net surplus be increased? If so, what investment will that growth require?

- Are there means to reducing the program's cost and improve the margin?

- Are there ways to achieve greater impact by making the program stronger?

- Is it aligned with our brand?

Assessment of Revenue Potential and Ability to Fund Future Program Portfolio

Before starting to create your future business model, financial and fund development staff and board will need to spend some time looking at the overall future cost of the proposed program portfolio and the feasibility of future funding of that portfolio. Obviously, revenue and cost considerations have been involved from the beginning. Now is the time to finalize projections.

Financial projections can not only serve as a reality check about the cost of implementing the strategic plan and where that money will come from. Be reasonable. The capacity to develop these forecasts in a meaningful way depends on the financial management skills and financial data available.

Develop Financial Projections

The long-range financial projections are not precise forecasts, and the focus of developing long-range financial projections should not be on budgets that are incredibly detailed. From a development point of view, however, it would be useful to know whether the additional staffing needed to support the strategic plan will cost in the neighborhood of $100,000 or $1 million, or whether the total budget to support the plan is closer to $1.5 million or $3 million.

Strategic Budgeting: How Much Is All of This Going to Cost?

Strategic budgeting focuses on the anticipated scale of each of the programs, the infrastructure needed to support that level of programming, and a realistic assessment of how the organization might be able to support this vision.

The expense side of the strategic budget is most easily derived by looking at the big-ticket items that make up the organization's budget (typically staff is 80 percent or more of a program's costs).

Program managers or department managers who have responsibility for the development of annual operating budgets should be involved in the development of projected expenditures to support any long-range goals and objectives that have been articulated in the strategic plan. What you are really trying to accomplish is to get a *broad-stroke estimate* of how much it will cost to implement your strategic plan.

The Long-Range Fundraising Plan: How Much Do We Need to Raise?

Estimating future revenues will also serve as a reality check for your plan. Given your proposed future program portfolio, is it realistic to secure the resources needed, or is it possible you will need to modify the time horizon for achieving those goals given the resources you are likely to be able to raise? This plan can be integrated into the final strategic planning document, or it can be a stand-alone document.

Steps in Estimating Revenues

1. *Review your fundraising performance from the previous two to three years.* When reviewing your fundraising performance from the previous two to three years, note any trends in previous support.

2. *Gather and analyze funder stakeholder information: Interview current donors and funders.* If you have not already interviewed current donors and funders during Step 2, this is a good time to involve your current and potential external stakeholders or go back to the ones with whom you have already talked to discuss your future vision.

3. *Assess your current and potential fundraising vehicles.* Assess your current fundraising and their potential to maintain or increase revenue. After assessing the full potential of each revenue source, decide on strategies to realize the full potential of each vehicle.

4. *Set fundraising targets.* Based on the previous analysis, you can estimate financial targets for each funding source.

DEVELOP SUMMARY FINDINGS

Using the results of the historical review of your revenue and expenses, insights from the matrix map, and the first draft of a long-term fund development plan, step back to look at the major implications of all of this on the creation of your future business model. These reflections are the basis for worksheet 6.1.

1. What are the implications of your financial analysis for your future program portfolio? Do you anticipate you can cover all of the future program portfolio's costs? Are there programs to change, drop, grow? What is that future funding mix?

2. What are the initial implications for capacity and for leadership? Are your revenue development efforts hampered by inadequate information technology, or staff without proper skills? If there are significant changes to be made in certain programs—what support will leaders need to succeed?

   The purpose of this worksheet is to distill your findings from your analysis and to identify the strategies and realistic goals for your business model in the strategic plan.

CAUTIONS FOR FACILITATORS

Facilitators should be aware of and work to avoid the following pitfalls during the strategic planning process:

Step 6: Business Model

Mission and Money. While there is much more openness to the intersection of finance and mission than before, help planners remember two things: mission comes first, *and* there is truth to the adage "no money, no mission."

Have the hard discussions. Facilitators need to be prepared for hard discussions in this step. There is often a tension between funders' interests and the organization's priorities that must be managed, if not resolved. The financial reality that not all programs can, or will, be continued is often stark and painful to accept. Keep the discussions grounded on the question of how to achieve the greatest impact toward mission—rather than whether or not a particular program has inherent value (they always do!).

WORKSHEET 6.1   Business Model Summary

❏ Using the results of your historical review, the revenue and expenses, the articulation of your business model, and insights from the matrix map, step back to look at the major implications of this business model step.

1. What are the implications—*from a financial point of view*—for the *program portfolio*? Are there programs to change, drop, grow?

   There is nothing we want to change about our plans, but it is going to be tough to both expand service and to increase the level of organization capacity. Still, that is what we are going to shoot for.

2. What are the initial implications for *capacity*? If there are significant changes to be made in certain programs—what support will *leaders* need to succeed?

   Our board has stepped up in the last few years and what seems clear is that we need a top-notch effort from a small team of staff and board to develop plans for gaining support from law firms and increasing support from individuals. Getting a grants manager will help a great deal in terms of making the grant funding process more efficient and cost-effective.

3. Bottom line: Based on this analysis, what are the 3–4 top priorities for enhancing the sustainability of your overall business model during the course of your strategic plan?

   1. *Focus on Pro Bono—is critical to our success. It is both a core capacity strategy and a core fund development strategy.*

   2. *Get very clear on targets, and provide regular feedback to all staff who are managing expenses or in charge of attracting revenue.*

   3. *Enlist the board in a creative way to help us be more successful.*

   4. *Be smart and careful as our plans unfold to both reach for our goals and keep an eye on what is realistic.*

(continued)

Current Business Model	Future Business Model
Who do you serve?	
Low income individuals in Central County	*We need to think of ourselves differently in that we serve a truly multicultural community now—and need to become a multicultural organization.*
Where do you do your work?	
See above.	*Increased service to South County, and some increased support to neighboring counties*
What programs/services do you provide?	
Housing, Health Care, Family Law, Public Benefits, modest attention to Advocacy	*All the same plus an increased emphasis on Advocacy.*
How is this work financially supported? % Government % Corporate and Foundations % Individuals % Earned Revenue % Other	
Government *45%*	Government *36%*
Corporate & Foundations *30%*	Corporate & Foundations *31%*
Individuals *20%*	Individuals *26%*
Earned *5%*	Earned *7%*
Other *0%*	Other *0%*

CURRENT YEAR BUDGET

	Housing	Health Care	Family Law	Public Benefits	Advocacy	FR and Admin.	Shared Costs	Total
Government	520,000	235,000	75,000	150,000	0	0	0	980,000
Foundation and Corporation Grants	150,000	50,000	200,000	100,000		150,000		650,000
Individual Contributions	0	0	0	50,000	0	400,000		450,000
Earned Revenue	0	60,000	0	50,000				110,000
Other	10,000	0	0	0	0	0	0	10,000
Total	680,000	345,000	275,000	350,000	0	550,000	0	2,200,000
Direct expenses	548,000	493,000	420,000	365,000	0	224,000	150,000	2,200,000
Allocation of Shared and Admin	112,241	100,976	86,024	74,759	0	−224,000	−150,000	0
Total	660,241	593,976	506,024	439,759	0	0	0	2,200,000
Net	19,759	−248,976	−231,024	−89,759	0	550,000	0	0

(continued)

PROJECTED BUDGET IN 3 YEARS

	Housing	Health Care	Family Law	Public Benefits	Advocacy	FR and Admin.	Shared Costs	Total
Government	520,000	250,000	175,000	175,000	0	0	0	1,120,000
Foundation and Corporation Grants	200,000	200,000	200,000	100,000		260,000		960,000
Individual Contributions	0	0	0	50,000	150,000	600,000		800,000
Earned Revenue	0	60,000	0	150,000				210,000
Other	10,000	0	0	0	0	0	0	10,000
Total	730,000	510,000	375,000	475,000	150,000	860,000	0	3,100,000
Direct expenses	750,000	500,000	450,000	600,000	150,000	400,000	250,000	3,100,000
Allocation of Shared and Admin	198,980	132,653	119,388	159,184	39,796	−400,000	−250,000	0
Total	948,980	632,653	569,388	759,184	189,796	0	0	3,100,000
Net	−218,980	−122,653	−194,388	−284,184	−39,796	350,000	0	0

CHAPTER 7

Step 7: Organization Capacity

FIRST STEPS	STRATEGIC ANALYSIS	SET YOUR COURSE
1. Set up for Success	4. Environmental Scan	9. Complete the Strategic Plan
2. Stakeholder Engagement	5. Theory of Change and Program Portfolio	10. Use Your Plan Successfully
3. Mission, Vision, Values	6. Business Model	
	7. Organization Capacity	
	8. Leadership	

In Step 7 we look at the broad range of supporting systems and infrastructure that keeps your organization running. This work is subordinate to the program work in terms of strategy, but it is essential to being effective. In fact, many in the strategic planning field think this aspect of nonprofit management does not get its due. For example, the Bridgespan Group stated:

> Disciplined management, rigorous analysis of performance data, accounting for true costs, relentless efforts to improve processes and programs, the hiring and development of great people—these are essential to ensuring that what is promised in theory is realized in practice, but simply don't seem to get due attention or respect.[1]

One of the tricky things about the topics in this step is that much of the work here has to do with day-to-day operations and is not thought of as the stuff of strategic planning. It rises to the level of strategic planning when there is either an outstanding strength or a glaring deficiency. An outstanding strength may create an opportunity for greater leverage; for instance, unusual depth in technological expertise may allow experimentation with new ways of serving clients or communicating with constituencies. A significant deficiency may create a liability or require significant funding.

---

[1] The Bridgespan Group Blog, July 2014, www.bridgespan.org/Blogs/Aligning-Government-Nonprofits-and-Philanthropy/July-2014/In-Praise-of-Operations.aspx#.U_OWAOsl4_E.

For example, you may have an urgent need for capital investment to attend to deferred facility maintenance, or you may require a large increase in the operating budget to address a compensation policy that is too low and has become a barrier to effective staff recruitment and retention.

This step begins by providing a few choices about how much depth to go into in assessing organizational capacity. We don't try in this chapter to give guidance on what optimal performance looks like for each of these areas. We do provide a few starting points for thinking about whether this area of organizational capacity is meeting your needs. Each of the seven areas of organizational capacity has its own extensive suite of resources, including books, websites, training programs, and, in some cases, national professional associations. And, frequently the strategic planning committee will have a general understanding of the strengths and weaknesses of your organizational capacity.

For example, if you know your compensation policy is pegged too low, you may need to know *how* low and determine what it would cost to make changes in salaries and/or benefits. Or, if you know your financial management function is inadequate, making an informed decision may require engaging an external expert to provide a deeper assessment during the course of the strategic planning process. If the general understanding is that there is a need but that it is unlikely to materially affect the strategic decision-making process, organizations frequently prioritize both a deeper assessment and subsequent action to address the function as a part of the strategic plan itself.

ELEMENTS OF ORGANIZATION CAPACITY

Eight areas of operations are most relevant for strategic planning: (1) human resources, (2) organizational structure and culture, (3) financial management, (4) resource and business development, (5) external communications, (6) information technology, (7) facilities and equipment, and (8) planning and evaluation.

Human Resources

Human resource management has a great deal to do with organizational performance. It is a dynamic area requiring ongoing attention. As we have said, the goal here is to see if any part of your human resource management function is so strong, or such a problem, that it needs to be prioritized in the strategic plan. Goal:

- Attract and retain qualified paid and volunteer staff for all services and activities.

  Key questions to consider:

- Are your people a strength and a reflection of sound recruitment and retention programs?

- Is supervision and performance management carried out well?

- Is your compensation policy competitive enough to attract and retain the people you need?

- Is a proactive professional development orientation part of performance management?

Organizational Structure and Culture

The degree to which the people in your organization uphold and are guided by your shared values, are dedicated to doing a great job, accept responsibility, and are welcoming toward and support each other can be a great strength or a major hindrance. If this is not a clear area of strength, where are the opportunities to build a more functional or productive structure and culture?

Goal:

- Sustain an organizational structure and culture that supports clear lines of accountability and a culture that rewards creativity and new ways of doing things.

Key questions to consider:

- Are internal communications and decision making efficient and effective?

- How effective is the existing structure, including reporting structure, program management structure, and so on?

- Can you say you have a high performance culture?

- Is your organization intentional and successful in managing diversity and developing a welcoming and inclusive environment?

Financial Management

This is one area where nonprofit boards often have expertise. It is also an area that, for most nonprofits, receives an annual external assessment in the form of an audit. The audit is an excellent indicator of how well the financial management function is structured and operated. However, even if your organization routinely receives "clean audits" without any findings, the quality of the information produced for managerial decision making and governance may be lacking. If there are deficiencies, it may be necessary and helpful to engage an expert in nonprofit financial management to provide input.

Goal:

- Produce timely, accurate financial reports for the organization as a whole, and for all departments.

Key questions to consider:

- Does the basic work of bookkeeping and accounting happen smoothly?
- Does the quality, timeliness, and completeness of financial information support oversight, decision making, and management needs?
- Is the financial management function responsive to the needs of other departments?

Resource and Business Development

It is likely that in Step 6 you will have touched on organizational capacity available and needed for your organization in this area. Just make sure this is the case, or see if any additional help is needed.

Goal:

- Acquire stable, broad-based, financial and nonfinancial resources to support the programs and growth envisioned in this strategic plan.

Key questions to consider:

- Is the function of resource and business development carried out successfully? (This may well depend on the participation of several people—not just the work of the "Development Department.")
- Are foundational activities such as grant writing and management taking place effectively?

- If relevant: is your organization effective and disciplined about soliciting individual contributions—small and major gifts, including relationship cultivation, sending prompt thank you acknowledgments, and so on?

- If relevant, are events managed successfully (including goals such as net revenue, public communications, and constituency engagement)?

- If relevant, is earned revenue managed proactively and successfully?

External Communications

In the past decade, nonprofits have generally begun paying more attention to external communications. External communications has primarily been thought of in connection with resource development. However, the ability to influence the larger system in which an organization works, through direct advocacy or by contributing expertise to policy development, is the basis of an effective strategy. Furthermore, successfully engaging constituencies in a comprehensive way requires integrated and efficient external communications.

Goal:

- Increase the visibility and community awareness of our organization and function to support engagement of our constituencies, through social media, participation in our work, and fund development.

Key questions to consider:

- Are we clear about the goals for all online communications, including website, social media, e-mail newsletters, and so on?

- How well are our efforts meeting our goals?

- Is the role for print communications and other graphic materials clearly defined?

- How well are our efforts meeting our goals in print communications?

Information Technology

The rate of development in information technology is astounding. Some of this development is not particularly relevant to the general nonprofit community. However just a few examples of relevant technology are the emergence of social media, advances in health care technology, and the need for more sophistication in data collection and analysis are all critically important to nonprofits.

Goal:

- Increase the operations and management efficiency and effectiveness of our organization.

Key questions to consider:

- Do we understand our needs in this area (for accounting, development, program management and evaluation, internal and external communications, etc.)?
- Do we have the right tools with appropriate level of technical functionality?
- Do our people know how to use the tools well?

Facilities and Equipment

The cost, performance, and management of facilities are a central management priority for many nonprofits. Whether a site is owned or controlled by the organization or a location simply hosts the organization (such as schools, in the case of after-school and many community programs), this is an important area to assess.

Goal:

- Increase the operations and management efficiency and effectiveness of our organization.

Key questions to consider:

- Do we understand our needs in this area (for office space, client service, performance space, storage, etc.)?
- Do we have the right facilities and equipment with appropriate level of functionality?
- Do our people know how to use the equipment and facilities well?

Planning and Evaluation

Planning is something that takes place across the organization at several levels and that shows up in other areas. The point of including this as a dimension of organization capacity is to step back and look at how well various planning systems are serving staff and board and how well they are integrated. Similarly, evaluation is the other side of planning. Program evaluation is one specific aspect of evaluation, but having systems in place for monitoring plans and learning from experience is a critical capacity for continuous improvement.

Goal:

- Ensure that our planning and evaluation systems are serving their respective purposes and are integrated appropriately.

Key questions to consider:

- Do we have a comprehensive understanding of the various types and settings in which we are doing planning and evaluation—from strategic planning to department planning to individual performance?

- How can we increase the efficiency, effectiveness, and transparency of our planning and evaluation processes?

- Do our staff and board members have the requisite skills to perform successfully in this area?

ACTIVITIES FOR THIS STEP

In this step, you must first decide on the level of independence and depth needed. Next, you should:

- Identify the performance requirements of each element of the systems.

- Determine whether any outside assessment or recent work has taken place to strengthen any of the particular areas listed in this step.

- Assess strengths and weaknesses against performance requirements.

- Determine priorities for investment and/or additional attention.

Finally, you should summarize implications for the strategic planning committee.

IDENTIFY REQUIREMENTS FOR EACH CATEGORY OF CAPACITY

How elaborate this initial step is will depend a great deal on the size of the organization and its particular needs. It may be that you don't actually know what your requirements are because you do not have the expertise to make that determination. In that case, getting assistance in identifying requirements and assessing current capacity is in order.

The level of depth on this step can range from a simple SWOT analysis to an intensive external assessment of your organizational capacity and systems.

DETERMINE HOW TO CARRY OUT ASSESSMENT

By independence, we mean the objectivity of the assessment. It can be a delicate decision for the strategic planning committee. The first questions are, What information do we need? Do we know our requirements and can we self-assess? Is the complexity in certain areas such that we need help with both understanding requirements and assessing current capacity?

Whether outside assistance is required depends on how much confidence you have in staff to provide an accurate and complete assessment. This is particularly true when there have been performance problems with a function, because this inquiry automatically raises questions about the competence of the responsible staff member. In many cases, existing staff will welcome outside assessment—often because they expect it to reveal inadequate resources dedicated to their department! We offer three approaches to assessment in increasing levels of objectivity and dependence on outside expertise.

Organization Self-Assessment

Using an instrument like the one we have included in Appendix B: Elements of an Effectively Managed Organization (EEMO) is one way to do this assessment. As was mentioned in Step 2 Stakeholder Engagement, this can be a great way to involve the full board and even all staff members in identifying organizational strengths and weaknesses. In that chapter we also identify three other online resources that each offer slightly different approaches and which we recommend highly.

Department Self-Assessment

The advantage of department self-assessment is that you are likely to get more detail. You also involve the people closest to the work and those who will need to do the most to strengthen the individual function. The key here is whether the department staff and leadership are competent to undertake this assessment. Sometimes you will trust the staff to identify where the problems are but know that they will need help in figuring out how to address the problems.

SWOT Analysis by the Strategic Planning Committee

A SWOT (Strengths, Weaknesses, Opportunities, and Threats) analysis is probably the place to start. Referring back to the SWOT done with internal stakeholders is a good place to start. You will most likely need to go into more detail at this point with respect to operational capacity then you originally did. This will help you see what you already know and where you have greatest confidence in what you know. This is a minimum requirement to complete the strategic plan. In our experience, the problem spots are generally common knowledge, but that does not mean it is obvious how to address the problem spots or what it will cost to tackle them.

External Expert Assessment

The Strategic Planning Committee may build on an internal task force by recruiting external expert assessment, either pro bono or contracted. For example, the staff and board may have confidence that they can conduct an internal SWOT analysis with a high degree of success, but they may know ahead of time that they will need to invest in outside help to select more robust financial management systems or program evaluation software. As part of the strategic planning process, or as part of the plan itself, this external assessment is prioritized.

WHEN TO USE OUTSIDE EXPERTISE TO ASSESS THE ADEQUACY OF SPECIFIC ORGANIZATION CAPACITIES

There are several issues to consider when deciding whether to employ an outside expert:

- If you have appropriate expertise on staff, then the department is either already running smoothly or any developmental needs have been identified and are in the works. In this case, no outside expert is needed.

- If you have appropriate expertise on the board, be a little more careful. Sometimes a board person doesn't know what they don't know, but because they know more than anyone else on staff or the board, they may be accepted as an expert. And, ensure that they have the time and necessary support to do what needs to be done.

- A third and increasingly available option is to hire a consultant who works in the area to do a checkup. This is similar to what you might do when buying a used car: Have an auto mechanic check it out and let you know what needs to be done. Depending on the complexity of your operations, this can vary in expense. Although the cost to get an expert assessment may give you pause, remember that inadequate financial management, information technology, or facilities can be greatly limiting your effectiveness as an organization, but it may not be completely clear there is a problem because the staff and board have adjusted to the limitations.

- Finally, there are volunteer associations in many regions for each area of expertise. You may be able to get guidance, and perhaps checklists, from them.

Understand that any external assessment may not be welcomed; a staff member whose department is being assessed may feel threatened. This is often easier to do when there is a new executive director, chief operating officer, or departmental manager. Regardless of the discomfort, however, if you see signs that there are problems in one or more of these areas, it is important to look into and resolve them.

AGREE ON PRIORITIES TO INCLUDE IN THE STRATEGIC PLAN

If everything is running smoothly or you have the necessary internal know-how and access to needed resources to get a particular capacity up to the performance level you need, then there may be little that belongs in the strategic plan related to capacity investment/development. However, if the analysis of one or more areas reveals a substantial drag on performance or even liability, and it will require a significant effort of time and/or money to fix, this belongs in the strategic plan as a priority. Examples of issues that rise to the level of inclusion in the strategic plan include the following:

- Your compensation is in the 25th quartile of the region, and you cannot hire competent staff. It will require significant additional funding to bring your compensation to the desired level.

- Your performance evaluation system is not connected to your program work, and outside assistance, new software, training for personnel, or other major investment will be required.

- Your online communications are so antiquated that you are reluctant to publicize your website, or you can't depend on your e-mail lists for important communication distribution.

- Your financial information is not organized to give you real-time updates on program-by-program spending, cost of service, or cash flow projections.

In such cases, you will not be able to execute your strategy successfully, and the most brilliant plan in the world will be for naught. The priorities need to be identified, budgeted, and planned for with a clear timeline. Or the plan may be to do a thorough assessment of a given function (e.g., Information Technology). Either way, this set of plans will become one section of the strategic plan.

CAUTIONS FOR FACILITATORS

Facilitators should be aware of and work to avoid the following pitfalls during the strategic planning process:

Step 7: Organization Capacity

Consider the leverage of capacity. Discounting the value of, and consequently underinvesting in, organization capacity characterizes the nonprofit sector. Once needs are clearly identified and cost estimates developed, facilitators may need to help planners avoid the trap of pitting one investment against another (e.g., increasing salaries, *or* adding a position, *or* improving technology), when frequently some combination is possible.

Make trade-offs clear. Discussions may mirror the tension in the business model step—the quantity of services may need to be limited while capacity is built to improve quality (and impact) or achieve efficiency to subsequently increase volume of service (and impact) after some period of time. Thinking about a longer time frame that one year helps planners better appreciate the importance and value of a longer-term benefit that will result from near-term "sacrifices."

WORKSHEET 7.1 Organizational Capacity Priorities

☐ For each organizational capacity area, list the overall goal or goals for each function and any long-term objectives to be included in the strategic plan.

☐ List any significant expenditures that may be needed to implement the objectives.

☐ (optional) Are there questions that need further discussion or research?

Organizational Capacity	Goal(s)	Long-Term Objectives	How Adequate Are Current Resources? Are There Significant Expenditures That May Be Needed in the Next 3 to 5 years?
Human Resources	Attract and retain qualified paid and volunteer staff for all services and activities.	Increase number of paid staff from 22 full-time and part-time employees to 31 full-time and part-time employees. Double the number of pro bono lawyers from 105 to 175 lawyers. Assess overall salary structure and benefits package, develop and implement a plan to increase staff salaries, and offer a competitive benefits package, including retirement benefits. Analyze fringe benefits package on an ongoing basis. Review personnel policies annually. Establish and maintain a more formalized ongoing training program for all staff and volunteers.	Salaries for additional 9 staff As soon as financially possible, bring on a grant writer/grants manager; bring half-time Volunteer coordinator position up to full time Need further discussion about whether we need a full-time director of advocacy or assign advocacy role to an advocacy/public policy matrix manager, whose job it is to coordinate all of the advocacy efforts across programs and work with external organizations

(continued)

			Resources needed to hire consultant for executive transition and succession planning
		Implement and maintain a new staff evaluation system that establishes overall objectives for positions and specific objectives for all employees.	Resources to improve salaries and offering of a more competitive benefits package
		Develop an agency-wide management training program.	
		Implement a successful and orderly transition to a new executive director and establish a succession plan for all long-term leadership.	
		Develop emergency succession plans for all leadership positions.	
		Increase number of spanish-speaking staff and improved capacity to work with other non–English-speaking clients	
		Continue to work with local law schools so as to increase number of interns serving our clients.	
Organizational Structure and Culture	Sustain an organizational structure and culture that supports clear lines of accountability and a culture that rewards creativity and new ways of doing things.	Review current organization chart and ensure that structure supports clarity of decision making and accountability.	
		Encourage staff to be open to new and different ways of doing things (breaking away from the "we have never done it that way") and acknowledge that we are no longer a mom-and-pop small organization, and our decision-making processes need to change.	
Financial Management	Produce timely, accurate financial reports for the organization as a whole, and for all departments.	Maintain computerized accounting system capable of producing detailed and accurate reports for both internal and external stakeholders.	As mentioned above, need to hire a full-time grants manager
		Assess organization's internal controls annually to ensure adequate safeguard of all resources.	
		Improve our grants management processes.	

Resource and Business Development	Acquire stable, broad-based, financial and nonfinancial resources to support the programs and growth envisioned in this strategic plan.	*Decrease our dependency on government funding: Within the next three years, at least 40 percent of CLAS's annual operating budget will be raised through private-sector philanthropy. The development of this subsidy is critical for the maintenance and growth of our programs.*	*As mentioned above, need to hire a full-time grants manager*
		Explore donations in kind (e.g., printing, equipment, etc.) to help support our services.	
		Increase the money that the organization receives from private individuals to a minimum of 10 percent each year.	
		Raise a minimum of $50,000 annually from special events and fundraisers.	
		Bring on a new grants writer as soon as budget allows or as funding can be raised.	
		Establish and maintain a computerized donor history file and increase the personal contacts made with donors.	
		Maintain a board-giving policy that requires all board members to contribute financially.	
		Increase the board's participation in all aspects of fundraising.	
External Communications	*Increase the visibility and community awareness of CLAS.*	*Build public awareness of CLAS in the community through increased media coverage and public service announcements.*	*Work with PR firm to augment our internal external communications efforts.*
	Make sure that CLAS is properly recognized for its achievements and closely identified as a	*Update brochures regularly and make sure they are available in English, Spanish, and perhaps Cantonese.*	
		Increase outreach to underserved populations.	

(continued)

	premier provider of legal services to disenfranchised populations.	*Implement branding plan so we have a recognizable logo and material that is consistent in appearance.* *Maintain an up-to-date online calendar of upcoming clinics and seminars.* *Develop a resource-rich website, capable of assisting individuals to access information for self-helps as well as being made aware of other community resources that are available.*	
Information Technology and Management Information Systems	*Increase the operations and management efficiency and effectiveness of CLAS.*	*Improve our system for tracking all necessary information required for funding sources and management decision making.* *Put in place a new client intake and tracking system.* *Develop technological capacity to reach remote areas not currently served. Explore creating a virtual assistance program and using technology to serve clients in hard-to-reach areas.*	*Developing and implementing a technological capacity to reach remote areas will be expensive.*
Facilities and Equipment	*Ensure that we have up-to-date equipment for increased efficiency and effectiveness of staff and service delivery.* *Ensure that all of our facilities are sufficient for staff needs.*	*Develop and implement a facilities master plan for our office and satellite offices.* *Explore the option of getting a building donated—we need to move the Central Office.* *Maintain facilities that are attractive to clients.* *Ensure that any satellite offices are easily accessible to public transportation and are sufficient to meet staff needs.*	*Significant resources will be required for moving Central Office, as well as facilities in other parts of our service area.* *If we merge with Valley County Legal Aid, considerable resources will be needed to bring their technology and facilities needs up to our current standards. This needs to be a critical part of any merger assessment.*

			Cost to implement remote legal assistance could be prohibitive, but perhaps we could get a grant to research and implement such a program.

| | | Continually assess technology needs and update computers and other technology as needed. | |
| | | Explore how much it would cost—and how it would work—if some of our legal assistance was done remotely. | |

Planning and Evaluation	Make sure that we have appropriate systems in place and are meeting the needs of our constituencies and that all of our programs provide the highest quality service.	Establish and maintain a board/staff ongoing planning committee to review the strategic plan at least quarterly and, as needed, make necessary changes that support the ability of the organization to achieve its mission.	
		Assign responsibility for the leadership team and managers to develop detailed annual operating plans.	
		Establish an ongoing evaluation process for all programs to assess program results, quality of services, and our ability to address the (changing) needs of level of service to our clients and the community.	
		Hold an annual board/staff retreat to plan for future needs and assess current capabilities.	
		Review the strategic plan quarterly and make changes as needed.	
		Ensure that detailed annual operating plans are developed.	
		Establish and maintain protocols for data collection, data entry, and outcome evaluation.	
		Annually look at how well we are meeting individual legal needs versus overall systems change that address issues of poverty and equal justice.	

171

CHAPTER 8

Step 8: Leadership

FIRST STEPS	STRATEGIC ANALYSIS	SET YOUR COURSE
1. Set up for Success	4. Environmental Scan	9. Complete the Strategic Plan
2. Stakeholder Engagement	5. Theory of Change and Program Portfolio	10. Use Your Plan Successfully
3. Mission, Vision, Values	6. Business Model	
	7. Organization Capacity	
	8. Leadership	

Leadership is central to any organization's success, and there may be more management books and articles written about leadership than all other aspects of organizational effectiveness combined. A brilliant, well-funded strategy with adequate resources cannot be successfully executed without shared, clear vision and direction—something the top leadership needs to accomplish. But how? And how does one know when good leadership is taking place?

Our approach to leadership refers to the broad notion of the leadership function, as well as to the effectiveness of individuals in specific roles, starting with the board president and the executive director. The simplest definition of leadership is "mobilizing others to take action." Leadership in this broader sense includes the work carried out individually and collectively by staff and board members.

One of the most famous books on leadership, *The Leadership Challenge*, by Jim Kouzes and Barry Posner, now in its fifth edition, identifies five practices and several attributes of exemplary leadership. The five practices of exemplary leadership are as follows:

1. Model the way

2. Inspire a shared vision

3. Challenge the process

4. Enable others to act

5. Encourage the heart

There also are attributes we look for and admire in leaders, according to Kouzes and Posner. Such leaders are:

- Honest—This is the single most important factor in the leader—constituent relationship.

- Forward-looking—They have a sense of direction and concern for the future.

- Inspiring—They are enthusiastic, energetic, and positive.

- Competent—They have relevant experience and sound judgment.

However, there is a tension in this construct. There are individual people in specific roles, who we hope embody the practices and attributes identified, yet we are looking for results that are brought about through the interdependent and coordinated efforts of a group of people. Any orchestra, sports team, or space shuttle has actors who are visible to the outside world, people who are in charge, and many more people behind the scenes who also have to make decisions every day and help each other if the collective enterprise is to succeed.

Tom Peters, the legendary management guru, famously observed, "Leaders don't create followers. Leaders create more leaders." Although individual people must play key leadership roles well, it is important to think about building a *culture of leadership*. Effective organizations encourage and support leadership by many people at all levels.

The archetypal top-down approach to management has given way to what some people call "leaderful" organizations. Leaderful organizations have people with formal authority, known as positional leaders, but more importantly, they have an orientation toward pushing decision making and the potential for initiative down through the organization. This approach requires intention and that training, job description designs, planning processes, and so on are organized to support the broader exercise of initiative and leadership.[1]

This book is about strategic planning and not about how to build effective boards, strong staff leaders, or a culture of leadership. What is crucial in the strategic planning process is to think carefully about the importance of leadership to the success of the organization, and to consider ways in which leadership can be enhanced and strengthened.

The first objective of this step is to assess at a high level the depth and effectiveness of your current leadership. The second objective is to identify opportunities to strengthen the leadership function in your organization, in light of new initiatives or demands that will need to be met to support strategy, funding, or capacity initiatives.

---

[1] For a discussion about how to create a Leaderful organization see: Allison, Misra, Perry; "Doing More with More: Putting Shared Leadership into Practice," *The Nonprofit Quarterly*, Summer 2011; published by Nonprofit Information Networking Association, Boston, MA.

After discussing the interrelationship among leadership and the topics of strategy and program, business model, and organization capacity, the planning team will be in a position to prioritize opportunities for strengthening leadership.

ASSESS LEADERSHIP, SUMMARIZE IMPLICATIONS

The Walter and Elise Haas, Jr. Fund in San Francisco has been a national leader in strengthening leadership in nonprofits. The fund developed an eight-part leadership assessment tool as part of their Flexible Leadership Awards Program and has generously agreed to share this tool. The authors of the survey note that its genesis was informed significantly by the work of others. At the top of the first page of the survey you will see: "In developing this tool, we reviewed and were guided by many other organizational assessments including those of REDF, San Diego Foundation, TCC Group, and particularly, RoadMAP's My Healthy Organization tool."

The premise of the assessment is that there are eight essential responsibilities where effective leadership is demonstrated. We like that this tool addresses together the roles of staff and board as components of an "organization's leadership." The assessment tool is designed to enable board and staff members to gather perceptions about how effectively the leadership team, including board and senior staff, is fulfilling these responsibilities. The eight areas are as follows:

1. *Vision, mission, and values.* The degree to which these foundational sets of ideas are understood and upheld.

2. *Strategy and assessment.* How clear and widely understood are strategic priorities, to what degree are priorities and plans reviewed regularly, and how consistently does the organization achieve its targeted goals and impact? By asking each respondent to name the priorities independently, it quickly becomes clear to what degree the group as a whole shares a common understanding.

3. *Board leadership and governance.* This section asks about eight dimensions of board effectiveness.

4. *Executive director and senior staff leadership.* Direct questions about the effectiveness of these key positional leaders.

5. *Staff development, organization culture, and succession planning.* The level of intentionality and organized action in these areas is an important manifestation of a sound leadership culture.

6. *Diversity and cultural competency.* Virtually all nonprofits work in multicultural communities; effective leadership is skilled at working with people of varied cultures, backgrounds, identities, and experiences.

7. *External communications.* Effective communication with the community and broader public to which an organization relates.

8. *Fundraising and planning for sustainability.* Organized and effective resource development.

A few people working together, the members of the strategic planning committee, or even the full board and staff can complete this assessment tool. The resulting data do not *prove* the presence or absence of strong leadership, but they provide a very good indication about what the respondents think. The survey process and results will likely spur new thinking and raise additional questions. If several people complete the Assessment Tool, you will want to tabulate the multiple-choice answers and have someone summarize the narrative answers. The survey is easily converted to an online survey using publicly available services such as SurveyMonkey. Thanks to the generosity of the Haas, Jr. Fund, the survey is available in Appendix F of our book and will be on the website along with other resources.

Worksheet 8.1 corresponds with the Leadership Assessment Tool in asking about short-term and long-term implications and priorities for leadership development. In essence, the worksheet asks the "so what?" questions. What are the implications of the current assessment of leadership, and what is relevant for the strategic plan?

FLA 2.0 - LEADERSHIP DIAGNOSTIC

Flexible Leadership Award (FLA) Leadership Diagnostic—Introduction

This survey was developed for the Flexible Leadership Awards (FLA) Program, a Project of the Tides Center and the Evelyn & Walter Haas, Jr. Fund. In developing this tool, we reviewed and were guided by many other organizational assessments including those of REDF, San Diego Foundation, and TCC Group, and particularly, RoadMAP's My Healthy Organization tool. Please feel free to further adapt and develop this tool for your purposes.

This tool is intended to help your organization gather the data it needs to develop a strong leadership development plan. Completing this tool is the first step in an integrated and multistep process intended to help you develop a plan that will strengthen your leadership to achieve your most important strategic priorities.

Your responses, along with those of others in the organization and in concert with the data collected from interviews and other organizational documents, will be used to help identify leadership opportunities and needs. The survey covers the following eight key leadership topics:

1. Vision, Mission, and Values
2. Strategy and Assessment
3. Board Leadership and Governance

4. Executive Director and Senior Staff

5. Staff Development, Organization Culture, and Succession Planning

6. Diversity and Cultural Competency

7. Communications

8. Fundraising and Planning for Sustainability

In each of the sections, you will find a series of statements. Please review each of these statements and check the box that best reflects your perspective—remember there are no right or wrong answers and that you are assessing this statement from YOUR point of view. (If you feel you do not have information about any of the statements, then check "unable to judge.")

It is not necessary to use this tool, or any formal tool, to think carefully about an organization's leadership. The important thing is for the strategic planning committee to understand what is needed from board and staff leadership to be successful and to identify any significant areas for attention. The ultimate goal of the strategic planning process is to identify the opportunities for making the best use of and strengthening the leadership at your organization.

If significant changes are decided upon as priorities, then these decisions about how to strengthen leadership and governance will become a section of the strategic plan.

CAUTIONS FOR FACILITATORS

Facilitators should be aware of and work to avoid the following pitfalls during the strategic planning process:

Step 8: Leadership

Leadership matters. The strategic planning process is an opportunity to look at its future leadership (management) needs. As this is not a topic many nonprofits spend a lot of time on, facilitators should be careful not to skip too quickly over this step—encourage exploratory discussion. What has helped individual planners grow as leaders? How might those experiences be institutionalized? Etc.

SAMPLE WORKSHEET FOR CASE STUDY: COUNTY LEGAL AID SOCIETY (CLAS)

> **WORKSHEET 8.1   Leadership Capacity**
>
> The following is a list of board and staff leadership attributes.
>
> For each category, set long-term priorities for ensuring that there is effective leadership to maximize the organization's mission.

Ensuring Impact

1. Clarity of Vision, Mission, and Values

The board and staff understand and share the vision of the organization.

The board and staff understand and can articulate the mission.

Everyone in the organization understands and can communicate a common set of values.

In all parts of their work, staff and board act in accordance with the organization's values.

2. Effective Strategy Setting, Planning, and Monitoring

The organization has clear strategic priorities that define the impact staff and board want to achieve over the next three to five years.

The organization has specific organizational and program goals that advance its strategic priorities.

The organization has an ongoing strategy review process in place that enables it to revise plans as needed and respond to changing circumstances so as to better meet needs of the community and achieve the organization's mission.

The organization regularly assesses its programs in order to maximize learning and ensure programs are operating effectively and efficiently.

The organization regularly achieves the goals and impact that the organization has agreed upon.

For the long term, what should the board do same as, more of, less of, or differently to ensure clarity of vision and mission and effective strategy setting, planning, and monitoring?	For the long term, what should senior management do same as, more of, less of, or differently to ensure clarity of vision and mission and effective strategy setting, planning, and monitoring?
• *Need to do a better job of orienting new board members about the organization's mission, vision, values, and what is in the strategic plan.* • *Board must provide a revised mandate to the current Board/Staff SP Committee so that it has a new role as a Monitoring and Evaluation Committee.*	• *Review current program evaluation mechanisms that are in place and make sure that in the future there is greater attention being placed on documenting successes and focusing on greater impact—as defined in our strategic plan.* • *Make sure that all new staff are oriented on the organization's mission, vision, and values.*

WORKSHEET 8.1 *(continued)*

• *The entire board needs to commit to meeting—at the very least—with the ED and Senior Management Team in an annual planning session to review, and if necessary to make fundamental changes to, the current strategic plan.*	• *Continue annual planning that involves all staff and all departments, once the board, ED, and senior management team have met to review current strategic plan and made any changes to reflect current environment.*

Board, Executive Director, and Senior Management Accountability

3. Effective Board Leadership and Governance

The board has the experience and skills the organization needs.

The board is fully engaged in governance of the organization, including setting strategy and direction, ensuring fiscal oversight, and ensuring there are evaluation and control systems to maximize the achievement of the organization's mission.

The board regularly evaluates the performance of the executive director.

The board actively supports the executive director and his or her leadership development.

The board focuses on board development and self-assessment, including the effective recruitment, training, and integration of new members.

The board members work well together.

The board and staff leadership are clear about and agree on their respective goals.

The board and staff communicate effectively with each other, with mutual respect and support.

Board member engagement is high: Board members contribute their time and expertise within the organization, help support the organization through their personal financial contribution, and engage in outreach to raise funds and build the organization's reputation.

4. Effective Executive Director and Senior Staff Leadership

Given where the organization envisions going over the next few years, the executive director has the skills and expertise the organization needs.

The executive director is self-aware, seeking opportunities to grow as a leader and increase the impact of the organization.

Given where the organization envisions going in the next few years, the senior staff members have the skills and expertise the organization needs.

Our senior staff members are self-aware and consistently seek opportunities to grow and increase the impact of the organization.

The staff leadership structure makes sense, with a shared understanding of who is responsible for what, decision-making processes, and lines of accountability.

The organization has a management team that takes responsibility for ensuring accountability, coordination, and implementation of programs and operations.

(continued)

WORKSHEET 8.1 *(continued)*

The senior team members not only represent their departments or functional areas, but also work well together to effectively lead the "whole" organization.

The senior leaders inspire, motivate, and challenge the full staff to work successfully toward our mission.

For the long term, what should the board do same as, more of, less of, or differently to ensure board, ED, and senior management accountability?	For the long term, what should senior management do same as, more of, less of, or differently to ensure board, ED, and senior management accountability?
• Board needs to do a better job of orientation and training of new board members, including clarity of expectations (participation, personal contribution, help with fundraising, etc.). • Board used to evaluate the executive director on a regular basis but has not done so of late. Board needs to make sure that it sets goals for the ED, and evaluates her or him against those goals. • Board development function has been done by the board executive committee over the last few years. This has not proven to be an effective process for board recruitment and training. The board should consider establishing a board development committee that will develop and implement a formal board recruitment plan. • Greater opportunities for board and staff to meet each other. • Board members have been good about not micromanaging. They should continue to provide support to the ED but not get involved in day-to-day operations.	• Succession plan put into place that results in new executive director being brought in within next 12 months. • Leadership structure needs to be revised to support greater collaboration among departments: Institute some form of matrix management, add advocacy as a formal program, and bring representative of that program into the management team. • All staff, including senior leadership, need professional development plans that include budgeted resources for training and development.

WORKSHEET 8.1 *(continued)*

Sustaining a Leaderful Organization

5. Intentional Staff Development and Succession Planning

Management nurtures leadership throughout the organization and intentionally develops staff through relevant training, coaching/feedback, and consistent performance appraisal.

The organization is able to attract and retain competent and committed staff members who represent the diversity of the community and our organization's stakeholders.

The organization anticipates the skill sets needed on staff in order to achieve its strategic priorities.

Staff engagement is high, and the organization's culture encourages experimentation and learning.

Challenges and conflicts are handled in a way that does not stifle effective problem solving.

There are emergency succession plans in place for all key positions.

6. Attention to Issues of Diversity and Cultural Competency

The organization assesses community needs on a regular basis.

The organization develops plans with input from its constituencies and holds itself accountable to its constituents.

The board reflects the community the organization serves.

The staff reflects the community the organization serves.

The organization's staff and board engage in organization learning in order to work well with people and issues of varied cultures, backgrounds, identities, and experiences.

For the long term, what should the board do same as, more of, less of, or differently to sustain a leaderful organization?	For the long term, what should senior management do same as, more of, less of, or differently to sustain a leaderful organization?
• Develop and implement a diversity plan. • Approve budget with staff development as a critical line item. • Reinstate annual evaluation of the ED. • As part of board development, design a process for succession planning for board leadership. • Institute term limits.	• Develop and implement a diversity plan. • Regular attention to, and training where appropriate, in becoming a more culturally competent organization. We currently do a fair job at this, but could be better. • Professional development training plans for all staff, not just senior management and attorneys. • Raise salaries and benefits to support staff retention. • Develop emergency succession plan and review yearly to ensure all key functions are covered if there was an unplanned absence. • Continue regular annual evaluations of all staff.

(continued)

WORKSHEET 8.1 *(continued)*

Communicating Impact and Ensuring Sustainability

7. Effective External Communication

The board has the skills to effectively promote the organization.

The board members are committed to acting as ambassadors for the organization.

The staff has the skills to effectively promote the organization.

The organization has clear communications goals designed to support its strategic priorities.

The organization has a clear and realistic communications plan.

The organization communicates effectively about its work and the impact of its programs.

8. Effective Fundraising and Planning for Sustainability

The organization has a realistic, well-developed fund development plan.

Senior staff members have the skills to raise sufficient funds to support the organization's programs.

Senior staff members consider fundraising a core leadership capacity.

The organization's board pulls its weight in fundraising.

Staff and board leaders work together effectively to raise the funds the organization needs.

The organization has the skills and systems to understand and manage our financial situation.

The organization has a clear business model that promotes sustainability.

The organization's budgets reflect our strategic priorities.

For the long term, what should the board do same as, more of, less of, or differently to ensure the organization is communicating its impact to current and future clients and supporters, and ensuring the long-term viability of the organization?	For the long term, what should senior management do same as, more of, less of, or differently to ensure the organization is communicating its impact to current and future clients and supporters, and ensuring the long-term viability of the organization?
• All board members should participate in regular trainings on how to effectively market the organization and how to ask for money. • Approve a long-term plan for financial sustainability and include a section as to the board's role in that sustainability plan.	• Create better collateral material that can be used to market the organization. • Develop a long-term plan for financial sustainability, making sure that CLAS's current business model can be used to support the expansion envisioned in the plan.

Set Your Course

All of the work you have done to date comes to fruition in the final steps, 9 and 10. A strategic plan is a set of ideas. You want these ideas to reside in two places: (1) summarized in a document and (2) alive in the hearts and minds of your board and staff members.

In Step 9, we focus on finalizing the ideas of the plan through completing a document and building commitment and alignment. Creating the document requires discipline in sharpening your thinking and preparing to communicate the plan to other people. The review process provides a final opportunity to ensure that a deep understanding of the plan exists and to get your board and staff excited about putting the plan into action.

In Step 10, we focus on taking proactive steps to prepare the way and ensure that people know how to put these ideas into action. The first steps of implementation involve translating the strategic plan into first-year annual operating plans and the annual budget. Thinking about how to help people manage the changes required and setting up an ongoing monitoring and response process help you begin navigating your course with confidence!

FIRST STEPS	STRATEGIC ANALYSIS	SET YOUR COURSE
1. Set up for Success	4. Environmental Scan	9. Complete the Strategic Plan
2. Stakeholder Engagement	5. Theory of Change and Program Portfolio	10. Use Your Plan Successfully
3. Mission, Vision, Values	6. Business Model	
	7. Organization Capacity	
	8. Leadership	

CHAPTER 9

Step 9: Complete Your Strategic Plan

FIRST STEPS	STRATEGIC ANALYSIS	SET YOUR COURSE
1. Set up for Success	4. Environmental Scan	9. Complete the Strategic Plan
2. Stakeholder Engagement	5. Theory of Change and Program Portfolio	10. Use Your Plan Successfully
3. Mission, Vision, Values	6. Business Model	
	7. Organization Capacity	
	8. Leadership	

You're in the home stretch! In this step you will finalize your decisions, ensure alignment and commitment, and complete the strategic plan, making sure the plan is clear, compelling, and supported. It is the strategic planning committee's job to make sure all of the important questions have been asked and answered, and that engagement in the process has built sufficient buy-in and alignment with stakeholders.

There are five substeps. The time it takes to go through each of the following substeps can vary from a few weeks to a month or two, depending primarily on how intensively the draft plan is reviewed with board and staff. It is the committee's job to strike the balance between having "enough" input and getting the job done. The substeps are as follows:

Summarize strategic decisions, agree on core strategies
Draft the complete strategic plan
Conduct a thorough review process
Begin to prepare a document for public distribution
Reflect and celebrate!

SUMMARIZE STRATEGIC DECISIONS

During the strategic analysis section of this process, each of the five key elements of the content of strategic planning has been investigated. At the conclusion of each step, the group prepared a summary of its proposals using worksheets, and subsequently made sure to connect the dots to ensure tight connectivity between each dimension. At this point the majority of strategic decision making should be done.

Don't be surprised if the planning process refuses to follow a straightforward path at this point. To do this job with integrity, the strategic planning committee must *seek out* doubters and pockets of resistance. You will already be familiar with the doubts of the people who feel able to speak up. But you will want to seek out the newer and quieter board members, the administrative staff, the program folks who really hoped that certain changes would be adopted, and maybe those who voiced questions early on, but have not "pounded on the table" to make sure their point of view was heard.

Momentum is building to complete the plan, and it is the strategic planning committee's role to swim against that current if necessary. Although it may be exhausting to contemplate reopening one or more questions, if there is good reason to do so—and it is not just rehashing a decision that really was settled—this is a time to "go slow to go fast." Absolute *consensus* is not necessary. However, overlooking meaningful gaps or objections has the potential to undermine all of the hard work that has been done. The risk is that the plan will be made less relevant, and therefore less valuable, through insufficient commitment.

You also want to look back at your original goals for strategic planning, and the vision that was drafted (and perhaps refined) along the way to see if anything important has been overlooked. A temptation will lurk to add a "few things" back into the plan that had been deemed lower priorities. The easy part of planning is choosing what to do; it is harder to explicitly choose what you will *not* do, or at least not do now. This step involves a combination of intuition and analysis, using facts and judgment to bring the plan to completion. Don't lose the focus on the *most important* work.

The strategic planning committee as a whole will want to review the full package of decisions and ask the following litmus test questions:

1. Have you identified the top three or four external **environmental** forces or trends to which your plan needs to respond?

2. Do you have confidence that your **core program strategies**—articulated in your theory of change and your program portfolio—will achieve the results you are seeking?

3. Do you have confidence that your **business model** not only supports and builds on your core program strategies, but that taken as a whole it is structured for sustainability?

4. Have you assessed your organization **capacity** needs thoroughly and planned to provide the people and infrastructure necessary for your strategy to succeed?

5. Is your senior staff and board **leadership** ready to lead the way?

6. Bottom line: Can you explain, briefly and clearly, how your program, business and other core strategies are different from other choices you could have made? In other words—what you chose not to do?

If the answer to these six questions is yes, then you have developed a plan in which you can have confidence. If one or more answers is no, it is time to go back to the drawing board. You may need to trim your aspirations or squarely face difficult trade-offs about resource allocation. Do what it takes to get to yes!

→ SEE WORKSHEET 9.1 TO SUMMARIZE YOUR CORE FUTURE STRATEGIES.

WORKSHEET 9.1	CORE FUTURE STRATEGIES

Process Notes

How to do this activity	Consider strategies that may have emerged from each of the five dimensions of strategic analysis. Narrow your choices to three to five core future strategies. After selecting the best strategy, respond to the rest of the questions on the worksheet: What assumptions, facts, and values support the proposed strategy? What possible obstacles may the organization face in implementing the strategy? And what triggers might encourage the organization to reevaluate the suggested new strategy?
Why do this activity	After all this thinking and brainstorming, it's time to make some decisions!
Who to involve in the process	Planning committee members and selected others develop draft core strategies. Once there is overall agreement, draft strategies may be reviewed by the entire board for sign-off and by the staff (either as a whole or by department) to generate ideas as to how to implement these strategies.

DRAFT THE COMPLETE STRATEGIC PLAN

(Note: A sample strategic plan is included at the end of this chapter following the material developed in the worksheets for the case study through the book.)

Most of the content of the plan has been generated, but it will likely need additional narrative and fleshing out into the structure of goals and objectives. We suggest you use some variation of the following outline:

1. Introduction by the board president and/or executive director

2. Executive summary

3. Mission, vision, and values statements

4. History of organization (optional)

5. External environmental themes

6. Summary of core strategies

7. Program portfolio and plans

8. Business model and financial plans

9. Organizational capacity development plans

10. Leadership development plans

11. Appendixes

Strategic Plan Content and Format

A strategic plan is a document that summarizes why an organization exists, what it is trying to accomplish, and how it will go about doing so. Its audience is anyone who wants to know the organization's most important ideas, issues, and priorities: board members, staff, volunteers, clients, funders, peers at other organizations, the press, and the public. It should make clear the direction in which the organization is headed and provide enough rationale for this direction to be compelling. The more concise and ordered the document, the greater the likelihood that it will be used and be helpful in guiding the organization's operations.

STRATEGIC PLAN: INTERNAL OR EXTERNAL DOCUMENT?

There are two distinct audiences for the strategic plan: internal stakeholders and external stakeholders. At the point of completing the plan for internal circulation and discussion, the audience is strictly *internal*. In this version, you can afford to include more detail and be more direct about the rationale behind your decisions. In order to produce a document to distribute to many others outside of the organization, it will be helpful to boil down the plan to its essence at the conclusion of the process.

The written plan should reflect the nature and extent of the planning decisions and should provide the level of detail needed to communicate clearly to your audience. Form follows function; the format should serve the message. The following are some common elements of a written strategic plan:

- The *introduction* is a one-page cover letter that introduces the plan to its readers. It gives a stamp of approval to the plan and demonstrates that the organization has achieved a critical level of internal agreement. This introduction is often combined with the executive summary.

- The *executive summary* of the strategic plan is usually one to three pages. The executive summary should reference the organization's mission and vision, and highlight its core future strategies and major program and organizational priorities. This summary should enable readers to understand what is most important about the organization's plan—the storyline you are planning to pursue. A version of this executive summary can become a public document, published in the organization's newsletter or website or distributed to supporters and participants in the planning process.

- *Mission, vision, and values statements* can stand alone without any introductory text, because essentially they introduce and define themselves. However, if there is additional narrative about what these statements mean to your organization, or specific elements to be highlighted, a brief commentary on each is also appropriate.

- *History and Current Context* tells the reader, in one or two pages, the story of the organization—key events, triumphs, and changes over time. This section also summarizes the environmental context in which this plan is written. The core strategies need to explicitly respond to the environmental context.

- The *summary of core strategies* section makes explicit the strategic thinking behind the plan and tells readers where the organization will be focusing its resources over the next few years. The section might be presented as a summary of the theory of change or a brief listing of the organization's three to five core future strategies. It may also include an explanation of each strategy, including relevant environmental context, so that the outside reader has a better understanding of the "why" of that strategy. This section can be thought of as an introduction to the program plans.

- The *program plans* (including goals and objectives) are the plan of action—what the organization intends to accomplish over the next few years. As such, this section serves as a guide to annual operational planning and as a reference for evaluation.

- The section on *business model* and funding strategy is foundational, as it explains the strategy and actions for financing the program plans and supporting infrastructure. We recommend that organizations include high-level, pro forma budget projections for the full period of the plan (typically three to five years), describing the arc of growth that is planned and how the organization will pay for any planned increase in expenses.

- The section on *organization capacity* highlights the most significant capacity building initiatives planned. These initiatives to increase efficiency, effectiveness, and resiliency will likely, although not always, require additional investments. Subordinate plans for each department (such as human resources or finance) need to be completed for the term of the plan, spelling out any particular changes required to support the implementation of the strategic plan. Typically, these will not all be included in the strategic plan, in favor of a summary of organizational capacity priorities.

- Discussion of *leadership* development goals should be oriented toward the strategic perspective and need not include all of the leadership development activities planned. Board development and steps to restructure or strengthen leadership at the staff level is the content of this section.

- Any *appendices* are included to provide the documentation needed by interested readers. No appendices may be necessary; many organizations opt for brevity. They should be included only if they will truly enhance readers' understanding of the plan, not just burden them with more data. Many organizations will at least summarize strengths, weaknesses, opportunities, and threats here, and paraphrase the results of any client/customer surveys. Appendices may be a few pages or considerably longer.

Finalize Goals and Objectives

Writing of goals and objectives is one aspect of planning with which most people have experience. Every grant proposal that has been written has some form of goals and objectives (see Table 9.1). Writing goals and objectives should not be a group project. For a large organization, each program and administrative manager should take the lead on drafting his or her unit's objectives. For a smaller organization, one or two individuals should take responsibility for drafting the initial goals and objectives. Two or three versions may be required before a final document is agreed upon. While this step may seem simple, important questions often arise and insights emerge in precisely describing a goal and its objectives. Do not shortchange this process. Clear and tightly written goals and objectives greatly improve the quality and utility of the document.

Goals are outcome statements (ends) that guide the organization's programs and its financial, organizational, and leadership functions. Goals and objectives must be written so they can be monitored. "Improve the well-being of the community" is a laudable goal, but it would be difficult to determine whether such a broad goal had been achieved. Work done now to ensure clearly articulated goals and objectives will save hours of frustration later, during implementation of the plan. Clear goals and objectives are the building blocks of successful program evaluation. Each goal usually carries with it two or more objectives.

The standard form for an objective is [verb noting direction of change] + [area of change] + [target population] + [degree of change] + [time frame]. So, for example, assume an organization's:

- Direction of change is *to reduce*
- Area of change is *unemployment status*
- Target population is *graduating students*
- Degree of change is *75 percent gain full-time employment*
- Time frame is *within six months of graduation*

The sum of the components of the equation yields the organization's objective: *To reduce the unemployment status of our graduating students so that 75 percent are fully employed within six months of graduation.*

All objectives should be SMART—specific, measurable, actionable, relevant, and time-phased. Objectives can focus on either process *or* outcomes. *Process objectives* typically begin with phrases such as "to develop," "to implement," "to establish," or "to conduct." These phrases all describe *activities* that will be undertaken by the organization. Process objectives guide implementation. *Outcome objectives* describe *changes* that advance your mission (improving the lives of individuals or a condition in the community). Outcome objectives typically begin with phrases such as "to increase," "to decrease," or "to improve." Outcome objectives define milestones in achievement.

Remember that if an objective describes something a staff person or volunteer is going to *do*, it is a process objective. If the objective describes a *change* in behavior, skills, awareness, health status, and so on, it is an outcome objective. Both types of objectives are useful as long as the writer is clear that they refer to different things: One is a means statement and the other is an ends statement.

TABLE 9.1   SAMPLE GOALS, OBJECTIVES, AND TASKS

Examples of Program Goals	Examples of Related Program Objectives (Process/Outcome)
Family Workshop Program To increase coping skills of families in stress (Martha's Shelter offers workshops to family members who need to acquire healthy coping skills.)	• Present two workshops for 20 families in July [process objective]. • Increase performance on self-administered test in coping strategies by an average of 50 percent for all participants as a result of the two workshops [outcome objective].
Volunteer/Victim Advocate Program To decrease the immediate trauma of victims of crime (This program of the Victim's Assistance Fund provides victims of crime with volunteers who will accompany them and speak for them at police and legal proceedings.)	• To match 200 victims of crime with 200 volunteers to provide support during police interviews in year 1 [process objective]. • Using provider-administered surveys, achieve a significant decrease in the immediate trauma reported by victims as a result of this program; "significant" to be defined once a baseline is established in year 1 [outcome objective].
Traveling Exhibition Program To increase the public's awareness and appreciation of photography (This program of the Museum of Modern Art makes a collection of world-class photography pieces available to the finest museums in the world.)	• To cosponsor with another museum one showing per year outside of our geographic area [process objective]. • Using attendance as a measure of cultural awareness, increase the number of people attending cosponsored photography exhibitions by 10 percent per year compared to previous year [outcome objective].

CONDUCT A THOROUGH REVIEW PROCESS

The process of review and ultimate approval is fundamental to the success of the strategic planning process. The review provides a measure of quality control, and you have your last opportunity to build commitment before approval. The planning committee should decide in advance who will review and respond to the draft plan. The guiding principle of participation in the strategic planning process is that everyone who will help execute the plan should have some input in shaping it. Whether this includes review of the final drafts of the plan is a judgment call that depends on an organization's particular circumstances.

The big ideas have been debated and resolved, so that revisions amount to only small matters of adding detail, revising format, or changing wording in a particular section. Some text editing can be helpful, but reviewers should be looking at how the whole plan holds together and whether it is appropriately ambitious.

The planning committee must exercise leadership in setting a realistic time frame and in bringing the review process to a timely close. The committee needs to choose the level of review appropriate for the organization, provide review copies to the selected individuals, and set a deadline for submitting feedback (usually allowing one to two weeks is sufficient).

This is an excellent opportunity to pull the whole organization together for a retreat to discuss the strategic plan and the implications for every member of the organization in terms of its implementation. A retreat held before approval also provides an opportunity for final changes based on discussion with the full team. Upon receiving all feedback, the committee must agree on which suggested revisions to accept, incorporate these changes into the document, and submit the strategic plan to the full board of directors for approval.

DRESSING UP YOUR STRATEGIC PLAN FOR PUBLIC DISTRIBUTION

With the advent of simple software and the facility of many younger people in creating graphically appealing documents, many of our clients are producing strategic plans that are beautiful documents, without having to send them out to a graphic designer. The power of color, a few photographs and tables, and visually interesting formatting can make a strategic plan an excellent communication vehicle.

STRATEGIC PLANNING COMMITTEE CELEBRATION AND DEBRIEF

It is time for celebration and reflection! Take some time at a final meeting of the strategic planning committee to look back on your process and identify what went well and where you might do things differently next time. Finally, begin the work of Step 10 to operationalize your plan by developing first-year workplans, tying the annual budget to the strategic plan, and establishing the process by which you will monitor and update your strategic plan.

Share the Plan

After the plan has been approved, you should, at the very least, prepare and send out the executive summary or a condensed version of the plan to key partners, funders, and other individuals whose knowledge of the organization's future is key to their support. Most external stakeholders do not need a copy of the full strategic plan, although they do need to know the hopes, aspirations, and priorities of the organization. Some detailed strategies and priorities (such as those that talk about beating the competition) may be best kept among internal stakeholders.

Of course, copies of the strategic plan should be made available to all staff and board members, and the key components should be presented at staff or management meetings.

Thank Participants

Along with the executive copy of the strategic plan, you should thank any stakeholder whose input was sought from surveys, interviews, or focus groups. Have a party to thank the strategic planning committee. In short, celebrate the accomplishment and choose an appropriate way to convey the message that this plan represents an important consensus about where you are going together for the future of the organization.

CAUTIONS FOR FACILITATORS

Facilitators should be aware of and work to avoid the following pitfalls during the strategic planning process:

Step 9: Complete the Strategic Plan

Push for clarity. Facilitators have to balance the need to drive to conclusion and keep fidelity to the original goals. Encourage the involvement of several reviewers. This both increases ownership and helps to identify sections that need clarifying.

Value of Plain Speech. Facilitators can also serve groups by asking planners and reviewers to summarize sections of the plan in their own words. If this is difficult to do, either the decisions have not been focused sufficiently or they have not been explained clearly.

County Legal Aid Society (CLAS) Strategic Plan, 2014–2017

TABLE OF CONTENTS

COVER LETTER FROM CHAIR OF THE BOARD AND THE EXECUTIVE DIRECTOR

Since 1977, County Legal Aid Society (CLAS) has been committed to making "Liberty and Justice for All" a reality. When we first opened our doors, we had 3 staff members and served 35 clients. Currently, our staff of 20 attorneys, post-graduate fellows, and other staff partner with volunteer lawyers and law school interns throughout the county to ensure that low income and other disenfranchised individuals in Central County have counsel and representation. Today, we serve over 3,500 clients, a number we are proud of, while recognizing that there are communities that we have limited ability to serve and numerous individuals who would benefit from our services. The support of our clients, donors, law firms, and the community is extremely important to our present success as well as our future vision.

While we have done some good strategic thinking during annual planning retreats, we have never engaged in a formal strategic planning process. Over the last several months, our board and staff devoted a great deal of time and critical thinking to envision what we hope to accomplish over the next three years and to create this strategic plan.

Through a thorough review of our operations, client evaluations, focus groups, and discussions with community leaders, government representatives, and law firms, one consistent theme emerged: we are doing good work but we are not doing enough to make sure that all disenfranchised and poor people in our county, as well as those in surrounding counties, have access to free quality legal assistance. The challenge we accept is to decide to help as many individuals as possible, while keeping in mind our commitment to excellence and our limited resources. This strategic plan is the practical roadmap that can help us better accomplish our mission and serve more individuals.

Signed:
Jane Doe, Executive Director
Miguel Rodriguez, Board President

EXECUTIVE SUMMARY

The County Legal Aid Society has been dedicated to Making Justice for All a Reality for more than three decades and in this plan we are preparing to do this work for more people, in both established and new ways.

The world around us is changing. Income inequality, demographic shifts, decreasing governmental support for low-income people, and changes in technology and the field of law all present both challenges and opportunities.

In our strategic plan we reaffirm our core three-prong theory of change: combining direct legal service and representation with education and system changing advocacy to ensure more people truly have access to justice and better lives as a result.

In this strategic plan we commit to:

- expanding our service region to include South County and support for neighboring counties

- increasing the resources we devote to advocacy and harnessing the many ways in which we can help, and force, the legal system and government in general to deliver justice

- using technology externally to facilitate and extend our ability to communicate and serve more people more efficiently, and internally to improve our operations

- finding new ways to connect those in our community who share our commitment to help all people live with justice on their side to support our work—through increasing opportunities for individual financial support

- maturing as an institution through improving systems and overall management, and supporting our staff more effectively to do their life-changing work.

MISSION, VISION, AND VALUES

Mission Statement

County Legal Aid Society's (CLAS) mission is to promote equal access to justice by providing counseling and legal representation for disenfranchised and low-income people in the Central region.

Vision

All residents of our Central region are protected from discriminatory and illegal treatment and benefit from all services available to them because they have access to justice with appropriate representation.

Values and Principles

- Clients deserve to be treated at all times with respect, dignity, compassion, and fairness.

- By providing legal assistance to low-income and other disenfranchised people, we can help ensure that all people, regardless of their economic or social situation, can have equal justice under the law. We believe legal help can change lives.

- We can have a greater impact if, in addition to providing legal services, we challenge policies and laws that are detrimental to people who are poor or disenfranchised.

- It is important for vulnerable populations to have their fundamental rights protected, including access to basic necessities such as housing and access to health services.

- We assume that we can better achieve our mission by seeking opportunities to empower our clients to advocate for themselves.

HISTORY AND CURRENT CONTEXT

Our organization has a proud and scrappy history of work for the past 35 years working to provide access to justice for low-income people in our community. We have seen many victories and helped many people. We also have continued for too long to operate as the "mom and pop" organization that characterized our beginnings.

The current environment is challenging and requires a proactive and bold stance in order to serve our mission. A few of the most important changes include:

- Demand: The economy, and decline in government safety net programs has left more and more members of our community behind even as the "economic recovery" has been taking place. The demand for our work has far outpaced our capacity. At the same time we have seen mergers of other legal aid organizations diminishing capacity in neighboring communities.

  Implication: we need to both prioritize and be creative about ways to expand service capacity.

- Demographics: In addition the demographics of our community have changed dramatically in the past few decades becoming much more diverse in background, ethnicity, and primary languages spoken.

  Implication: we need to invest in our internal capacity to work with different communities' needs to catch up.

- The Law: Law schools and law firms, our traditional partners and a major source of our capacity to provide services are both changing. At the same time, advances in the law with respect to immigration status, LGBT rights, and increased awareness of racism have given us new opportunities to serve our clients.

    Implication: we need to adapt in order to maintain an effective relationship with both groups and to keep abreast of the legal expertise required to take advantage of new opportunities.

- Technology: new case management software and communication technology, including the advent of nearly ubiquitous mobile technology, has made many things more possible in terms of communication and service delivery.

    Implication: Using technology is not free—CLAS must invest in equipment, skills development, and restructuring our service delivery model to tap these opportunities.

- Funding: government funding for our work continues to decline and law firms are being more selective in their charitable giving; on the other hand, individual giving has rebounded since the recession.

    Implication: our business model needs to continue to shift toward more support from individuals and we need to be more "customer-focused" in our relationship with law firms to continue to recruit both pro bono assistance and funding support.

ABOUT OUR ORGANIZATION

Founded: 1977

Current Operations: 3,500 clients served

Current Budget: $2,200,000

Current and Future Programs:

Housing: CLAS work in this area includes helping individuals resolve landlord–tenant disputes, assisting renters who are facing eviction, and helping people maintain housing subsidies.

Public Benefits: CLAS assists people to obtain and maintain government assistance, such as TANF (federal benefits for families), food assistance benefits, Social Security, General Assistance (GA), Supplemental Security Income (SSI), and so on.

Health Care: CLAS has always been committed to helping individuals access timely, affordable, and quality health care, as well as health coverage through government assistance programs.

Family Law/Domestic Violence: CLAS assists victims of domestic violence by obtaining restraining orders, helping parents obtain and keep custody of their children, and assisting family members in obtaining guardianship for children without parents.

Advocacy: This is currently a very small area of work that we plan to grow into a full program during this strategic plan. Advocacy will include both work on legislation as well as effective administration of existing laws and policies at the state, county, and municipal levels.

CORE FUTURE STRATEGIES

1. **Expand our service region (Program Portfolio)**
   Dramatically increase our impact by expanding the delivery of legal counsel and representation to all parts of Central County, and to explore options for ensuring that low income and other disenfranchised populations in neighboring counties have access to legal services. Inherent in this strategy is a commitment to increase our capacity to serve non-English-speaking clients, specifically the Hispanic and Asian Pacific Islander communities.

   Background to This Strategy
   Currently we have two offices, our main office in the northeast region of the county and a satellite office in the Central region. We have limited capacity to serve residents of the southern part of the county. In addition, during our planning process, neighboring counties' two small legal aid programs both asked us for assistance in supporting their capacity to provide services in their respective counties.

   Highlights in the Strategic Plan
   - Location: Conduct feasibility study for leasing new office space in South County and/or colocating with a partner organization.
   - Staffing: As resources become available, hire more bilingual staff.
   - Communications: Develop resource/educational material in different languages.
   - Technology: Experiment with technology as a means to reach underserved communities.
   - Partnership: Create joint task force to explore options for how to best support neighboring counties' legal aid programs.

2. **Formalize and increase our policy and advocacy work (Program Portfolio)**
   We will add one full-time position by the end of the first year of this plan. This director of advocacy will work with our board and other staff to work on

legislation and administration. We will continue to work in coalitions and to seek ways to engage our constituents in advocacy.

Background to This Strategy

Over the years, the need to do policy and advocacy work has become more apparent. Many of the external stakeholder interviews addressed increasing our advocacy work: while we are being successful in meeting individual's legal needs, they recognize that in order to better accomplish our mission we need to focus on changing—or having enforced—laws that impact low income and other disenfranchised groups.

Highlights in the Strategic Plan

- Hire a full time policy and advocacy director.
- Increase our advocacy collaborative efforts through our work in coalition and in partnership with other nonprofits.
- Ensure training on policy and advocacy skills for all attorneys, regardless of department.
- Develop a policy and advocacy plan for each program area, under the direction and guidance of the director of advocacy.

3. **Continue our work of diversifying our revenue streams and building a new business model (Business Model)**

We believe we have three key areas to make meaningful increases in our revenues to help pay for increased personnel and capacity.

Background to This Strategy

While we have had some success in diversifying our revenue streams, we need to anticipate that government funding will likely continue to decline at the same time that we are facing an increased demand for services.

Highlights from the Strategic Plan—Priorities include

- Expand our efforts to bring in additional law firm and other corporate support.
- Increase involvement of the board in raising money.
- Bring on additional staff to assist with fundraising.
- In select contracts and grants negotiate for higher rates of reimbursement/ funding to cover more of associated overhead.

4. **Strengthen Internal Operations and Infrastructure (Organization Capacity)**

We will upgrade our facilities and information technology. We will also add new manager positions and develop a better system of performance and support for staff.

Background to This Strategy

Neither our facilities nor our technology are able to support our current program activities, let alone our plans to expand our geographic reach. Our computer software programs, especially those that enable us to track clients, are in serious need of updating. Finally, we need to move beyond the "mom and pop" level of management infrastructure in order to provide clearer lines of authority and improved support for staff from supervisors.

Highlights from the Strategic Plan—Priorities include

- Move to another larger office at our central office.
- After we have completed our feasibility study (whether it supports independent offices or colocation), begin operations in the southern part of the county.
- Implement a new case management software system.
- Improve staff supervision, professional development, and support.

5. **Complete Successful Executive Transition (Leadership)**

Successfully transition to new leadership since our long-term executive director plans on retiring by the end of 2015.

Background to This Strategy

Our current executive director has given us notice that she intends to leave at the end of 2015.

Highlights in the Strategic Plan

- Prepare board through training and external assistance to lead this process.
- Implement a successful and orderly transition to a new executive director.
- Establish a succession plan for all long-term leadership.
- Develop emergency succession plans for all leadership positions.

PROGRAM GOALS AND OBJECTIVES (SAMPLE OF ONE OF THE PROGRAM GOALS)

	Goal(s)	Long-Term Objectives
Health Care	Increase enrollment of uninsured individuals in Central County.	• Expand the number of partners whom we support in providing legal assistance required to help enroll uninsured individuals through the Affordable Care Act. • Assist with legal and administrative advocacy to produce more productive and

Goal(s)	Long-Term Objectives
	proactive support from relevant government offices. • Assess overall salary structure and benefits package, develop and implement a plan to increase staff salaries, and offer a competitive benefits package, including retirement benefits. • Establish and maintain a more formalized ongoing training program for all staff and volunteers. • Implement and maintain a new staff evaluation system that establishes overall objectives for positions and specific objectives for all employees. • Develop emergency succession plans for all leadership positions. • Increase number of Spanish-speaking staff and improved capacity to work with other non–English-speaking clients. • Continue to work with local law schools so as to increase number of interns serving our clients.
Increase access to health care.	• Continue existing litigation to expand provision of community clinics in more rural areas of the county. • Partner with other agencies to educate and assist our clients in accessing needed health care services for their families. • Support local coalition working to expand delivery of preventive health care through schools.
Expand litigation services to prevent discrimination based on long-term disabilities.	• We have taken on several cases in the past few years on an ad hoc basis. Now that staff has developed increased expertise in this area, we can formally offer these services. • Educate partner agencies and advocates about this expanded service.

BUSINESS MODEL GOALS AND OBJECTIVES

	Goal(s)	Long-Term Objectives
Fund Development	Increase individual donations.	• Our objective is to increase the proportion of our funding coming from individuals from 20 to 26 percent; and to grow in absolute dollars from $450,000 to $800,000 in a budget targeted to grow over 40 percent. • We will develop a tight planning team of board and senior staff to work year-round on this goal. • Our tracking will be reported monthly to all board and staff, as we hope staff will be able to help in recruiting new supporters as well (though we do not have high expectations for dollar return there). • We will review our collateral and overall approach—potentially seeking outside consulting support at some point.
	Increase foundation and corporate giving.	• We are optimistic that expanding our service region and supporting our neighboring counties will open new possibilities for support. • There are a few foundations that may be supportive of our increased advocacy, and collaborative leadership strategy, as well.
	Maintain government funding.	• Maintain excellent relationships with government agency representatives. • Engage board members where appropriate to let them know how important their funding is to our communities.
Cost management	Improve cost accounting and reporting to department leaders.	• Our directors need better information in order to manage costs more proactively—this is already in the works and is an important priority. • Our senior team will also review overall costs quarterly and consider, in an ongoing way, how we might achieve efficiencies or economies of scale or work allocation among staff.

ORGANIZATION CAPACITY GOALS AND OBJECTIVES

	Goal(s)	Long-Term Objectives
Human Resources	Attract and retain qualified paid and volunteer staff for all services and activities.	• Increase number of paid staff from 22 full-time and part-time employees to 31 full-time and part-time employees. • Increase the number of pro bono lawyers from 105 to 175 lawyers. • Assess overall salary structure and benefits package, develop and implement a plan to increase staff salaries, and offer a competitive benefits package, including retirement benefits. • Establish and maintain a more formalized ongoing training program for all staff and volunteers. • Implement and maintain a new staff evaluation system that establishes overall objectives for positions and specific objectives for all employees. • Develop emergency succession plans for all leadership positions. • Increase number of Spanish-speaking staff and improved capacity to work with other non–English-speaking clients. • Continue to work with local law schools so as to increase number of interns serving our clients.
Organizational Structure and Culture	Sustain an organizational structure and culture that supports clear lines of accountability and a culture that rewards creativity and new ways of doing things.	• Review current organization chart and ensure that structure supports clarity of decision making and accountability. • Encourage staff to be open to new and different ways of doing

(continued)

	Goal(s)	Long-Term Objectives
		things (breaking away from the "we have never done it that way") and acknowledge that we are no longer a mom-and-pop small organization, and our decision-making processes need to change.
Financial Management	Produce timely, accurate financial reports for the organization as a whole, and for all departments.	• Maintain computerized accounting system capable of producing detailed and accurate reports for both internal and external stakeholders. • Assess organization's internal controls annually to ensure adequate safeguard of all resources. • Improve our grants management processes.
Resource and Business Development	Acquire stable, broad-based, financial and nonfinancial resources to support the programs and growth envisioned in this strategic plan.	• Decrease the percentage of our funding coming from government sources: Within the next three years, at least 40 percent of CLAS's annual operating budget will be raised through private-sector philanthropy. • Increase in-kind donations in kind (e.g., printing, equipment, etc.) to help support our services. • Increase the money that the organization receives from private individuals to a minimum of 10 percent each year. • Bring on a new grants writer. • Establish and maintain a computerized donor history file

	Goal(s)	Long-Term Objectives
		and increase the personal contacts made with donors.
		• Increase the board's participation in all aspects of fundraising.
External Communications	Increase the visibility and community awareness of CLAS. Make sure that CLAS is properly recognized for its achievements and closely identified as a premier provider of legal services to disenfranchised populations.	• Build public awareness of CLAS in the community through increased media coverage and public service announcements. • Update brochures and ensure they are available in English, Spanish, and Cantonese. • Implement branding plan so we have a recognizable logo and material that is consistent in appearance. • Create and regularly update an online calendar of upcoming clinics and seminars. • Develop a resource-rich website, capable of assisting individuals to access information for self-help, as well as being made aware of other community resources that are available.
Information Technology and Management Information Systems	Increase the operations and management efficiency and effectiveness of CLAS.	• Improve our system for tracking all necessary information required for funding sources and management decision-making. • Install new client intake and tracking system. • Develop technological capacity to reach remote areas not currently served: Explore creating a virtual assistance program and using technology to serve clients in hard-to-reach areas.

(continued)

	Goal(s)	Long-Term Objectives
Facilities and Equipment	Ensure that we have up-to-date equipment for increased efficiency and effectiveness of staff and service delivery. Ensure that all of our facilities are sufficient for staff needs.	• Develop and implement a facilities master plan for our office and satellite offices. • Maintain facilities that are attractive to clients. • Ensure that any satellite offices are easily accessible to public transportation and are sufficient to meet staff needs. • Continually assess technology needs and update computers and other technology as needed.
Program Evaluation	Make sure that we are meeting the needs of our constituencies and that all of our programs provide the highest quality service.	• Improve evaluation process for all programs to assess program results, quality of services, and our ability to address the (changing) needs of level of service to our clients and the community. • Ensure that detailed annual operating plans are developed. • Establish and maintain protocols for data collection, data entry, and outcome evaluation. • Annually look at how well we are meeting individual legal needs versus overall systems change that address issues of poverty and equal justice.

LEADERSHIP GOALS AND OBJECTIVES

Board of Directors	Ensure that CLAS Board of Directors fulfills its leadership role of governance and support.	• Support Governance Committee in taking leadership for training incoming board members, and working with Executive Committee to use board meeting time more creatively. • Work with search consultant to train board in their hiring responsibility and in ways they may be able to assist with recruitment and managing the transition.
Leadership	Hire a new ED.	• Assemble the Search Committee in the first quarter of the new year. • Hire a search consultant to work with us. • Develop a highly proactive recruitment process.
	Invest in supervision training.	• Select a training program to use in giving all staff who are supervisors, or who want to become supervisors better preparation. • Align our performance review and feedback processes with the new organization-wide orientation to better supervision and staff support.

WORKSHEET 9.1	Core Future Strategies

Identify and assess your core future strategies.

Proposed Strategy	Assumptions, facts, and values that support this proposed strategy	What possible obstacles do we face in implementing this strategy?	How to respond to possible obstacles: how to overcome obstacles— shorter term priorities to overcome obstacles	What triggers might encourage us to reevaluate this strategy
1. Expand service region	We already experience unmet need and have received requests from neighboring counties.	Funding, and mastering new technology to increase service reach	Seek technical assistance from one of our law firms on technology?	If the funding doesn't materialize.
2. Formalize and increase our advocacy work	There is a need for leadership in this area and we are well positioned to work with others.	Funding—we have the know how and the access.	Aggressively seek independent donations for this work.	We will do this one way or another— the growth might have to be tempered if funding does not come in rapidly.
3. Continue to balance our revenue mix	We have had success reducing the percent of government money—we are optimistic about growing individual contributions.	This is hard no doubt, but we will find a way—main obstacle would be giving up.	We know what to do, just have to do it and keep learning!	No trigger will change this direction—only the pace and specifics.
4. Strengthen organization capacity	We have identified several specific opportunities to increase our	Some of these objectives require funding—however, taking steps to increase our	Look for support from board, other agencies and perhaps our pro bono friends who are familiar with legal	Only way is up!

WORKSHEET 9.1 *(continued)*

	sophistication and effectiveness.	approach to management can proceed no matter what.	administration issues.	
5. Complete successful executive transition	Our ED has announced retirement—this is a major change.	We should be prepared for a lengthy recruitment process with interim management options.	Support board in playing this role— be ambitious in getting the best possible person for this role.	Again—as they say in the movies "failure is not an option!"

CHAPTER 10

Step 10: Using Your Plan Successfully

FIRST STEPS	STRATEGIC ANALYSIS	SET YOUR COURSE
1. Set up for Success	4. Environmental Scan	9. Complete the Strategic Plan
2. Stakeholder Engagement	5. Theory of Change and Program Portfolio	10. Use Your Plan Successfully
3. Mission, Vision, Values	6. Business Model	
	7. Organization Capacity	
	8. Leadership	

Congratulations! You have completed your strategic plan. Your long-term direction is clear, and ideally two important things have been accomplished. First, because various stakeholders have been engaged in the process in many ways, there is a high level of commitment to major decisions within the stakeholder communities. Second, thanks to the work of the committee, various authors, and reviewers, the written document presents your direction and priorities in organized and compelling language.

Now is the time to make sure that your strategic plan is closely synched and translated into the processes of annual budgeting and annual program and departmental planning. Ensuring that your team is ready to go is the other critical step in this juncture.

Although the process of planning has energized and focused the organization members, the full value of the planning effort will only be realized through its implementation. Barriers to implementation come in many guises and include failure to translate strategies into operational plans, resistance to change, lack of specificity, losing focus, and failure to adapt to external developments.

Step 10 has four substeps focusing on (1) managing change, (2) developing annual implementation plans and budgets, (3) drafting an overall dashboard to track progress,

and (4) developing ongoing monitoring and evaluation systems to manage inevitable course corrections along the way.

HELP PEOPLE MAKE REQUIRED CHANGES

To avoid being stymied by resistance, part of planning for the implementation of your strategic plan includes identifying the new skills requirements, systemic and structural changes, and organizational culture changes that will bridge the gap between the old way of doing things and the new ways things need to be done.

First, think about new skills board and staff members will need to successfully implement the strategic plan. A plan that includes greatly increasing foundation grants and individual contributions will likely require board and staff members to increase their skills in such areas as foundation research and grantwriting and individual solicitation.

Second, look at how current structures and systems need to change in order to support your new vision. As organizations grow, their internal systems need to keep pace. Has the plan taken into account new accounting, IT and other management systems, and the training that may be needed for staff?

Finally, but perhaps most importantly, you should look at how the organization's culture or mindset might need to change to support new core strategies. Management guru Tom Peters famously said "culture eats strategy for lunch." If the people aren't working together the way they need to (perhaps greater openess to innovation, fewer silos, comfort with more transparency, etc.) business as usual will likely prevail. Increasing delegation and sharing leadership more broadly requires a mindset change. Letting go of control can be difficult for the executive director and senior managers. Middle managers may have a difficult time assuming more authority. An organization that has realized it needs to shift its culture from program centered to client centered requires a deep cultural change. Proactive steps to support these types of transitions can ease the transition and reduce predictable resistance.

In their 2010 *New York Times* bestseller, *Switch: How to Change Things When Change Is Hard*, Chip and Dan Heath present a very accessible three-part framework for helping people accomplish change.[1] They use the metaphor of a person riding an elephant along a particular path. (Each member of your organization has within them both the rider and the elephant!) The rider needs to be convinced, the elephant needs to become motivated, and the path needs to be cleared so that the duo can successfully move down the road.

1. "Direct the Rider" refers to helping individuals understand and accept the logic and urgency of the needed change.

2. "Motivate the Elephant" refers to developing commitment by helping individuals both get enthusiastic about the potential a particular change can bring to the organization and to them and to see how it is possible for them to make the needed change.

3. Finally, "Shape the Path" focuses not on the individual but on the systemic forces that may impede change that individuals are willing and even want to make. ("Systemic" factors include things like accurate accounting and other information needed to support new managers in successfully taking on additional authority.)

The Heaths cite several dramatic examples of leaders, even those without significant positional authority, who enlist large numbers of people to make dramatic changes. One famous example is a doctor who used this three-part approach to mobilize hospitals nationally to save more than 100,000 lives in an 18-month period by adopting six very specific procedures to reduce infections—changes that confronted inertia and active resistance throughout the hospital industry.

The inertia, fear, and systemic barriers may not be as extensive in your organization as they were in the national hospital industry, but they can be powerful enough to undermine change in "the way we do things" needed to execute your strategies successfully.

---

[1] Chip Heath and Dan Heath, *Switch: How To Change Things When Change Is Hard* (New York: Random House, 2010).

→ **SEE WORKSHEET 10.1 TO ASSIST WITH THIS STEP.**

WORKSHEET 10.1	MANAGING THE TRANSITION: THE CHANGES REQUIRED FOR SUCCESS

Process Notes

How to do this activity?	• Identify the changes that are inherent in the strategic plan: changes in focus, changes in ways of doing things, etc.
	• For each of the changes, list any new skills that may be needed, any structures that need to be modified or introduced, and changes in culture—behaviors and beliefs of staff and board—that are needed to support the changes articulated in the strategic plan.
Why do this activity?	• Supporting actions to implementation of the strategic plan can be identified through this activity, and thereby overcome obstacles and/or resistance.
Who to involve in the process?	Both the staff and board should do this activity separately, because both will be responsible for, and affected by, the decisions reflected in the strategic plan.

WRITE DETAILED ANNUAL OPERATION PLANS

The next step in implementing the strategic plan is to develop a first-year operating plan based on the strategic plan. This step is critical to ensure that the strategic plan is implemented in a coordinated and effective manner. It must be translated into specifics: The strategic plan must be converted into an annual operating plan, with a supporting annual budget.

The operating plan describes what services will be provided, what types of action will be conducted to provide these services, and who is responsible for taking the actions. The budget describes how much it will cost to carry out the plan.

Because the operating plan should begin the implementation of the strategic plan, the structure of the operating plan must be congruent with the priorities outlined in the strategic plan. As the year unfolds, choices will arise about whether and how to modify the original objectives. All of the work that goes into the strategic planning process will be more useful to decision makers if choices in the middle of the year can be easily placed in the context of the long-term priorities of the organization.

Just as monthly financial statements often present a budget for revenue and expenses and compare the budget with actual figures for a given time period, operating plans should allow for a similar type of comparison. The plan defines the work in terms of goals and objectives for each program, area, and management/operations function and reports the actual progress on a monthly or perhaps quarterly basis. This operating plan budget-to-actual report, along with the financial budget-to-actual report, gives a clear reading of how the year is going.

An effective operating plan states the strategic goal to be addressed, clearly breaks out the activities or action steps required to accomplish the goal, establishes time frames and who is responsible, and notes the progress thus far. Many organizations already have some tracking system in place that might be adapted for the purposes of the operating plan, or perhaps you will want to customize the suggested format to best suit your purposes.

What Level of Detail Is Necessary in an Operating Plan?

Imagine you are driving a car while going on vacation. It is important to have a destination in mind, your long-range goal. The destination alone, however, is not enough to get you there successfully. You need to have detailed information about which roads are most likely to get you there, estimates about the distance to be covered and the time it will take, estimates of how much money will be needed for meals and gas for the car, and warning systems to tell you if the engine gets overheated or other systems fail.

Now imagine that you are not driving the car alone. Instead, you have 20 people doing different jobs simultaneously: Your organization's executive director is at the steering wheel with a couple of board members looking over her shoulder; staff members are stationed at each tire making them spin; other people are pooling their money for gas; and someone else is in the back making sandwiches. It is going to take an impressive plan to move this crew in the same direction efficiently!

Such is the stuff of annual operating plans and annual budgets: Which programs and management/operations functions are going to be implemented for the upcoming year, by whom, by when, and how much "gas" (money and person power) will they require? This level of detail is unnecessary in a strategic plan. In fact, it would clutter up the presentation of the long-range vision. The strategic plan focuses on the destination you are going to, and the overall direction and route to get there, not which gas station to stop at along the way. The annual operating plan needs to provide enough guidance for the travelers to move ahead at full speed, so there is no need to constantly discuss where to go next or why the driver took the last turn.

What If You Don't Have All of the Information You Think You Need?

Organizations typically have more developed routines around the annual budgeting process than they do around annual program planning. It is a rare board that approves a budget with vague information about planned expenses and little detail about projected revenue. (For this reason, and because there are many useful resources already available, this book does not go into detail about the mechanics of the annual budgeting process.) There are three important characteristics of a useful annual operating plan:

1. An appropriate level of detail—enough to guide the work, but not so much detail that it becomes overwhelming, confusing, or unnecessarily constrains flexibility

2. A format that allows for periodic reports on progress toward the specific goals and objectives

3. A structure that allows a user to easily see that it is consistent with the priorities in the strategic plan

The process of developing detailed operating plans is much less precise than budgeting. Perhaps for this reason, some organizations have fairly informal planning processes that are not tied into their strategic plan. We've seen many instances where the only "operating plan" is the narrative of a grant agreement. Program planning is often not as coordinated on an agency-wide basis as the budgeting process nearly always is. The potential for staff to waste effort, or worse, to work at cross-purposes, is much greater when program planning is not coordinated and detailed enough to ensure that objectives get met in a timely manner.

This does not mean including every detail. To go back to the vacation metaphor, the operating plan does not need to include instructions on how to make sandwiches, but it does need to mention that someone is in charge of feeding the travelers. What if you do not know who is in charge of feeding the travelers, or what the travelers' dietary needs are, or what route to take that will get you to your destination on time? The operating plan mentions the fact that these jobs have to be done or the information gathered and assigns responsibility for figuring them out.

For example, organizations doing strategic planning for the first time may never have conducted in-depth program evaluation. If there isn't time to do this work before the strategic plan is to be completed (and often there isn't), doing program evaluation work can become an objective of the operating plan: "We think our programs are doing a good job, but we do not know as much as we'd like, so our objective this year is to conduct a thorough program evaluation. When we get new information, we will adjust our strategic plans accordingly."

The appropriate level of detail depends on how much authority or latitude staff members have to use their judgment in pursuing objectives. Jack Welch, CEO at General Electric for many years, said he didn't even want to know about any decisions that cost less than $25 million to implement. Below this expenditure level, his staff had the authority to use their own judgment in pursuing corporate objectives. Few nonprofit staffs will have quite this much authority! Typically, more detail is useful when a program is new, staff members are inexperienced, or actions in one program area have extensive implications for the operation of other programs. In general, the more concise the operating plan, the easier it is to implement and to monitor. Provide only as much detail as is appropriate.

The format of an annual operating plan is important. A confusing format implies confused thought and inevitably leads to confused implementation. There are two questions to ask yourself about your annual operating plan format:

1. Can everyone who needs to use the plan make sense of what it says?

2. Are the objectives and action steps written and organized in a way that makes it easy to monitor?

Just as monthly financial statements often present a budget for revenue and expenses and compare the budget with actual figures for a given time period, so should operating plans allow for the same type of comparison: The plan defines the work in terms of goals and objectives for each program, area, and management/operations function and reports the actual progress on a monthly or perhaps quarterly basis.

Two sample operating plans are included as follows. The first is for a program goal at an economic development agency, and the second is for a development effort at a museum. Both examples meet all four characteristics of an effective operating plan: They state the strategic goal to be addressed, clearly break out the objectives, the activities or action steps required to accomplish the goal, establish time frames and who is responsible, and note the progress thus far (obviously, the information in this last column would change with each report).

These are the requisites for the operating plan. Many organizations already have some tracking system in place that might be adapted for the purposes of the operating plan, or perhaps they will choose to customize the suggested format to best suit their purposes. The point is to develop a format that keeps the organization on the right track.

What if you already have program operating plans written for specific grants? No problem. In an organization with more than one program, it makes sense to have two levels of operating plans. The level of detail required in a program plan by many funders is often specific. It is not practical or useful to compile several of these plans into one large operating plan. In the first place, they are usually too long to be useful to individuals who are not directly involved with the particular program. In the second place, the funding cycles are often different from the organization's fiscal year.

For both of these reasons, the answer is to create a less detailed organization-wide annual operating plan, which serves as the one-year implementation version of the strategic plan and as the umbrella plan for more detailed program plans. The organization-wide plan is useful to the board and to all staff members who are interested in gaining a better understanding of the work of a program in the context of the work of the entire organization.

Finally, make sure to set a regular schedule for reviewing progress against the operating plan—at least monthly or bimonthly, both with staff and with your board.

SAMPLE (ANNUAL) OPERATING PLAN: PROGRAM GOAL FOR AN ECONOMIC DEVELOPMENT AGENCY

Overall agency goal: Increase economic development capacity to foster job creation and business investment in our city.

Enterprise zone unit goal: Enhance the application of the tax incentive programs by:

- Completing the designation process for approval of new zones

- Offering suggestions for the improvement of the programs of those previously approved

Task	Measure	Staff	By When
1. Select and train scoring team for final enterprise zone application	Select two sets of five scorers	AB/PM	Jan 1st
2. Print and distribute scoring materials and final applications	Distribute materials to scorers	AB/PM	Sept to Dec
3. Conduct technical review	Complete six technical reviews	AB/PM	Sept to Jan
4. Conduct substantive review	Complete six substantive reviews	PGN and scorers	Oct to Feb
5. Tabulate results of scoring team	Compile two sets of results	PGN	Oct to Feb
6. Announce winners of competition	Two press releases and two e-mails	JW and PM	Feb

FUND DEVELOPMENT GOAL FOR MUSEUM (FROM ANNUAL OPERATING PLAN)

Annual goal (the same as the strategic plan goal): Acquire a stable, broad base of financial and nonfinancial resources to support our museums' programs.

Long-term objective (the same as the strategic plan objective): Double the amount of foundation or corporate support that we receive from $XX to $YY.

Annual operating plan objectives (what needs to be accomplished this year to support the long-term objective):

- Secure $25,000 for the new children's art program by the end of the calendar year.

- Maintain foundation and corporate contribution levels at least at the current level.

- Raise at least a total of $150,000 in unrestricted revenue from new foundation and corporate sources.

Feedback mechanisms (check-in mechanisms to ensure that the work is being accomplished): Director of development will provide a monthly status report of all proposals pending, accepted, or declined.

Resources required: One-half FTE Development Associate; $5,000 to produce annual report

Detailed action plan (what activities need to happen, who is responsible for making sure they happen, and by when; status report updated quarterly):

Action Steps for Securing $25,000 for New Children's Art Program	Responsible Personnel	Time Frame or by When	Status as of 3/31/15
1. Develop proposal to describe program	Selena Garcia, Program Director	January 1– February 1	Done: It looks beautiful!
2. Research possible funders and develop list of at least ten prospective funders	Susan Seeker and Pam Proposal* (*designated prime mover)	February 1	Completed 1/25/15
3. Arrange interviews with each prospect	Pam Proposal	February 15	3/1/15
4. Submit at least three proposals	Pam Proposal	April 15	Three proposals submitted as of 3/31
5. Follow up on proposals	Pam Proposal	Two weeks after submission	
6. Cash the checks!	Pam Proposal	As soon as the money arrives!	

CREATE A DASHBOARD TO MONITOR IMPLEMENTATION

A major barrier is simply maintaining focus on the strategic plan. The most important antidote to losing focus is having a plan that is compelling and relevant. We have clients joyfully tell us they are "working their plan." They are excited and challenged by putting their plans into action. The point is not the plan, of course; the excitement comes from their commitment to accomplishing the goals they have set for their organization and moving meaningfully toward their mission.

Even with the enthusiasm, in order to maintain focus and really *use* the plan, an organization must have a systematic review process. There is one level of review, *operational review*, that is straightforward and is analogous to tracking progress against your budget—regularly asking how you are doing against your goals and objectives.

To support this process, a tool called a dashboard can be extremely helpful. The name is drawn from the dashboard of a car: an instrument panel that quickly provides critical and current information, including speed, fuel, distance traveled, and warning lights for rare but potentially disastrous conditions.

CompassPoint Nonprofit Services has a free online resource (www.compass point.org/dashboard) to support the development of useful dashboards, with a wide array of potential measures to include on your dashboard. Check with other organizations in your field to see if they have dashboards, and what they focus on for tracking purposes.

The key is to identify a *few* measures that answer important questions. For example: Are we meeting our service delivery numbers? Is progress toward the new database system on track? Has the new staff training program been developed and implemented? Identify a target level for each measure that indicates success, or whether or not the organization is on track. This level is often shaded green for go. A midlevel that is below target, but not dangerous, is typically shaded yellow for caution, and a final level that indicates a dangerous situation is shaded red.

→ SEE WORKSHEET 10.2 TO ASSIST IN THE DEVELOPMENT OF A DASHBOARD FOR YOUR OWN ORGANIZATION.

WORKSHEET 10.2   NONPROFIT DASHBOARD

Process Notes

How to do this activity?	• Identify the most important goals or objectives that you want to track regularly.
	• For each of the target measures define three levels of performance: Good—green; Caution—yellow; Danger—red.
Why do this activity?	Creating this tool will greatly aid in the monitoring of the plan, and in specifying for all board and staff what are the key, dynamic measures of success for your organization.
Who to involve in the process?	Both the staff and board should separately do this activity, because both will be responsible for, and affected by, the decisions reflected in the strategic plan.

DEVELOP A DYNAMIC APPROACH TO WATCH FOR CHANGING TRENDS

There is a second level of review, *strategic review*, which can be more elusive. This level of review asks a different question: Has our world changed, or are we anticipating changes we did not expect? Because new developments in the environment, changing trends, demographics, and competition are not announced in the daily paper, it is harder to perceive their impending arrival. For this second level of review, a different process is needed.

Some organizations undertake a quarterly review by the strategic planning committee or the full board, where the floor is opened for observations, questions, and hypotheses about potential changes. Sometimes staff may get information about a new trend that it wants to share with the board. This second level of review involves stepping back to see the big picture and checking in on whether any major assumptions underlying your strategic plan should be questioned or reexamined.

John Kotter offers a more formal approach to ongoing strategic review in a 2012 *Harvard Business Review* article.[2] He describes a process that he helped several large for-profit companies develop, in which a parallel organizational unit is constantly testing and experimenting with new ideas. The innovation in this Skunk Works–like structure is that the people involved are also involved, most days, in the regular work of the company. The assignment for this ongoing body for which people volunteer, and by design is cross functional, is to be an ongoing "scouting" unit for new opportunities. This is one model for an ongoing, integrated structural approach to constantly looking down the road. The outcome of this particular model is formal, though brief, proposals for the organization to pursue a new course of action. The group is empowered to to recruit a department or unit put test the concept if they can persuade a "guiding coalition" to try it.

There are many different approaches. Ad hoc is often fairly functional—time at board or staff meetings for periodic reflection and discussion about "what's happening out there" is common and can be an effective practice. We have also worked with nonprofits that have appointed a task force, with staff, board members, and sometimes outside advisors meeting regularly as their futurist team. Sometimes the Strategic Planning Committee is re-enlisted to assist with both monitoring the implementation and progress of the strategic plan as well as to be on the look out for new opportunities. However you accomplish this second level of strategic review, it is helpful to engage more than just the top leadership in watching the dynamics of the world to see opportunities and threats as they materialize. And it is important to be intentional about incorporating a "looking down the road" practice into your ongoing operations.

---

[2] John Kotter, "Accelerate: How the Most Innovative Companies Capitalize on Today's Rapid-Fire Strategic Challenges—and Still Make Their Numbers," *Harvard Business Review*, November 2012.

CAUTIONS FOR FACILITATORS

Facilitators should be aware of and work to avoid the following pitfalls during the strategic planning process:

Step 10: Using Your Plan Successfully

Build strong bridges. If an organization is not used to doing strategic planning, it may require facilitators to help create enough bridges to operating plans and budgeting. Operationalizing the strategy is an excellent test of its clarity and relevance. Tweaks to the strategic plan itself should not be avoided if called for after this step.

WORKSHEET 10.1	Managing the Transition: The Changes Required for Success

List the major changes that may need to happen/will happen as a result of the strategic plan:

❑ Changes that will impact staff and the skills they may need in the future

❑ Changes that will impact the structures and systems that may need to be modified to support the changes

❑ Changes that will impact how the organization's culture (mindset) may need to be modified to support the changes

New skills that may be needed	Modified or new structures and systems that may be needed	New culture/mindset that may be needed
Delegation training Managing change training	The organization chart needs to be updated to reflect new programs, and we need to make sure that it's clear in terms of who gets to make what decision and who has meaningful input.	We currently operate a lot like a mom-and-pop organization and not at all like a fairly large organization with multiple sites and a much larger staff. We need to change the mindset of "but we have always done it that way" or "we have not done it that way so we shouldn't do it that way" to a mindset that is willing to look at new ways of doing things. We are committed to ensuring that staff who are impacted by a decision have an opportunity to give some feedback before the decision is made, but we can't continue to operate with the assumption that everyone needs to be involved in most decisions.
How to be an effective "matrix manager"	With a matrix management approach, we can continue to have programs that are organized by topic area (housing, health, benefits, etc.) but also will have matrix managers whose responsibility it is to think across departments (such as someone who is in charge of ensuring that all clients who are seniors get served well and that legal issues that impact seniors are monitored closely).	Programs don't collaborate/coordinate as much as they could/should. Each department tends to "do its own thing," so staff need to seek opportunities to collaborate/work together.

(continued)

WORKSHEET 10.1 *(continued)*

Training in how to use new technology.	*If we are truly committed to serving the entire county, then we need to figure out how the various offices/outposts can be better served by technology.*	*Currently, we have some old-timers who are not at all comfortable with using remote access/ technology to serve some of the remote areas of our county that don't record sufficient client notes for follow-up purposes and/or evaluation purposes.*

WORKSHEET 10.2	Nonprofit Dashboard

For each dashboard area[3] you want to monitor, develop appropriate indicators, target measures, and flags (yellow light and red light indicators): Staffing and Benefits, Marketing, Infrastructure: Financial Management Systems, Technology, and Facilities Planning/Evaluation/Quality Control, Governance Functions/Board of Directors, Finances, Resource Development

At least quarterly, update dashboard to individuate actual status and light (green, yellow, or red)

Indicators	Target (Green)	Flag (Yellow)	Flag (Red)	Status (as of:___)	Indicate Collor: Red/ Yellow/ Green Light
Program: xxxxx (sample for one program)					
Staffing and Benefits					
Staff retention	90%	80%	70%		
Professional Development Plans for all staff	100%	90%	80%		
Sufficient funding for all Professional Development Plans (per staff)	$250– $750	$150–$500	$0–$150		
Yearly Staff Evaluations	100%	80%	75%		
Staff Satisfaction on Annual Survey (survey scale 5–1)	5	3.5	2.5		
Competitive salary and benefit packages	50 percentile	40 percentile	30 percentile		``
Bring on full time volunteer manager and grants manager	hired within 6 months	hired within 12 months	not hired		

[3] Adapted from CompassPoint Nonprofit Services resource materials on Dashboards (for a more complete list of indicators, see http://www.compasspoint.org/sites/default/files/docs/560_libraryofindicatorsjune09.pdf).

(continued)

Marketing				
Community Events	10	9-Jul	less than 6		
Marketing and outreach goals met by committee	100%	80–99%	less than 80%		
Advocacy presentations/ articles/events	5	4-Mar	2 or less		
Infrastructure: Financial/MIS, Technology and Facilities				
Technology System for Remote Clients Implemented	within 12 months	within 18 months	within 24 months		
Move to new location	by January	by March	not move		
Planning/Evaluation/Quality Control				
Install new client tracking system	within 9 months	not finished by end of year	not started		
Regularly scheduled meetings of Planning and Evaluation Committee of board and staff representatives to monitor the SP and review in-depth annual workplans and dashboard	meets every two months	meets quarterly	does not meet		
Governance Functions/Board of Directors				
Attendance at board meetings					
Total board members	15	13–14	12		
% of board member giving	100%	80–99%	less than 80%		
Advisory Board	12	10 or less	not active		

WORKSHEET 10.2 *(continued)*

Board satisfaction Survey on Governance and Support Roles	score of 5	score of 4–3.6	score of under 3.5		
Finances				
Total Revenue	$2,750,000	$2,500,000	less than expenses		
Total Expense	$2,500,000	10% less than target	maintains at current level		
Months operating reserve	3.5	3.0+	less than 2 months		
Resource Development				
New major donors	6 or more	3–5 donors	less than 3		
Board giving	100%	80–99%	less than 80%		
Fundraising event revenue net	$40,000	$30,000– $39,999	less than $30,000		
Number of Individual Donors				
Number of new law firms supporting us	9 or more law firms	6–8 law firms	less than 6 firms		
Fundraising goals met by Development Dir & Committee	100% or more	85–99%	less than 85%		
Volunteer Management				
Hire full time director for our pro bono activities	hired within 6 months	hired within 12 months	not hired		
Increase number of pro bono lawyers	150 lawyers or more	maintain existing number of 105	less than 105		

Conclusion
A Word to Leaders

If we had reliable crystal balls, strategic planning would be a snap. Because there is uncertainty about the future, however, strategic plans are more like roadmaps to a new land that were drawn up before the journey has been made. No one has been to where we want to go; it is in the future. We can ask many people their advice about how best to make the journey. We can do extensive analysis to forecast the conditions we will encounter and to assess our capabilities to handle various situations. We can dream about how we would like the journey to go. All of this work can be discussed and written down in the form of a strategic plan. Once the journey begins, a strategic plan will remind us where we want to go, as well as where we don't want to go.

In *Alice's Adventures in Wonderland*, the Cheshire Cat says to Alice, "If you don't know where you are going, any road will take you there." The strategic planning process helps the leaders of an organization to articulate their vision about where they are going and to choose the best road to take the organization there.

Still, things change. In the external environment, the economy is better, or worse, than expected, and this has a ripple effect on your clients or your field. Science finds a new way to deal with an issue you have long worked on. A new organization begins offering services that compete with one of your programs. A longtime funder changes its priorities. Any of the many assumptions you have made as part of the planning process turns out to be wrong. Internally, the executive director might move or become ill, a case of embezzlement might surface, or staff members may either do much more or much less than they thought possible.

There is no way to foresee these changes. They must be responded to as they arise. Ultimately, the end sought is to be effective in pursuing your mission, not to correctly predict the future. The strategic planning process is a means to that end. As the future unfolds, if the organization knows where it wants to go, it will be much easier to see whether the road is taking you there, and if not, to select a better road.

It is the responsibility of the leadership of every organization to ensure that a strategic plan is in place and that appropriate adjustments are made in the implementation of that plan as circumstances change. The strategic plan is a reference document, a map to assist with these responsibilities.

We hope this workbook will make it a little easier to put the process of strategic planning to good use in your organizations. Good luck. We are counting on you to succeed, because our world will be better for it.

Sample Workplans for Abbreviated, Moderate, and Extensive Planning Processes

HOW TO USE THE WORKPLAN TEMPLATES

We offer these workplan templates as guides to strategic planning processes of different levels of intensity. The three workplans are written to illustrate different levels of intensity in the planning process.

An abbreviated planning process is essentially a one-day board and staff retreat with preparation by a small group and follow-up anticipated by staff or ad hoc committees. We highly recommend engagement of an outside facilitator.

A moderate planning process is estimated to last two to three months. This time frame allows for a limited amount of research and stakeholder engagement. It also allows a strategic planning committee to meet a few times in addition to holding a board-staff retreat.

An extensive planning process is the level of intensity that this book describes. It is estimated to last from six to nine months and involves an extensive amount of internal and external stakeholder engagement, thorough analysis of the theory of change, program portfolio, business model, organization capacity, and leadership. The strategic planning committee will meet at least monthly during the period to steer the process and ensure that it is brought to successful completion.

Sample Abbreviated Planning Process Workplan

Participants include the board and staff.

Preparation requires a small group to plan the retreat and to gather and distribute ahead of time the agenda and any useful background information.

Proposed Agenda Topics	Process and Personnel Responsible	Time Frame
Introductions, meeting agreements, and agenda review	Facilitator	9:00–9:15 AM
State of the organization and report on the external forces affecting the organization	Short presentation by executive director	9:15–9:30 AM
SWOT: Strengths, weaknesses, opportunities, and threats	Facilitated discussion by full group of SWOT Identify key questions and issues raised through the discussion	9:30–10:15 AM
Break		10:15–10:30 AM
Reaffirm/create/revise mission statement: purpose statement; values, beliefs and assumptions; what services we offer	Facilitated discussion of each component of a mission statement by all attendees Delegate small group to complete write-up of statements after retreat	10:30–11:15 AM
Vision the possible: our preferred external and internal vision	Brainstorming session by board and staff, we suggest Headline News as useful vision exercise	11:15–11:45 AM
Strategy and program portfolio	Based on SWOT and discussions of mission and vision, identify key issues and possible changes or additions to current strategy and program	11:45 AM–12:30 PM

Sample Abbreviated Planning Process Workplan (*continued*)

Proposed Agenda Topics	Process and Personnel Responsible	Time Frame
Lunch		12:30–1:15 PM
Complete discussion of strategy and program portfolio	Revisit key issues and potential changes to program portfolio Agree on short- and long-term priorities for programs Delegate implementation planning to staff and/or small group after retreat	1:15–1:45 PM
Business model	Presentation by executive director and/or development staff regarding current business model Discussion by all regarding future business model, including agreement on how to best fund current and future programming	1:45–2:30 PM
Break		2:30–2:45 PM
Organization capacity	Brainstorm list of short- and long-term priorities for each organization capacity area such as staffing, marketing, management information systems, facilities, and so on Agree on needed changes and delegate follow-up to staff or ad hoc group	2:45–3:30 PM
Identification of issues that need further discussion by board or staff and any additional information needed to help clarify priorities (such as client survey, etc.)	All	3:30–4:00 PM
Review of next steps, responsible individual, time frame Adjourn	All	4:00–4:30 PM

Sample Moderate Planning Process Workplan

Proposed Format	Process and Personnel Responsible	Possible Worksheets to Support Achieving Outcomes	Time Commitment
Meeting to assess organization's readiness; begin to identify issues to be addressed as part of the planning process and who to involve in the planning process May start to discuss what information is needed to help inform the planning process and how that information should be gathered, or may wait until after planning retreat to see what information needs to be gathered	Executive director, board president or designated representative, and consultant*	• Worksheet 1.1: Identify Planning Process Issues and Outcomes • Worksheet 1.2: Set Up Your Planning Process for Success • Worksheet 1.3: Develop a Plan for Gathering Information from Internal and External Stakeholders • Worksheet 1.4: Choices to Consider When Developing a Planning Workplan	One or two meetings, each 2 to 3 hours long
Internal stakeholder engagement	• Online survey for board and staff to fill out: mission, vision, values, organization SWOT • Summary of results	Worksheet 2.1	Approximately two to three weeks for this to be accomplished
Timing of planning retreat	Strategic planning committee to decide whether retreat should be at the beginning or toward the end of the process; this workplan assumes retreat will be toward the end of the process		
Review of strategic issues from online internal stakeholder surveys and decision on what ad hoc groups will be created to discuss issues and present findings at retreat	Ad hoc committees to meet and develop three- to five-page white papers on their particular issue: white papers contain summary of recommendations or presentation of scenarios/options that		Ad hoc committees to meet two to five times, either face to face or via electronic means, to discuss issue and agree on

Sample Moderate Planning Process Workplan (*continued*)

Proposed Format	Process and Personnel Responsible	Possible Worksheets to Support Achieving Outcomes	Time Commitment
Ad hoc committees (made up of board and staff) may include program portfolio; resource development/business model; organization capacity; marketing[†]; board leadership	must be discussed at an upcoming retreat. Chair of ad hoc committee to write white paper		recommendations or scenarios/options to consider
Meeting to plan retreat and review white papers	Executive director, board president, planning committee (and outside facilitator of retreat)		One meeting, 2 hours long
Board-staff retreat	Retreat agenda will vary but usually will include state of the organization report, review of previous strategic plan results, revision or affirmation of mission statement, brief summary and discussion of online surveys, and then review of white papers	Some of worksheets contained in this book may be used by ad hoc committees to guide their discussions	Full-day retreat
Identification of steps necessary to complete strategic plan	Meeting of planning committee to review notes from planning retreat and assess what additional information needs to be gathered before agreement on future goals and objectives	Possible worksheets that may be used include 1.3 and 1.4	One meeting, 2 hours long
Additional discussions	If additional discussions are needed, strategic planning committee itself may discuss those issues or delegate to groups of individuals		Unknown number of hours; will depend on whether ad hoc committees and retreat adequately addressed the issues

(*continued*)

Sample Moderate Planning Process Workplan (*continued*)

Proposed Format	Process and Personnel Responsible	Possible Worksheets to Support Achieving Outcomes	Time Commitment
Write the plan	Designated writer (and others as needed) write the first draft of the strategic plan		5 to 10 hours to complete the first draft
Meeting of planning committee to review strategic planning document Second draft of strategic planning document circulated to staff and board for final comments	Planning committee		One to two meetings, each 2 to 3 hours long Additional time for designated writer to complete second draft of plan
Meeting of board of directors to approve strategic plan	Board of directors		At regularly scheduled board meeting
Develop annual operating plan to implement strategic plan	Program and organization managers (such as development director, technology director, etc.)		Amount of time will vary
Celebrate the completion of the planning cycle	Planning committee		
Monitor the strategic plan through the use of an annual planning retreat for the planning cycle	Planning committee coordinates and plans retreat		

Total estimated hours and time frame: Many variables will affect the number of hours for a moderate strategic planning process, but normally the estimated consulting hours is about 50 to 70 hours over the course of three to four months.

* The organization may choose not to use an external consultant to facilitate the entire planning process but instead may choose to have a consultant act as a neutral facilitator during some of the large-group meetings.

† Actual topics for ad hoc committees will be dictated by results of the online surveys.

Sample Extensive Planning Process Workplan

First Steps:

Step 1: Set Up for Success

Key Deliverable: Final Strategic Planning Process Workplan

Estimated Consultants' Hours: 6–12

Activities	Process	Time Frame
• Define and agree on strategic issues • Clarify expectations and roles of consultants, executive director (ED), other staff, board, and strategic planning (SP) committee • Clarify and agree on deliverables and timeline • Agree on how to ensure effective communication among and between consultants and ED, board president, other staff and board, and SP committee • Review key planning concepts • Agree on "nonnegotiables" • Agree on initial discussions/actions to identify data needed to inform SP conversations (these conversations about data gathering to continue during step 2) • Evaluate previous strategic planning efforts and success/effectiveness of previous core strategies • Agree on makeup of SP committee	Phone calls and consultants' face-to-face meetings with ED and other key staff; initial conversation with board president Consultants to review CLAS materials (previous strategic planning efforts, financials, annual reports, sample proposals, etc.) SP committee to review and if necessary revise workplan and clarify consultants' role, timeline, deliverables, and so on	January 2015
If needed, revise workplan/summary of strategic planning process	Consultants to revise and submit final workplan	January 2015
Orient consultants	Provide consultants with background information on organization, its programs, and prior planning efforts	January 2015

Steps 2 and 3: Engaging Stakeholders and Articulating Mission, Vision, and Values

Key Deliverable: In-depth understanding of CLAS's strengths, weaknesses, opportunities, and threats as well as board's and staff's vision for the future

Estimated Consultants' Hours: 25–45

Activities	Process	Time Frame
Finalize additional data-gathering plan	Consultants meet with SP committee (either face to face or via phone) to review data-gathering plan and discuss possible additional stakeholders to interview and questions to ask and ask follow-up questions with stakeholders previously interviewed	February 2015
Gather input from internal stakeholders regarding perceptions of CLAS's strengths, weaknesses, opportunities, and threats, and vision for the future	• Develop and manage online surveys for staff and board • Place follow-up phone calls if needed to clarify survey answers • Consultants to summarize findings from data collection for review with leadership team and with SP committee • Facilitate follow-up discussions to "make sense" of the data	February 2015
Gather input from external stakeholders regarding perceptions and expectations of the organization	• Decide on whether we should gather input from external stakeholders now or wait until the strategic analysis stage of our work • If we decide to interview external stakeholders now, consultants and/or members of SP committee do one-on-one (phone) interviews with 5 to 15 external stakeholders (governmental agencies, funders, other partners, other nonprofit organizations doing similar work, etc.) • Consultants to summarize findings from interviews	February 2015
Affirm CLAS's mission statement Develop consensus on CLAS's values and guiding principles/assumptions Define CLAS's vision for the future	Facilitated discussions at board and staff level	March 2015

Strategic Analysis:

Steps 4–8: Environmental Assessment, Strategy and Program Portfolio, Business Model, Organization Capacity, and Leadership

Key Deliverable: Consensus on CLAS's long-term (and short-term) program, organization, financial and leadership (management and governance) priorities, and overall core future strategies for the organization

Estimated Consultants' Hours: 45–80

Activities	Process	Time Frame (Date)
Research "environment" to understand external trends and issues that affect the organization—important issues that are or may become significant, those to which we must respond or be prepared to respond—whether these are helpful or are obstacles to be overcome	Consultants and/or staff members to research current trends in the environment that may or will affect CLAS's ability to achieve its mission	April 2015
Engage in internal assessment of CLAS's programs and services and needs in the community Analyze your competitive environment: How well is your organization doing its job, relative to others?	Consultants, with guidance of ED and senior leadership team, to take lead in designing internal "assessment" instruments for all programs Staff discussions focus on assessing their program's effectiveness/impact as well as its competitive strength, and discuss programmatic changes/priorities for the future	April 2015
Start to set program and administrative priorities and outline alternative scenarios for programs and services and, as well as possible, organizational structural changes	Consultants to present/debrief data findings to leadership team and SP committee (and possibly entire board and staff) for reactions to surveys and identification of emerging themes Consultants to facilitate discussion in terms of implications for the future: program/service priorities, administrative priorities, organizational structure options	May 2015

(continued)

Strategic Analysis: (*continued*)

Activities	Process	Time Frame (Date)
	Possible follow-up to discussions with creation of staff or ad hoc board and staff committees (or other interested/informed parties) charged with responsibility of writing white papers that outline alternative scenarios for programs and services and other ad hoc planning committees whose job it is to make recommendations to the staff and board at upcoming retreat	May 2015
Write white papers (three- to five-page documents that outline alternative scenarios—program choices, organizational structure options)	Ad hoc committee chairs take lead in writing white papers Consultants available to review documents and provide guidance through facilitating discussions and suggesting formats for and content of these white papers	May 2015
Finalize material for strategic planning retreat, plan agenda for retreat, agree on participation	Meeting with SP committee to finalize agenda for planning retreat and review materials	June 2015
One-day board/staff retreat	Consultants to facilitate one-day retreat involving board and staff	July 2015
Debrief retreat	Consultants and SP committee debrief retreat and confirm CLAS's core future strategies and programmatic, administrative, and governance priorities	July 2015
Set short- and long-term business model and organizational capacity goals and objectives	Members of senior leadership team meet to agree on business model and organizational capacity goals and objectives	July 2015
Agree on board and staff leadership priorities—both short and long term	Based on results from board self-assessment survey and discussions at retreat, consultants to facilitate board discussion regarding possible long- and short-term priorities for future in terms of board membership, expectations, role, and so on Senior leadership team meets with consultants to set management short-term and long-term leadership priorities	

Set Your Course

Steps 9 and 10: Complete the Strategic Plan and Use Your Plan Successfully

Deliverables: Written five-year strategic, implementation-oriented plan that has been informed by internal and external stakeholder input and in-depth discussions; plan for ongoing implementation and monitoring—and, if need be, adjusting—of the plan

Estimated Consultants' Hours: 10–25

Activities	Process	Time Frame
Draft strategic planning document	Executive director (or other designated staff person), with support and assistance from consultant, starts to develop draft strategic plan	August 2015
Second draft of strategic planning document	SP committee and other appropriate staff and board give feedback on draft SP document Designated writer(s) drafts second version of the plan for review by staff and board	August 2015
Approval of strategic planning document	Final version of SP submitted to board for approval at board meeting	September 2015
Develop process for ongoing monitoring, evaluating, and revision of plan	SP committee and consultant meet to assess SP process and agree on process for ongoing monitoring, evaluation, and revision of the plan	September 2015

Estimated Consultants' Hours for **First Steps**	31–57 hours
Estimated Consultants' Hours for **Strategic Analysis**	45–80 hours
Estimated Consultants' Hours for **Phase 3**	10–25 hours
TOTAL ESTIMATED CONSULTANT HOURS: 86–162*	
TOTAL ESTIMATED CONSULTANT COSTS (number of hours times consultants' hourly fee plus travel-related expenses). For example, at $200 per hour, this workplan will cost $17,200 to $32,400 plus travel-related expenses.	

*Consulting hours will vary widely and will depend on amount of work done by staff or strategic planning committee versus using a consultant, amount of data that need to be collected, number of issues that need to be discussed, how much of the research and writing will be done by the consultant, and degree of consensus regarding core strategies and priorities.

Tips on Using Task Forces

If task forces are assigned to do some of the planning work, it is essential that the planning committee stay engaged to provide necessary guidance to the subgroups and ensure that all the pieces fit together. The planning committee should provide sufficient guidance to the task force up front to set up the committee for success. Before the ad hoc committees start their work, clarify membership and roles of committee members. The primary requirements for membership are (1) knowledge about the topic or interest in the topic and a willingness to become knowledgeable and (2) willingness to participate in meetings (either face to face or by phone).

Should an ad hoc task force be composed of only board or staff members or a partnership of both board and staff members? Staff members are often the most up to date and knowledgeable about a topic; board members may not be as well informed, but they are responsible for keeping the larger picture in mind—what is best for the community and helps the organization achieve its mission while remaining financially viable. As such, a task force's membership might have representatives from both board and staff. In addition, certain task forces might benefit from having nonboard or nonstaff members—interested external stake-holders whose knowledge of the topic would add depth and wisdom to the conversation; for example, if an organization needs to dramatically improve its public image, a marketing and public relations task force might invite someone from a marketing firm to provide guidance to the conversations.

Make sure that each task force is given a mandate regarding what it is supposed to accomplish: Generally speaking, most task forces are asked to develop specific recommendations about the topic at hand. These recommendations would then be brought back to a larger group (e.g., at an all-staff or all-board retreat) or to a coordinating body such as the strategic planning committee. Rather than presenting one option, some task forces might be asked to discuss and present a few options for consideration, with supporting analysis for the various choices.

For example, a task force might be given the following mandate: How should our agency respond to the unmet needs of housing for people with disabilities? In this example, the task force would be given a series of questions to answer or a request to collect data, such as the following:

- What statistics are available regarding the number of homeless individuals or individuals with substandard housing that is not accessible?

- Who in the county currently provides housing services?

- What type of services do they provide?

- Are there other organizations also facing this issue?

For many proposals being brought forth by a task force, they might be asked to not only propose what to do but also to look at the following questions: What are the costs? What are the risks? What are the advantages of moving in this direction? What are the disadvantages?

Regardless of the type of task force, each task force should have (1) a chair whose responsibility it is to call the meetings, facilitate discussions, and make sure that notes are kept and progress is made toward accomplishing the mandate; (2) clear timelines—a specific date by which should they have completed their work; and (3) clarity regarding its decision-making authority—ad hoc planning committee task forces are advisory and not final decision makers.

SAMPLE OF A MEMO CLARIFYING A TASK FORCE MANDATE

Strategic Plan Client Demographics Task Force

Goal: Develop recommendations in response to this mandate: Are our client demographics changing, and, if so, how do we respond to the new client base (i.e., best meet the needs of our clients)?

Task Force Membership: Two board members and three staff members. Committee should consider expanding membership to include interested external stakeholders whose knowledge of the topic would add depth and wisdom to the discussion.

Process: Begin by selecting a task force chair. This person will be responsible for setting up team meetings; facilitating team meetings, including setting meeting agendas; and making sure that notes are kept and progress is made toward accomplishing the mandate. Follow the timeline as described following in the development of the task force's recommendations.

Timeline

- Hold first task force meeting before December 12, 2015.

- Review mandate; discuss questions and research activities; identify task force members who will be responsible for gathering data needed for analysis in order to develop recommendations for the strategic plan.

- Complete research/data-gathering activities, along with task force meetings to develop recommendations, by January 9, 2016. Submit recommendations to executive director for review and clarification, if necessary, by January 9–16, 2016.

- Task force recommendations submitted to the board of directors at January 24, 2016 daylong strategic planning retreat for review, discussion, and approval.

Questions to Be Answered/Data to Be Gathered by This Task Force

- Have the client demographics changed during the past five years?

- If the client demographics have changed, why? Is the reason internal (i.e., the nature of our programs or change in programs)? Is the reason external (i.e., other agencies are narrowing the scope of whom they provide services to)?

- If the demographics have changed, what do staff members need to do to meet the needs of our consumers?

- Do we want to do targeted outreach to specific populations to change the existing demographics?

Outcomes

Based on the answers to these questions and research, develop specific recommendations—with supporting analysis—on how we could best respond to unmet needs of our client base over the next three to five years. The task force may suggest one option or more than one option. For any of the recommendations, answer the following questions:

- What are the costs?
- What are the risks?
- What are the advantages of moving in this direction?
- What are the disadvantages?

Sample Possible Recommendation

Our review of five years of client demographics shows that there has been a 40 percent increase in the number of clients with mental health disabilities, partly because mental health agencies in our area have narrowed eligibility for their services to individuals and our eligibility criteria are much broader. To better serve this population, one of our recommendations is that our staff need better training on working with clients with mental health issues. Potential costs for this proposal should average $200 per staff person and should include time to attend off-site training as needed. The advantage is that staff will be better equipped and more comfortable when handing the complex issues that are more often associated with persons who have mental disabilities. The disadvantage is that there is a possibility that by staff being better trained to assist this target population, we would continue to see an increase in services to this group.

External Stakeholders

When interviewing external stakeholders, first identify whether the reason to talk with them is primarily to assess your situation or to build relationships. If the reason is primarily information gathering, a consultant might be used to gather that information. If the reason is primarily to build a relationship, the interviewer should be a board or staff member.

INTERVIEWING AN EXTERNAL STAKEHOLDER

- Call the individual, introduce yourself, and explain that the organization is engaged in a strategic planning process and that the interviewee's input into this process would be invaluable. List the questions that you would like him or her to answer.

- Remember, you want to limit the number of questions that you ask because most busy people have limited time. You need to estimate how much time it will take to complete the set of questions; be upfront about the amount of time you are expecting the interview to take. The amount of time needed should range from 20 to 30 minutes. Under rare circumstances, the time might extend to an hour or more.

  The estimated time frame depends on the type and number of questions to be asked and the time needed for the answers. The actual time frame might be more or less than your estimate, but be respectful of the interviewee's schedule—the interview usually shouldn't take more than 30 minutes, and you should use that time wisely. Ask the person for a convenient date and time to speak with him or her on the phone (you might offer to meet in person, if appropriate).

- Make sure you indicate that the input of several individuals or organizations is being sought during the strategic planning process and that, although all of the input will be seriously listened to, differing input and limited resources may mean that not all ideas will be incorporated into the plan.

- If he or she wishes for confidentiality (i.e., no specific comment would be specifically attributed), then offer that confidentiality if it is possible to do so, but be clear that feedback will be included in the overall feedback you and others are getting from other individuals (unless you have come up with some other agreement with the interviewee). After you interview the individual, type up your notes.

- Follow-up: Send the people you interview a note thanking them for their participation, and make sure that you close the loop on their participation by sending them either a copy of the strategic plan or an executive summary of the plan once the planning process is completed.

SUGGESTED FORMAT FOR WRITING A STAKEHOLDER INTERVIEW

- Name of person interviewed (if confidential, only identify type of stakeholder, such as "major donor")
- Name of interviewer
- Date of interview
- Key points made by person being interviewed
- Interviewer conclusions: Aha! moments, such as suggested strategies or priorities; biggest surprise; most important information gleamed from the interview
- Any other comments/observations
- Optional: Attach detailed notes

SUGGESTED POSSIBLE QUESTIONS

Following are suggested possible questions for gathering specific information from all external stakeholders.

Assess an Organization's Situation: Strengths, Weaknesses, Opportunities, and Threats

- What do you think are the organization's strengths and weaknesses?
- What trends do you think are happening in the city, state, and nation that might have a positive or negative impact on the organization? What are the opportunities or threats facing the organization? How might the organization respond to those trends?
- What do you think are the major obstacles to our organization's success?

Assess Stakeholder Perception of the Delivery of Services in Terms of Quality and Competitive Position

- What do you [or your organization] expect from our organization—what are the criteria you use to judge our performance? How well do we perform against those criteria?

- What do you think are the best ways our organization can help our constituencies? Given the myriad programs and projects that we currently offer (provide list if appropriate), are there any on which you think we should primarily focus our resources (or are there specific projects and programs that you think we should be emphasizing over the next three years that you think would make a significant impact on our ability to achieve our mission)?

- Who are other groups that are doing similar work? What distinguishes our organization from the competition?

- What are the service gaps that you think might exist for our clients, and what role should we be filling in meeting those gaps? Are there additional or increased programs or services that you think we should be offering if resources were available?

- What do you think our organization should be doing more or less of?

- Who else should we be talking to who could inform our strategic planning process?

Assess Collaboration and Partnerships

- How can our organization best partner or work with you?

- How well do you think our current partnership is going? Are there ways we can increase our work together—or make it work better? How might we work together to accomplish our overlapping missions?

- Are there groups (national, regional, and local) we should be aligning ourselves with to help accomplish our purpose?

Understand How Your Organization Might Best Leverage Your Resources and Garner Additional Support

- How could we better utilize our members and/or the public to become advocates for our organization?

- Do you have any ideas about how we might increase our visibility and improve our image throughout our geographic location?

- How can we get our name out in the community so more people will avail themselves of our services?

- How good do you think we are at positioning ourselves in the political arena? Are there things we should be doing to be able to work with administrations from both political parties? How can we more effectively work with government officials and legislators? Are there some key allies we should be working more closely with?

Following are suggested questions for gathering information from specific types of external stakeholders.

Major Donors

- Why did you first get involved with our organization?

- What are the particular projects and programs of ours that are of the most interest to you? (Name or show list of all projects if they are not familiar with all that the organization does.)

- Are there some other projects and programs that you would be interested in having our organization support if resources were available?

- How would you prioritize our possible efforts to raise discretionary endowment funds versus using resources to raise funds for specific projects? (Depending on the relationship you have, you may or may not ask this question if you are considering starting an endowment fund.)

- What ideas do you have about how we might increase our membership and/or fundraising efforts?

- How do you best like to be communicated with? How might we best keep you informed of our organization's progress?

Foundations

- How do you think our organization is doing? How do you see the organization fitting in the overall service delivery system, and what do you think makes our organization unique?

- What are the prospects for funding from your organization? Are there other funders who might be interested in supporting our work? (Ask for names.)

- What do you think are most important issues facing our organization today?

- Who else should we be talking to who could inform our strategic planning process?

Media

- What major issues and challenges are affecting the constituencies served by our organization?

- How would you like us to keep you informed about what is happening in the field?

- Do you have any ideas about how we might increase our visibility? How can we raise our image and name?

Groups That Do Similar Work

Note: Much of this information can be found on the Internet, in IRS form 990, and in annual reports.

- What services do you offer?
- How are you funded?
- How many clients do you serve?
- How do you measure success?
- How are you structured?
- What are the main challenges you experience in delivering services?
- Where do you see our organization fitting in within the matrix of service providers?

How to Use the Matrix Map

The matrix map was published in the second edition of *Strategic Planning for Nonprofit Organizations,* under the name "The CompassPoint Dual Bottom Line Matrix." It is with the permission of the authors of two recent books that this article is reprinted: *Nonprofit Sustainability,* published by Jossey-Bass in 2010, by Jeanne Bell, Jan Masaoka, and Steve Zimmerman; and *The Sustainability Mindset: Using the Matrix Map to Make Strategic Decisions*, also published by Jossey-Bass, in 2014, by Steve Zimmerman and Jeanne Bell.

It's easy to embrace the concept of the dual bottom line but harder to apply it in a real-world board setting. For example, board members—and many staff—are seldom familiar with all of the programs and activities of the organization. Although there may be a strong sense that "all our programs are great," there may not have been any discussion about which programs are, in fact, those with the greatest or most important impacts. Even people with financial expertise may feel uncertain about how to make decisions that are more nuanced than "stick to the budget and at least break even."

Board meetings unintentionally support this kind of fragmentation. They take each subject on its own: first the financial report, then the program report, and then the fundraising report. The matrix map aims to change that.

The matrix map is a visual tool that plots all of the organization's activities—not just its programs—into a single, compelling image. By illustrating the organization's business model—through a picture of all activities and the financial and mission impact of each one—it supports genuinely strategic discussions.

Following is an example of a matrix map for a community center. Each circle represents a program. You can see that circles higher on the map have higher impact than those lower on the map. You can see the relative size of each activity, and which ones make money, which break even, and which require subsidy from the organization's unrestricted funds.

The resulting image often provides an "aha!" moment for board members. After years of hearing about the seemingly unrelated programs, they can now understand how they all work together to support the impact and viability of the organization they care about.

How to Make a Matrix Map of Your Organization

To create the matrix map there are four steps:

1. Identify your mission-specific and fund development programs,
2. Assess relative mission impact,
3. Determine profitability, and
4. Map the results!

Here is a more thorough explanation of each step.

1. *Identify your programs—all of them.* Programs, sometimes called business lines or activities, represent all mission-specific and fund development activities that require effort. Counseling, dance performances, citizenship classes, and forest restoration are all mission-specific programs. A fundraising phone-a-thon is a fund development program as is a special event or major donor solicitation.

2. *Assess relative mission impact.* In many nonprofits, there's an implicit assumption that all programs are effective and important—and that's typically true. But everyone also realizes—yet seldom says—that some programs have higher impact than others. We may not discuss impact levels in order not to sound as if we are criticizing a worthwhile program (or its director), but it's precisely these judgments about which programs have the highest impact that the management team and the board should discuss as strategic choices are made.

   Each organization will use two of the same criteria for impact—contribution to intended impact and excellence in execution—and have two different criteria for impact—after all, impact is defined by each nonprofit differently. And remember, this is an informed self-assessment, not an evaluation. We suggest a survey or discussion with the management team and the board that asks individuals or the group to rate each program on a scale of 1 to 4 using four criteria.

   • *Contribution to Intended Impact:* Relative to other programs, how well does this program contribute to what the overall organization aims to accomplish?

   • *Excellence in Execution:* Organizations are simply better at delivering some activities than others. A program may be important to our mission, but we may not have the right skills or financial resources to implement it with excellence. This is a nice way of separating planning from execution.

   After the first two criteria, organizations can identify more criteria for impact based on which resonate with your organization:

   • *Scale:* How many people are touched or influenced by this program?

- *Depth:* How profound is the level of intervention with this program?

- *Building Community or Constituency:* Does the program build community around the program or the organization as a whole?

- *Significant Unmet Need:* Is there significant competition or are there similar offerings of this program? Is there an adequate supply of services to meet the demand for them in our community?

- *Leverage:* Does this program benefit from and nurture important relationships and partnerships inside and outside the organization?

Remember, you only need to choose four criteria. After you've rated all of the programs, take an average of the scores each line receives across the criteria and that will be its mission impact score. For example, if tutoring were to receive:

- Contribution to Intended Impact: 4

- Excellence in Execution: 3

- Significant Unmet Need: 3

- Building Community: 2

- The mission impact score would be the average $(4 + 3 + 3 + 2)/4$ or 3.0.

3. *Determine profitability.* Look at how much a business line is contributing financially (profit) or how much it needs subsidy from the organization's unrestricted funds (loss). (Unrestricted revenue should be attributed to the fundraising program that was used to raise it, such as major donors or direct mail.)

4. *Map the results.* Once these steps are done, you can map each program on a grid. We put impact on the vertical or x-axis and profitability on the horizontal or y-axis.

Then using Excel's chart function, select "Bubble Chart" to create the matrix map seen at the beginning of this article. More than a picture, though, the matrix map can now help engage board members in strategic discussions about how to strengthen the organization's business model—understanding that the implications of their decisions will affect both the impact and finances. And staff can see the entire organization at a glance in a way that focuses attention on activities and impact rather than as an organization chart.

Financial Data for Our Youth Community Organization

	After-school Tutoring	Sports League	Summer Programming	Community Festival	Job Placement Services	Individual Donations	Community Theater	Admin	Total
Revenue	**41,488**	**60,560**	**56,473**	**145,258**	-	**40,750**	**15,000**	-	**359,559**
Direct Expense	51,360	49,500	52,890	79,500	17,860	21,052	22,000	36,251	330,413
Shared Costs	5,802	2,800	7,320	9,750	2,560	2,450	1,132	2,123	33,937
Administration	5,608	5,697	6,782	11,331	2,809	3,305	2,842	(38,374)	-
Total Expenses	62,770	57,997	66,992	100,581	23,229	26,807	25,974	-	364,350
Surplus/ (Deficit)	**($21,282)**	**$2,568**	**($10,519)**	**$44,677**	**($23,229)**	**$13,943**	**($10,974)**		**($4,791)**

These are the data that are entered in Excel in order to generate the bubble chart that follows.

Matrix Map Data

Business Lines	Profitability	Mission Impact	Expenses
After-school tutoring	($21,282)	3.85	$62,770
Sports league	$2,593	3.25	$57,997
Summer programming	($10,519)	3	$66,992
Community festival	$44,677	2.6	$100,581
Job placement services	($23,229)	2	$23,229
Individual donations	$13,943	1.5	$26,807
Community theater	($10,974)	1.8	$25,974
TOTAL	($4,791)		$364,350

Matrix Map

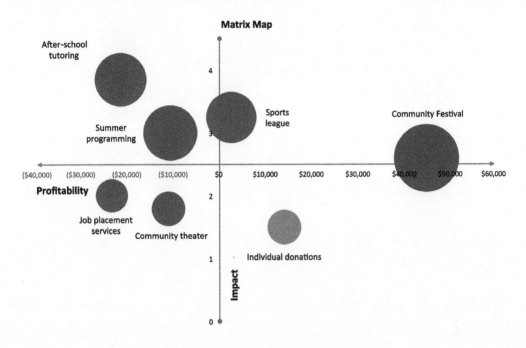

Leadership Assessment Survey

Haas, Jr. Fund

Leadership Diagnostic - Introduction

This survey was developed for the Flexible Leadership Awards (FLA) Program, a project of the Tides Center and the Evelyn & Walter Haas, Jr. Fund. In developing this tool, we reviewed and were guided by many other organizational assessments including those of REDF, San Diego Foundation, and TCC Group, and particularly, RoadMAP's My Healthy Organization tool. Please feel free to further adapt and develop this tool for your purposes.

This tool is intended to help your organization gather the data it needs to develop a plan that will strengthen your leadership to achieve your most important strategic priorities.

Your responses, along with those of others in the organization and in concert with the data collected from interviews and other organizational documents, will be used to help identify leadership opportunities and needs. The survey covers the following eight key leadership topics:

1. Vision, Mission and Values

2. Strategy and Assessment

3. Board Leadership and Governance

4. Executive Director and Senior Staff

5. Staff Development, Organization Culture and Succession Planning

6. Diversity and Cultural Competency

7. Communications

8. Fundraising and Planning for Sustainability

In each of the sections, you will find a series of statements. Please review each of these statements and check the box that best reflects your perspective—remember there are no right or wrong answers and that you are assessing this statement from YOUR point of view. (If you feel you do not have information about any of the statements, then check "unable to judge.")

The survey should take about 15 minutes to complete.

Please identify your role in the organization by selecting one of the following:

◯ Executive Director

◯ Leadership Team Member

◯ Other Staff Member

◯ Board Member

Haas, Jr. Fund

Section One: Vision, Mission and Values

Vision, Mission and Values

	Strongly Disagree	Disagree	Somewhat Disagree	Somewhat Agree	Agree	Strongly Agree	Unable to Judge
1.1 Our board and staff understand and share the **vision** of the organization.	○	○	○	○	○	○	○
1.2 Our board and staff understand and can articulate our **mission.**	○	○	○	○	○	○	○
1.3 Everyone in our organization understands and can communicate our **common set of values.**	○	○	○	○	○	○	○
1.4 In all parts of our work, we **act** in accordance with our **values**.	○	○	○	○	○	○	○

1.5 Any comments about strengths or gaps in this area? Any further information to explain your answers?

Please continue to Section Two: Strategy and Assessment.

Haas, Jr. Fund

Section Two: Strategy and Assessment

Strategy and Assessment

	Strongly Disagree	Disagree	Somewhat Disagree	Somewhat Agree	Agree	Strongly Agree	Unable to Judge
2.1 We have **clear strategic priorities** that define the impact we want to achieve over the next three to five years.	○	○	○	○	○	○	○
2.2 We develop and carry out **organizational and program goals** that advance our strategic priorities.	○	○	○	○	○	○	○
2.3 We have an **ongoing strategy review process** in place that enables us to revise plans as needed and respond to changing circumstances.	○	○	○	○	○	○	○
2.4 We regularly **assess our programs** in order to maximize learning and develop programs accordingly.	○	○	○	○	○	○	○
2.5 We **regularly achieve the goals and impact** that we set for our organization.	○	○	○	○	○	○	○

2.6 What are the top three strategic priorities for your organization over the next three years?

Strategic priorities are the primary objectives for your work—that is, the change or impact that your organization is working to achieve over the medium to long term in order to fulfill its mission.

Example 1: To shift from a reactive to proactive role in gaining significant policy and litigation wins for low-income immigrants

Example 2: To significantly increase school safety for all by expanding from 400 to 600 GSAs in California schools

Please identify the top three strategic priorities based on your knowledge of and intuition about your organization:

2.7 Any comments about strengths or gaps in this area? Any further information to explain your answers?

Please continue to Section Three: Board Leadership and Governance.

Haas, Jr. Fund

Section Three: Board Leadership and Governance

Board Leadership and Governance

	Strongly Disagree	Disagree	Somewhat Disagree	Somewhat Agree	Agree	Strongly Agree	Unable to Judge
3.1 Given where we need to go in the next few years, our board has the **experience and skills** the organization needs.	○	○	○	○	○	○	○
3.2 Our board is fully engaged in **governance** of the organization, including setting strategy and direction, and ensuring fiscal oversight.	○	○	○	○	○	○	○
3.3 Our board **evaluates** the performance of the **executive director**.	○	○	○	○	○	○	○
3.4 Our board actively **supports the executive director** and his/her leadership development.	○	○	○	○	○	○	○
3.5 Our board **focuses on board development and self-assessment,** including the effective recruitment, training and integration of new members.	○	○	○	○	○	○	○
3.6 Our board members **work well together.**	○	○	○	○	○	○	○
3.7 Our board and staff leadership are **clear about and agree on their respective goals.**	○	○	○	○	○	○	○
3.8 Our board and staff **communicate effectively** with each other with mutual respect.	○	○	○	○	○	○	○

3.9 Any comments about strengths or gaps in this area? Any further information to explain your answers?

Please continue to Section Four: Executive Director and Senior Staff Leadership.

Haas, Jr. Fund

Section Four: Executive Director and Senior Staff Leadership

Executive Director and Senior Staff Leadership

	Strongly Disagree	Disagree	Somewhat Disagree	Somewhat Agree	Agree	Strongly Agree	Unable to Judge
4.1 Given where we need to go in the next few years, our **executive director** has the **skills and expertise** the organization needs.	○	○	○	○	○	○	○
4.2 Our **executive director** is **self-aware,** seeking opportunities to grow as a leader and increase the impact of the organization.	○	○	○	○	○	○	○
4.3 Given where we need to go in the next few years, our **senior staff members** have the **skills and expertise** the organization needs.	○	○	○	○	○	○	○
4.4 Our **senior staff members** are **self-aware** and consistently seek opportunities to grow and increase the impact of the organization.	○	○	○	○	○	○	○
4.5 Our **staff leadership structure makes sense,** with a shared understanding of who is responsible for what, clear decision-making processes and lines of accountability.	○	○	○	○	○	○	○
4.6 Our senior team members not only represent their departments or functional areas, but also **work well together** to effectively lead the "whole" organization.	○	○	○	○	○	○	○
4.7 Our senior leaders **inspire, motivate and challenge** the full staff to work successfully towards our mission.	○	○	○	○	○	○	○

4.8 Any comments about strengths or gaps in this area? Any further information to explain your answers?

Please continue to Section Five: Staff Development, Organization Culture and Succession Planning.

Haas, Jr. Fund

Section Five: Staff Development, Organization Culture and Succession Planni...

Staff Development, Organization Culture and Succession Planning

	Strongly Disagree	Disagree	Somewhat Disagree	Somewhat Agree	Agree	Strongly Agree	Unable to Judge
5.1 We do a good job at **attracting and retaining** competent staff members.	○	○	○	○	○	○	○
5.2 We are **intentional about staff development** through relevant training, coaching/feedback, and consistent performance appraisal.	○	○	○	○	○	○	○
5.3 We **anticipate the skill sets** we need on staff in order to achieve our strategic priorities.	○	○	○	○	○	○	○
5.4 We have **planned ahead** for potential departures in order to facilitate smooth transitions.	○	○	○	○	○	○	○
5.5 Our culture encourages **learning and experimentation.**	○	○	○	○	○	○	○
5.6 Our **organizational pace** enables and encourages regular self-reflection and longer term thinking.	○	○	○	○	○	○	○
5.7 Our staff is **consistently informed** of key information.	○	○	○	○	○	○	○
5.8 We openly and directly **resolve conflicts**.	○	○	○	○	○	○	○

5.9 Any comments about strengths or gaps in this area? Any further information to explain your answers?

Please continue to Section Six: Diversity and Cultural Competency.

Haas, Jr. Fund

Section Six: Diversity and Cultural Competency

Diversity and Cultural Competency

	Strongly Disagree	Disagree	Somewhat Disagree	Somewhat Agree	Agree	Strongly Agree	Unable to Judge
6.1 We **assess community needs** on a regular basis.	○	○	○	○	○	○	○
6.2 We develop our plans with input from our constituents and hold ourselves **accountable** to our constituents.	○	○	○	○	○	○	○
6.3 Our **board** reflects our community.	○	○	○	○	○	○	○
6.4 Our **staff** reflects our community.	○	○	○	○	○	○	○
6.5 We engage in **organization learning** in order to work well with people and issues of varied cultures, backgrounds, identities and experiences.	○	○	○	○	○	○	○

6.6 Any comments about strengths or gaps in this area? Any further information to explain your answers?

Please continue to Section Seven: Communications (External).

Haas, Jr. Fund

Section Seven: Communications (External)

Communications (External)

	Strongly Disagree	Disagree	Somewhat Disagree	Somewhat Agree	Agree	Strongly Agree	Unable to Judge
7.1 Our **board** has the skills to **effectively promote** the organization.	○	○	○	○	○	○	○
7.2 Our **board members** are committed to acting as **ambassadors** for the organization.	○	○	○	○	○	○	○
7.3 Our **staff** has the skills to **effectively promote** the organization.	○	○	○	○	○	○	○
7.4 We have clear **communications goals** designed to support our strategic priorities.	○	○	○	○	○	○	○
7.5 We have a clear and realistic **communications plan.**	○	○	○	○	○	○	○
7.6 We **communicate effectively** about our work and the impact of our programs.	○	○	○	○	○	○	○

7.7 Any comments about strengths or gaps in this area? Any further information to explain your answers?

Please continue to Section Eight: Fundraising and Planning for Sustainability.

Haas, Jr. Fund

Section Eight: Fundraising and Planning for Sustainability

Fundraising and Planning for Sustainability

	Strongly Disagree	Disagree	Somewhat Disagree	Somewhat Agree	Agree	Strongly Agree	Unable to Judge
8.1 We have a realistic, well-developed **fund development plan.**	○	○	○	○	○	○	○
8.2 Senior staff members have the **skills to raise the funds** we need.	○	○	○	○	○	○	○
8.3 Senior staff members consider fundraising a **core leadership capacity.**	○	○	○	○	○	○	○
8.4 Our **board pulls its weight** in fundraising.	○	○	○	○	○	○	○
8.5 Staff and board **leaders work together effectively** to raise the funds the organization needs.	○	○	○	○	○	○	○
8.6 We have the skills and systems to understand and **manage our financial situation.**	○	○	○	○	○	○	○
8.7 We have a **clear business model** that promotes sustainability.	○	○	○	○	○	○	○
8.8 Our **budgets** reflect our **strategic priorities.**	○	○	○	○	○	○	○

8.9 Any comments about strengths or gaps in this area? Any further information to explain your answers?

Please continue to the Final Section: Conclusion.

Haas, Jr. Fund

Final Section: Conclusion

Finally, what do you think are the three most important <u>leadership issues</u> for your organization at this time? Please rank your top three issues, by marking the highest priority as #1, your second as #2, and your third priority as #3.

	1st most important	2nd most important	3rd most important
Mission, Vision and Values	○	○	○
Strategy and Assessment	○	○	○
Board Leadership and Governance	○	○	○
Executive Director and Senior Staff	○	○	○
Staff Development, Organization Culture and Succession Planning	○	○	○
Diversity and Cultural Competency	○	○	○
Communications (external)	○	○	○
Fundraising and Planning for Sustainability	○	○	○

Please share any reflections that occurred to you in this ranking process. Are there other leadership issues that you want to highlight?

Please share any other comments or observations on the leadership strengths, priorities and challenges for your organization at this time.

Selected References

Barry, Bryan W. *Strategic Planning Workbook for Nonprofit Organizations.* St. Paul, MN: Amherst H. Wilder Foundation, 1986.

Bell, Jeanne, Jan Masaoka, and Steve Zimmerman. *Nonprofit Sustainability: Making Strategic Decisions for Financial Viability.* San Francisco: Jossey-Bass, 2010.

Bryson, John M. *Strategic Planning for Public and Nonprofit Organizations: A Guide to Strengthening and Sustaining Organizational Achievement.* 3rd ed. San Francisco: John Wiley and Sons, 2004.

Chait, Richard P., William P. Ryan, and Barbara E. Taylor. *Governance as Leadership: Reframing the Work of Nonprofit Boards.* San Francisco: John Wiley and Sons, 2005.

Crutchfield, Leslie R., and Heather McLeod Grant. *Forces for Good: The Six Practices of High-Impact Nonprofits.* San Francisco: Jossey-Bass, 2008.

Drucker, Peter F. *Managing the Nonprofit Organization: Principles and Practices.* New York: HarperCollins, 1990.

Epstein, Marc J., and Kristi Yuthas. *Measuring and Improving Social Impacts: A Guide for Nonprofits, Companies and Impact Investors.* San Francisco: Berrett Koehler Publishers, 2014.

Heyman, Darian Rodriguez. *Nonprofit Management 101: A Complete and Practical Guide for Leaders and Professionals.* San Francisco: Jossey-Bass, 2011.

Johansen, Bob. *Leaders Make the Future: Ten New Leadership Skills for an Uncertain World.* San Francisco: Berrett Koehler Publishers, 2012.

Kotler, Philip, and Alan Andreasen. *Strategic Marketing for Nonprofit Organizations.* 4th ed. Englewood Cliffs, NJ: Prentice Hall, 1991.

Lafley, A.G., and Roger L. Martin. *Playing to Win: How Strategy Really Works.* Boston: Harvard Business Review Press, 2013.

LaPiana, David. *The Nonprofit Strategy Revolution: Real-Time Strategic Planning in a Rapid-Response World.* Minneapolis, MN: Fieldstone Alliance, 2008.

Mintzberg, Henry. *The Rise and Fall of Strategic Planning.* New York: Free Press, 1994.

Peters, Thomas J., and Robert H. Waterman Jr. *In Search of Excellence: Lessons from America's Best-Run Companies.* New York: HarperCollins, 1982.

Porter, Michael E. *Competitive Strategy: Techniques for Analyzing Industries and Competitors.* New York: Free Press, 1980.

Ross, Holly, Katrin Verclas, and Alison Levine. *Managing Technology to Meet Your Mission: A Strategic Guide for Nonprofit Leaders*. San Francisco: Jossey-Bass, 2009.

Schwartz, Peter. *The Art of the Long View*. New York: Doubleday, 1991.

Steiner, George A. *Strategic Planning: What Every Manager Must Know*. New York: Free Press, 1979.

Zimmerman, Steve, and Jeanne Bell. *The Sustainability Mindset: Using the Matrix Map to Make Strategic Decisions*. San Francisco: Jossey-Bass, 2014.

About the Companion Website

This book has a companion website, which can be found at www.wiley.com/go/strategicplanning. Enter the password: nonprofit123. The companion website provides resources to support the strategic planning process.

1. Blank worksheets are configured as PDF Form documents so that entries can be made directly into the worksheet in the course of using the book to support a strategic planning process.

2. Haas, Jr. Fund Leadership Assessment Survey

3. Business Model: How to Create a Matrix Map in Excel

4. Tips on External Stakeholder Input

5. Tips on Use of Task Forces

6. Organization Assessment Instrument: Elements of an Effectively Managed Organization

About the Authors

Mike Allison has been providing strategic and management consulting support to nonprofits and philanthropy for the last 25 years. Having started his career as a neighborhood organizer and executive director, Mike then served for 15 years as Director of Consulting and Research at CompassPoint Nonprofit Services, a consulting firm in Northern California. Mike received his MBA from the Yale School of Management, and his published work includes numerous nonprofit management articles and manuals. He works as an independent consultant nationally from his office in downtown Oakland, CA. Mike can be reached at Mike@MAconsulting.org.

Jude Kaye is an organization development and strategic planning consultant who has spent the last 35 years providing consulting and executive coaching services to the managers and staff of nonprofit organizations. Before starting her own company, Intention to Action, Jude was the senior staff consultant at CompassPoint Nonprofit Services.

Index

NOTE: Page references in *italics* refer to exhibits, figures, tables, and worksheets.